OCEANSIDE PUBLIC LIBRARY
330 North Hill Street
Oceanside, CA 9?

D0399183

OCEANSIDE PUBLIC LIBRARY

3 1232 00429 7000

LIEUTENANT RAMSEY'S WAR

Also by Stephen J. Rivele

The Plumber: *The True Story of How One Good Man Helped Destroy the Entire Philadelphia Mafia* (with Joseph Salerno)

940.5359
RAM

LIEUTENANT RAMSEY'S WAR

**Edwin Price Ramsey
and Stephen J. Rivele**

KNIGHTSBRIDGE PUBLISHING COMPANY
NEW YORK

OCEANSIDE PUBLIC LIBRARY
330 North Hill Street
Oceanside, CA 92054

Copyright © 1990 by Edwin Price Ramsey and Stephen J. Rivele

All rights reserved. Printed in the U.S.A.

No part of this publication may be reproduced or transmitted in any form
or by any means, electronic or mechanical, including photocopy,
recording, or any information storage and retrieval system now known or
to be invented, without permission in writing from the publisher, except
by a reviewer who wishes to quote brief passages in connection with a
review written for inclusion in a magazine, newspaper, or broadcast.

Published in the United States by
Knightsbridge Publishing Company
255 East 49th Street
New York, New York 10017

Library of Congress Cataloging-in-Publication Data

Ramsey, Edwin.
    Lieutenant Ramsey's war / Edwin Ramsey & Stephen J. Rivele.—1st
ed.
      p. cm.
    ISBN 1-877961-58-2
    1. Ramsey, Edwin. 2. World War, 1939–1945—Underground
movements—Philippines. 3. World War, 1939–1945—Personal
narratives, American. 4. World War, 1939–1945—Commando
operations—Philippines. 5. United States. Army—Biography.
6. Soldiers—United States—Biography. 7. Guerrillas—Philippines—
Biography. I. Rivele, Stephen J., 1949–   II. Title.
D802.P5R35   1990
940.53′599′092—dc20
[B] 90-36444
      CIP

Designed by Susan Shankin

Medal on preceding page: Distinguished Service Cross,
awarded to Edwin Ramsey in 1945 by General
Douglas MacArthur, for heroism in combat.

10 9 8 7 6 5 4 3 2 1
First Edition

JUL 2 7 1994

To Captain Joe Barker, and to all the other brave men and women of the Philippine resistance who sacrificed their lives in the cause of liberty.

*If you know the enemy and know yourself,
you need not fear the result of a hundred
battles.*

—Sun Tzu
The Art of War (c. 500 B.C.)

Contents

List of Maps

Acknowledgments

Without the incurable optimism and loving support of my darling wife, Raquel, this book would never have been completed. And the daring and indomitable courage of my sister, Nadine, probably set the stage for many of my later actions and decisions. But most of all, the constant love, unquestioning support, and faith in me expressed by my mother, Nelle Ramsey, formed the dominant factor in my life and the ultimate development of my character.

No matter how exciting a story may be, if it is not well written and properly introduced it dies aborning. Whatever success my story may have I owe to my coauthor Steve Rivele, and to my literary agent, Joel Gotler, for their efforts on my behalf.

Finally, to the management and staff of Knightsbridge Publishing and especially to its editor-in-chief, Shelly Usen, I am deeply indebted for their faith and their unstinting support in bringing this book to fruition.

—EPR

WICHITA
SWELL

1934–1941

MEDAL ON PRECEDING PAGE:
Purple Heart (AMERICAN)

The Legger

We could tell he had made a run into Oklahoma because the springs on his sedan were so depressed. The Oldsmobile lumbered down the main street and turned left in among the rows of respectable houses. Bobby Harrison and I waited a discreet interval and then followed.

I was seventeen years old, and possessed of a reputation. In the Wichita of 1934, a conservative big small town, I was known as a hell-raiser, the boy over whom neighbors wagged their heads, considering what a wonderful woman my mother was, and my sister's brilliant prospects. "That Ramsey boy," I was; "that Edwin."

We made our way between two hedges to the side door of the bootlegger's house. The old sedan stood gaping before the garage, its springs relieved of their burden.

"Gin, do you think?" I asked Bobby.

Whiskey, he was sure. He was not as stocky as me, and his fair hair hung in tousles over his forehead. "That's all they're makin' these days."

I knocked. It was midmorning and the town was at its work. Bobby and I had skipped school, and so the streets, with their trim, dry lawns and drawn curtains, were ours.

The front door cracked open and a long face appeared.

"Seen your car," I told it.

The door pulled back and we stepped into the parlor. There was not much furniture, and the house, which had been closed for several days, smelled of stale Lucky smoke. The legger, we knew, was a bachelor and lived alone. He gave us a sleepy, almost mournful look, and turned his back.

Bobby poked me in the ribs. "The money," he whispered.

I reached into my pocket and felt for it: eighteen dollars and some change I had earned as a waiter at the Palms nightclub on the east side of town.

The legger was in the backyard, rooting around.

"You think he's got it buried already?" Bobby asked.

I shrugged.

He shuffled back into the parlor, a Lucky between his lips, two bottles in his hands. He was a lengthy, slim man with thinning hair and garters on his sleeves, who could have been thirty-five or fifty, for all I could tell. Had it not been Prohibition, he would have sold hardware store to store, or clerked at the Beechcraft airplane plant. As it was, every other week he drove down to Oklahoma, where the sharecroppers' stills smoked whiskey in the Cookson Hills across the border. He was the spare, dry Wichita I chafed at; the kind of life I feared instinctively for its bland inevitability. Yet every week I made the secret trip to his clapboard house, sometimes with Bobby, sometimes alone.

He handed the bottles over and I slipped him the cash. It was folded in his pocket in an instant. The Lucky sizzled as he pulled at it, then he lifted it away and gave a long, dry cough.

"You shouldn't," he said, as if against himself.

"Huh . . . what?" I asked. I couldn't recall that he had ever spoken to me.

"Drink," the legger answered.

"Oh, yeah," I agreed. "You shouldn't either."

"Huh?"

"Smoke so much," I said. "S'bad for your health."

"Scram," he told us.

We took the bottles, bulging beneath our shirts, down to the railroad tracks and settled with them on the berm.

"Whiskey," Bobby sniffed. "Pretty smooth."

I watched him take a tentative sip. He was taller than me,

and thinner, and he had always been game for my adventures. I
was a thickset, combative kid, and had had my share of fights.
But I was also a swell, and when the Big Bands played at the
Palms, the women all wanted to dance with me around the dingy
clump of linen palm trees from which the club took its name.
The gawking Kansas bachelors would watch in awe, and then
pay me on the side to teach them the fox-trot and the paso
doble.

Bobby, I knew, envied me, and he also understood me. Like
me, he had lost his father, and like me, the loss had left him at
loose ends. The lack of a father forced us back upon ourselves,
increasing our sense of isolation. Marooned in Wichita, we had
no outlet for our energies. We needed an example to rein us in;
instead we had only our restless selves. And so, anxious to
become men, we stumbled through a wanton, manless youth.

My father had been a tragic soul. A wildcatter in the oil fields,
he had had no education and no prospects except a bent back
and dirty hands. He worked harder than any man I ever saw,
forcing iron into the earth and oozing oil out. Others made the
profits while he moved on to more pumps and pipes and the wet
black chains they slung around them like lashes on a slave's
spine.

But there was poetry in him, and he saw it in my mother.
He courted her in the carefree days before the Great War with
flowers and verse and inexhaustible attention, and he won her
over the bankers' and doctors' sons. She was the grace that his
laborer's life lacked, the antidote to the sweaty, grimy toil of
the fields.

But he was a brooding man, and away in the oil fields of
Texas and Oklahoma, he tortured himself with jealousy. She
was bright, she was musical, and every man in town admired
her. When he came home he eyed her accusingly and searched
the house for signs of unfaithfulness. He looked at the grit
indelibly under his fingernails and could not bring himself to

believe that he really possessed her. He seemed to yearn for proof of infidelity, and finding none, he felt doubly betrayed.

It was all in his mind, of course, which was warping. To Nadine and me as small children the transformation was a puzzle, and I tried for a time to think of it as a game he was playing. After his trips he would return from the fields with exotic gifts, arrowheads or lumps of turquoise or the intricate silver carvings of the Indians. Nadine and I would buzz around him, happy that he was home and eager for the prizes he brought.

But as time went on I watched him become sullen, then angry, then isolated. This was no game, I began to understand; it was a frightening intrusion in our lives, an alien presence that we were helpless to understand or control. We tried to ignore it, distancing ourselves from him and hoping that it would end of its own accord, but it only grew worse. He began to rail at Mother and accuse her, and despite her tearful denials he refused to believe her. Then he began to beat her.

To see Father hit Mother was terrifying to us, and at first Nadine and I cowered away from the sight. But it was not in our nature to run, and we began to intervene, crying and pulling at him to stop. Then, when he had stormed out in frustration and shame, we would console ourselves and Mother. We were just children—Nadine was fifteen and I was ten—and there was nothing we could do. It was chilling to watch the man we all loved turn into something else. Where we had once celebrated his return from the fields, we now learned to fear it.

As father became more and more unstable, Nadine and I drew closer together. We joined in a conspiracy aimed at protecting Mother and concealing our trouble from the proper Kansas world. When Father was home we avoided conflict with him, limiting our conversation to insubstantial talk. While he napped we tiptoed round the house so as not to wake him, and we spent as much time as we could with Mother away from him. Most of all we kept up appearances. We were determined that the town would not know of our trouble, and secretly I learned to hate the place all the more for its uncaring intolerance and my fear that we would be shamed.

Meanwhile, in the turmoil of my adolescence, the example of him threw me into confusion. I withdrew farther into myself, becoming sullen and rebellious. I was frightened of my father and deeply resentful of the unhappiness he was causing. I could not believe that any of my friends had to suffer what I did, and the conviction made me feel even more isolated and ashamed. It struck me as horribly unfair that I and Nadine and Mother had to pay the price of his loss of control.

Emotion was to blame, I told myself: brooding, doubt, suspicion, self-absorption, self-indulgence. I saw them destroying my father, and as I watched him ride the nightmare of his emotions I became terrified of my own. At a time when I should have been emulating him to define my own manhood, I found myself frightened by his. Instead of the support I needed in order to establish my direction, I faced a subtle, silent struggle to protect Mother from Father and Father from himself.

Father, no doubt, found fuel for his own fears in our behavior and became even more violent. He interrogated us about Mother and began to make threats against her. Nadine and I pleaded with him to stop, assuring him that there was no need for his suspicions, but his threats only grew more strident and explicit.

Then one night Nadine and I were awakened by shouting coming from our parents' bedroom. We both crept into the half-lit hall and listened, exchanging looks of embarrassment and fear. It was Father's voice, sounding more enraged than we had ever heard him. Suddenly there was mother's voice pleading with him to stop, and then we heard the word *gun*. We glanced at each other in alarm, and in the same instant we ran to their room.

Mother was struggling with Father, who was grappling to get at the shotgun he kept hidden behind the headboard of the bed. We called to her in panic from the doorway, but she yelled at us to run. Instead, Nadine and I threw ourselves at Father. I was twelve, Nadine seventeen, and between us we barely dragged him away.

He stared at us in a horror of recognition. He was gripping the barrel of the shotgun, his hands white and trembling. He glanced down at it, gave an animal groan of anguish and shame, thrust it aside, and shoved his way heavily out of the room. Mother lay panting in tears on the bed, and when we were sure that she was alright, Nadine called the police. They found Father near the house and arrested him. Mother was trembling so badly that she could not speak, and the police told us that they would hold Father overnight. The next day they found him hanged in his cell.

It was a terrible blow to us, but inevitably it was a relief. The scandal in the town stung me almost as much as his death, and in reaction I affected a callous, defiant manner. My demeanor dared anyone to speak to me about it or to mention my family. No one did, but the truth was that the years of silent warfare in the house and the sudden fearful outburst had shaken me to levels I did not know existed in myself. It was a stunning revelation that I could be hurt so deeply, and it frightened me and left me feeling all the more vulnerable and alone.

Father's death also meant hardship. There was no pension, no death benefit, and so all three of us went to work. Nadine left school and got a job as a secretary. I took on a paper route, trudging the barren streets before dawn in shoes that let the sidewalk in, and at nights I waitered and danced at the club. Mother enrolled in cosmetology school and worked in a beauty shop. An energetic and enterprising woman, before long she had a large clientele and was able to buy the business.

Meanwhile, I stumbled into my teenage years, becoming a source of concern to my mother, who watched my aimlessness with dismay. She was always ambitious for me, and I hated the idea that I was disappointing her. I had discovered moonshine and girls and I salved my hurts in them, but they were no cure for the loneliness I felt, nor for my deeper desires. What those desires were exactly I could not tell, but I was feeling a lack I could not fill and a longing I could not define.

Bobby and I finished half a bottle of the whiskey, feeling whoozy. "I'm gonna get home," I said, standing unsteadily. "You'll keep those?"

He slipped the bottles under his jacket. "Yeah, I got a place."

We followed the tracks to the grade crossing where we parted. That night, after dinner, Mother took me aside.

"Buddy," she said, using the name she had always called me, "I have been thinking about your future."

"Oh?"

She nodded. "I feel strongly that one of us should." Her face had a frown I had noticed more often, which knit her slender brows and was bringing wrinkles to her forehead. "I am concerned about your grades," she said, "and . . . other reports I have heard." There was a pause. "How would you like to go to military school?"

It was a calculated gesture, for she knew I was interested in martial things.

"Hadn't thought about it," I replied.

"I have inquired at Oklahoma Military Academy," she said. "It is a cavalry school."

I loved horses; she knew this also. I had always lived for the trips to my uncle's farm in Illinois, where I spent whole days on horseback. Riding was for me a release, a chance to merge my energies with the power of the horse, a challenge to master both the animal and myself. I had never taken lessons, but from my childhood I had ridden headlong with instinctual unconcern. Riding was a risk that I relished and the kind of freedom that my restless nature craved. Now mother was offering me both what I wanted and needed: horses and discipline. I fought to conceal the sudden eagerness I felt.

"I'll think about it," I agreed.

☆ ☆ ☆

Unlike me, Nadine was driven by a purposefulness that pointed her energies and propelled her ambition. Every evening after work she slipped secretly down to the little airfield at the Beechcraft factory to take flying lessons. It was her passion, and so unorthodox in the Kansas of that day that she swore me not to tell Mother for fear of scandal.

"What do you want to fly for?" I wanted to know.

"What difference is it to you?"

"Will you teach me?" I asked.

"Only if you keep your mouth shut."

I solemnly promised that I would.

She put out her hand for me to shake. "It's a deal," she said.

Over the next few weeks she gave me lessons in an old, squat biplane that she rented for two dollars an hour. I was amazed at what an expert, instinctive flier she was, throwing the little plane into neck-breaking loops, slicing straight up for thousands of feet and dropping again in hypnotic spirals that made the wires wail.

She bullied and browbeat me, her first student, and gave me grudging, mannish praise when at last I mastered the controls. I lacked her talent, but I refused to admit it. Nor would I let myself be defeated by her intimidating instruction. I learned to fly to spite her.

"Well," she drawled one day as she drove me home, "you can put in for your ticket now."

"My what?"

"Your pilot's license."

"Do you have one?" I asked.

"Course. I was the first girl in Wichita to get one. About the first girl in Kansas."

I affected disdain. "Not interested," I remarked.

"Oh?" she said, lofting her brows.

"I don't need it."

Nadine gave me a long, withering look. "Suit yourself," she said. "But flying's where the future is." She threw a sidelong glance: "Not horses, for Christ sake."

☆　☆　☆

It was summer, and I faced my senior year. There would be long, dry months of town—nights at the club, the pallid Wichita girls, visits to the legger, his mournful looks, and whiskey by the tracks. Then school again, and then . . . ?

I had no direction, and the fact frightened me. I was a restless, physical boy, but my father's legacy had left me with a terror of excess. I had watched him brood himself to death, slipping deeper into a dense web of self-doubt in which his sanity had been hopelessly entangled. And I had seen his feelings fester into violence. It was a lesson I swore myself never to forget—that emotion was weakness, and that obsession was death.

It was the practical side of me warring with the poetic, for it had been the poet in Father that had betrayed him. He had sought a beauty he did not believe himself entitled to, and the despair that resulted had become deadly. I was determined to save myself from that, even if it meant sacrificing a part of me in the process.

Such sacrifice, I instinctively felt, was not only necessary to protect myself but also would make me stronger. If I could not be a man in the example of my father, I could become one despite it. My goal was no longer the usual boy's desire to be like his father: I swore myself to be unlike him. His weakness would point the way to my strength; by avoiding the source of his suffering I would avoid my own. I would steel myself and strip myself of the vulnerability that had been bred into me, and what better training ground for that, I felt, than the army.

In midsummer I told Mother I would go. She seemed quietly relieved. I could finish high school there, and two years of college. She would see to the arrangements. It was settled.

From that point on, the romance began to grip me: military school, a uniform, the cavalry. . . . It was a chance to escape, to leave behind the bland face of Wichita, to construct my manhood free of confining Kansas. I would become a cavalier astride his charger, and when I returned to Wichita everyone would envy me for the warrior I had become and the worlds that I had seen, and that they, in their Kansas blinkers, could not even imagine.

"So you're leaving," Bobby Harrison said a few days later. "Sounds swell."

I admitted that it did.

"You wanna celebrate?"

We walked to the legger's. The Olds slouched at the back. He appeared in his garters and long face, a Lucky in his lips, looking annoyed to see us.

"You going to Oklahoma?" I couldn't resist asking as he handed us the swill. The legger squinted at me.

"So am I," I went on. "To military school."

"He's gonna join the cavalry, ride a big horse," Bobby added.

The legger grunted, with relief it seemed to me, and took my money. He gave me a long, dry look, tinged slightly with regret. "Don't fall off," he said, dragging on the Lucky. "S'bad for your health."

Chukkers

Oklahoma Military Academy, near Claremore, was a bastion of the old army. It worshiped the values of nineteenth-century warfare and informed them only slightly with the lessons of the twentieth. It was a West Point of the prairie with a righteous love for American military tradition embodied in the horse.

Discipline was strict, and adherence to the honor system was obligatory. This system was meant to teach loyalty to the institution above all, imposing on the cadet a responsibility to report dishonesty and rule violations. But it was shadowed by another, unwritten honor code that mandated loyalty to fellow cadets. Under this shadow code the upperclassmen preyed on plebes, searching out the least excuse to use the "board of education," a two-by-four applied to the backside.

I was not used to such treatment, but the renegade in me determined not to break. It was a will reinforced by my loneliness. I had never been away from home before, I knew no one at OMA, and I made friends with difficulty. In my first year I was crowded into a bunk-bed dorm with a hundred other cadets; there was no privacy and little time to myself. If I was to survive I would have to adjust quickly, and I accepted the new system as a challenge to prove that I could take it as well as anyone. That challenge soon took on a human form.

He was a senior, a huge Osage Indian named Victor White-law. His size and fearlessness had earned him a position of authority among the cadets, and he exploited it regally. A native of Oklahoma, he resented interlopers, which included whites in general and out-of-staters in particular. With my stocky frame and will to succeed he must have feared me as a competitor, for he took an instant dislike to me. "You're mine, Ramsey," he warned me one day, apropos of nothing.

Conflict meant demerits, which I was determined to avoid, and so I resisted his taunts as long as I could. But at last the inevitable confrontation came.

"Ramsey!" he barked to me one day in a corridor outside of class. I shot to attention, as the rules required.

Whitelaw looked me up and down disapprovingly and offered several insults regarding my appearance and demeanor, each of which he asked me to confirm.

I was used to it, and I merely snapped, "Yes, sir!" looking straight ahead.

There was a pause, and Whitelaw eased himself around behind me.

"I understand your sister's a flier," he said slowly. I felt myself begin to tremble. He leaned closer to my ear. I could hear the malicious leer in his voice. "How about it, Ramsey . . . you think she'd take me up for a ride?"

I pressed my lips together, trying to master my anger.

"Well, Ramsey?" Whitelaw said.

"No, sir," I answered quietly.

He stepped around and pressed his face into mine. "What's that?" he asked in a tone of threat and triumph.

"No, sir."

"Oh, and why not?"

I looked him in the eyes. "Because you're a goddamn son of a bitch, sir."

Whitelaw smiled faintly. "I told you that you were mine," he said.

He called me up before the upperclass discipline committee, an informal—if not illegal—affair, which met in the boiler room of the seniors' dormitory, and accused me of insubordination. The committee duly found me guilty, and Whitelaw took the board and beat my backside until it bled. As the rules required, I left in silence.

Word of the beating—or rather, of its severity—reached the commandant, and he summoned me to his office. He made it clear that such conduct was unmilitary, and he asked that I identify the cadet who had beaten me. I refused, both from pride and because to do so would have violated the unofficial honor code of the cadets.

The commandant made a tight, rueful face. "I understand what you're doing, Ramsey," he said. "Loyalty is an admirable thing, but the military is run by rules. When somebody breaks those rules, everyone suffers. I'm not asking this for you personally; I'm asking for the good of the corps."

It was my first encounter with the conflicting demands of regulations and revenge, the competing obligations of the officer and the injured self. I kept silent.

"Very well," the commandant sighed. "I'm not going to order you to answer. However, if you expect to be a leader, you're going to have to learn that you have a responsibility higher than yourself. You're not in this alone, Ramsey: What you do affects all of us, because we're all in the same fight."

I brooded over it all the next day. To do nothing was unthinkable. Inaction would make me vulnerable, and besides, it was not in my nature to suffer an insult in silence. Yet an open conflict with Victor Whitelaw was also out of the question. I had agreed to live by the rules of the academy, and like it or not, I also had to live with Victor. The commandant, I realized, was right: I had an obligation as an officer. But I also had one to my pride.

That evening I reached a decision. After mess I went alone to the prairie behind the stables. There, on maneuvers the day before, I had seen a dead rattlesnake. I searched in the moonlight until I found it, a lengthy, rigid thing, and stuffed it into a sack. Then, while the upperclassmen preened at the sinks, I sneaked into their barracks, slipped the snake into Victor Whitelaw's bunk, and withdrew.

The explosion could be heard in our dorm across the parade ground. I was later solemnly assured by his bunkmates that Victor nearly died of a heart attack. He too was summoned before the commandant and, in his turn, declined to name his tormentor. But everyone knew who had done it, and from that moment my reputation among the cadets was secure. I had bested an upperclassman without breaking the code: I had balanced honor and revenge. The other plebes began looking up to me as a leader, and I found myself making friends. What was more, Victor Whitelaw never interfered with me again.

It was at OMA that I learned properly to ride. Our bible was the cavalry's two-volume *Horsemanship and Horsemastership*. It taught me how to train the horse and train myself and then the two of us together until we were a unit. There were days of drill, mounted and dismounted; we learned animal care and weaponry and covered the rolling countryside with our lightning maneuvers.

I was training as an officer as well. I studied military history and science, the handling of weapons and of men. Cavalry officers were expected to take the van, to set the direction and the pace. It was a role that fit my character, with some modifications. I learned that individuality was an asset but that willfulness was not. Willingness to take risks was rewarded, but foolhardiness was punished. And though the history of the cavalry was steeped in romance, its work was as pragmatic as I had set myself to be.

Nonetheless, I absorbed into my brain and blood and bones the spirit of the cavalry. The cavalry was elite, the crown of the service. Its history was the schema of the nation. The cavalry had been born in the Revolution, opened the frontier, fused the Union, and conquered the West. America was made on horseback, carved by mounted soldiers; our identity as a people was dictated from the saddle.

For the military, cavalry was mobility, shock, and speed; it was firepower compounded with flesh, the commingled flesh and fury of man and mount. There were no equals, only followers, for the cavalry was always first, the cutting edge of steel and spirit. Youngbloods sought the same spirit in airplanes; the more sluggish, in armor. But all of them envied the horsemen, and we were they.

We knew we were better than anyone; we understood that we had to be better. We had to have the dash to get in ahead of everyone else, the discipline to do our job, and the brains to get out alive. And because we moved faster and farther than the rest of the army, we had to think faster and farther than them too. The lead belonged to us by right; we brought on the battle, and what followed did so in our dust.

Our elitism extended even to the afterlife. As cadets we were taught the tradition of Fiddler's Green, the meadow on the borders of hell reserved for the souls of troopers. The legend was conveyed from one generation of cavalrymen to the next in a poem that was as artless in its verse as it was grim in its message. While the foot soldiers trudged to the inferno, troopers would get a last drink and a final visit with friends on Fiddler's Green.

"When horse and man go down/Beneath a sabre keen," the poem concluded, "And the hostiles come to get your scalp/Just empty your canteen/And put your pistol to your head/And go to Fiddler's Green." The cavalryman never surrendered. This was an idea that appealed to me and to my own half-formed character.

Our professor of Military Science and Tactics at OMA was a square-faced, gruff-voiced cavalryman of the old school, Colonel Glenn S. Finley, and he trained us to the tradition. An army without horses was obscenity to him, as it became to us—fight without flourish, combat without *anima,* the animal soul. So long as there was a nation there would be an army, and so long as an army, there would be a cavalry, and the cavalry, Finley taught, was horse and man and pride.

Colonel Finley was a strict, paternal teacher, shaping our characters as much with regulations as with a carefully guarded concern. The plebes were terrified of his outbursts and scowls, but the upperclassmen referred to him as Uncle Glenn. Colonel Finley was a fixture at OMA, and he brought not only pride to his cadets, he brought polo.

I had never been much of a sportsman, and I viewed the prospect of polo with a disdain informed by ignorance. What kind of game was this, to chase a ball with hammers and a horse? And how to take seriously a sport measured out in "chukkers"? It was a pastime for snobs, the plaything of the idle rich.

Colonel Finley recruited me for the team. I was by now becoming an expert horseman, and by reputation a rough customer. I had developed the upperclassman's stern demeanor, and my teenage stockiness had turned solid. I took risks, some of them ridiculous, to test myself. I slid down rubble cliff faces a hundred yards sheer, forcing the horse back onto his haunches, balancing myself in the stirrups. I took jumps at full gallop that should have broken the horse's back and mine. But I could ride formation as well as anyone, stirrup to stirrup at a jaunty trot. Colonel Finley knew it even if I did not: Polo was the game I was made for.

The ostensible reason for schooling us in the sport was to sharpen our equestrian skills, improve our teamwork, and hone our spirit of competition. But inescapably the game was also an outlet for our pure unbridled verve.

For me polo was the perfect blend of my native recklessness and the discipline I was acquiring. It meant teamwork, control, and a careful regard for the rules, but it also entailed risk, danger, and a headlong disregard for consequences. Hearing about the broken bones and the fact that two cadets had been killed in matches fueled my interest; I devoted myself to a full year of mastering the sport.

By my second year at OMA, I was on the team, and by my last, 1937, I was playing varsity Three. Of the four-man team, Three plays the pivot, by turns aggressor and defense, the chief handler of the ball. When the opponent has the ball, Three joins Four in the defense, pulling back, guarding goal, looking for an opportunity to steal and drive. On offense, Three maneuvers the ball downfield with Two, creating an opening for One, who leads the charge.

The charge is the epitome of the game. In our military training we had learned to shoot pistols from horseback, hitting at a gallop targets that infantry strained at prone. And we had rehearsed the ancient arts of saber play, the slash and stab, the wrist-breaking lunge and disengage. But polo concentrated the charge upon that scudding sphere, a melee of mallet shafts and legs, tons of headlong horses and men pounding the air, pounding the earth, pounding at one another.

I loved polo as surely as I loved horses, and because I loved horses. I was never a top player, but I was a devoted one. Polo became my passion, and when I graduated from OMA after three years, it determined my decision. I enrolled in the law school of Oklahoma University. The law was largely incidental; OU had a polo team.

My mother, meanwhile, had been building her career. Her business had flourished, and her reputation for innovation had spread throughout the state. She was appointed by the governor as the first president of the Kansas State Board of Cosmetologists, and within a few years she had been elected president of the National Association of Cosmetologists.

More than her own success, however, Mother valued my transformation. I was a successful graduate with a bachelor's degree, a reserve officer in the army, and a law student. I discreetly kept her unaware of the fact that I spent most of my time playing polo and chasing women. The latter interfered with my grades, which were average. Though I had completed half of my studies, I still had not chosen a specialization. In fact, most of the law simply bored me. I gave little thought to my career, and supposed I would join a firm in some city or work for the government. Of wider concerns I remained steadfastly unaware.

War had finally broken out in Europe, a fact that neither surprised nor animated me. From my boyhood I had been a staunch conservative, and I regarded Roosevelt and the New Dealers with the same disdain that I reserved for the isolationists and the appeasers. The Fascists, however, I viewed with alarm.

There was a German exchange student enrolled at OU, a strident Nazi of the Hitler Youth, and his incessant tirades infuriated and disgusted me. Some of my friends and I had tried at first to debate with him, but ideology made him immune to reason. My experience of him confirmed my belief that only the threat of massive force could hold tyrants in check, and in this, I felt, the free world was woefully failing. Weakness had made war inevitable; we could only hope that the oceans would keep it away.

☆ ☆ ☆

By September of my last year of law, Nadine had declared her decision to make her living as a flyer. Mother took the announcement calmly. What was harder for her was Nadine's insistence that there were no opportunities for fliers in Kansas: She would move to California. It was a heartfelt blow. Though she was a busy, prominent career woman, Mother had never been without her family. Now she faced the prospect of living alone. But, understanding that Nadine's ambition could no more be restrained than her own, she helped her prepare, and gave her the means to establish herself on the Coast.

Within a few months, Nadine was working as a stunt and racing pilot in California and had become the first woman to fly the air mail. She was rapidly making a name for herself and hobnobbing with film stars and the leading aviatrices. Her courage was unshakable, even brash. She would fly the mail through snowstorms with the same aplomb she displayed in aerobatics. She was a popular, robust, irrepressible girl with restless auburn hair and the flaming, red-lipped smile that marked the sportswomen of the day.

With her growing celebrity, Nadine was soon asked to represent a line of airplanes. On a sparkling San Diego morning in 1940 she took a potential buyer up over the bay for a spin. The passenger asked Nadine to buzz his home.

Nadine threw the plane into a dive, gathering speed, and swooped in low over the housetop. The passenger was delighted.

"Go round again," he said.

She whipped through a turn and tore back, pulled up slightly to avoid some trees, and nosed in.

It happened in an instant. A downdraft seized the little plane and shoved it, and it clattered into the trees. Fabric ripped away, the engine went spinning with a thud into the house, the tail fin crumpled, legs twisted off, nearly severed.

Nadine, splayed among the branches, never cried.

"Ramsey, telephone!" one of the students yelled down the dorm corridor. It was September, the start of polo season, and I was looking forward to a semester filled with horseplay. I grabbed the receiver. It was Mother.

"Buddy," she said, steadying her voice, "there's been an accident."

For me, the polo, and the law that went with it, were over.

Remounting

It took me four days to drive from Kansas to California in Mother's aging Chrysler. She had intended to go herself, but I had talked her out of it. Her prominence in the National Association of Cosmetologists had prompted two Swiss doctors to travel to Kansas to train her in the new science of dermatology. It would not be, I realized, a good time for her to leave. Instead, I promised to call her as soon as I saw Nadine.

I had no idea what I would find, except that Nadine was said to be near death. After the crash, she and her passenger had been taken to a hospital in San Diego, where doctors had removed one of the passenger's legs and had decided to take off one of Nadine's as well.

A friend of hers, a movie actor, heard of the crash on the radio and rushed to the hospital. Claiming that he spoke for the family, he had refused permission for the amputation. Instead, he had Nadine transferred to Los Angeles, where a friend of his, a famous surgeon, managed to save the leg.

She was still critical by the time I arrived. "She's in bad shape," her doctor said as he led me to the room.

"Will she live?"

"Only if she wants to."

He pushed open the door and I entered the room. There were flowers everywhere, and the stifling smell of alcohol and bandages. Nadine lay on her back, her eyes closed. Her face was bruised and lacerated almost beyond recognition, and I winced to look at her. Her back was broken, as were most of her ribs, she had several concussions, and her left leg was wound in a tube of bandages from her foot to her thigh. She groaned occasionally and twisted her neck, the alternating tides of pain and morphine tossing her back and forth from shock to stupor.

The sight of her stunned me. She had always been graceful, athletic, and defiantly self-sustaining. Now she was scarcely recognizable, either as my sister or the combative spirit I knew. I stepped to the bed and told her quietly hello.

She looked at me, her dark brown eyes clouded by morphine, struggling to remember me. At last she gripped my hand on the iron bedrail.

"Oh, Buddy," she whispered, and tears came into her eyes. I asked how she felt.

"I don't want to live," she moaned. "I know I'll never fly again, and if I can't fly I won't live."

Her doctor, also a pilot, told her it was not so. "You'll both live and fly," he scolded her, "but only if you make up your mind to it." I promised I would stay with her as long as it took to get her back on her feet, as long as it took to get her back into the air.

"She's going to need a lot of nursing," the doctor said to me outside. "It won't be easy. Are you up to it?"

I told him that I supposed I was. Nadine and I had been through a lot together; we had a conspiratorial strength against adversity.

"She's a tough customer," the doctor continued. "Otherwise she wouldn't be alive. What happens now is up to her, and you."

I moved into Nadine's apartment on the beach at Playa del Rey and phoned Mother. I assured her that Nadine would live, but that it might be a year, maybe more, until she was well again.

"I'm withdrawing from law school," I told her. "She's going to need me to look after her."

"I'll come out," Mother said. "You go back and finish school."

I told her no. She would soon qualify as a dermatologist, and I convinced her that Nadine and I would need the money from her practice to support us through her convalescence. Reluctantly, she agreed.

Nadine came home after a few weeks and began the long process of recovery. But she was a total invalid, and it was a difficult business for us. I was a bachelor and unused to cooking, cleaning, and shopping. Nor was I a nurse, and learning the profession caused anguish to us both. Every movement, no matter how practiced, fired her with pain. The dressings on her leg had to be changed continuously, and my having to wash her and clean after her was as wearing on her ego as on mine.

That ego, which we shared, sustained us. Through the difficult days with Father, we had developed the habit of supporting each other. And through all our battles we had emerged victorious, not just from pride but from spite as well, for neither of us wanted to be the first to surrender. It was a strength born of a deep hurt that we had suffered together, expressed in a determination to preserve each other against the odds. Neither of us would let the other go down, but in the process we spared each other nothing in the way of anger and stubbornness.

"Why are you putting me through this?" she would yell at me.

"You?" I hollered back. "How about me? Do you think this is any easier on me?"

"You should have let me die when I wanted to!"

"Well, I'm damned if I do," I railed. "I'm going to get you back into a plane if I have to drag you by the hair." It was harsh, even cruel, but her spirit, like my own, I knew, needed to be prodded to defiance.

By Christmas she was walking again—to spite me, she said—and by the end of January 1941, she could care for herself. There was still a lumbrous cast on her leg, but she was already making plans to fly.

"Are you sure?" I taunted her.

"Just get me to the plane," she snapped. "I'll do the rest."

On a gray February afternoon I drove her to an airfield on the coast. It was early morning, and no one was around. I helped her from the car to where a little monocoupe was waiting, and with an effort she fitted herself, cast and all, into the cockpit. I stood back and watched the engine sputter to life. Nadine taxied onto the runway, turned her wings into the wind, and took off. She was whole again.

For me there was the problem of what to do. It was far too late in the academic year to return to law school, and Kansas had nothing to offer. I was virtually broke, living at my sister's, supported by money from Mother, with no immediate prospects and no skills except those I had learned at military school. Under normal circumstances I could have waited until fall and finished my studies, but the circumstances no longer were normal.

For years I had watched the policy of appeasement in Europe with dismay, while the Nazis jawed the continent piecemeal and the liberals in Washington blinkered their eyes. Now the war in Europe had been on for over a year, and though it seemed a distant, grudging storm, I was sure that we would be drawn within it. Even if I returned to OU in September, with my reserve commission in the cavalry I would probably be yanked out again. And so I traveled to the federal building in downtown Los Angeles and applied for active duty.

I was posted as second lieutenant to the second squadron of the Eleventh Cavalry Regiment, which was based at Camp Moreno in the mountains above San Diego. With my horsemanship skills I was assigned as remount officer, in charge of training both the draftees and unbroken mounts that were filtering into the camp from across the country.

Preparing such raw material for war was hard work but welcome to me, for it meant whole days of breaking and training horses. There was no polo, but the Eleventh had a show jumping team, which I quickly joined. I was keen for competition and savored the skill, but I missed the aggressiveness and risk of polo.

The life of the old cavalry was unique to itself. We wore riding breeches and high boots, and our round campaign hats were tilted at a meaningful rake across one eye, the strap stretched beneath the chin. I was twenty-three years old, proud and invincible. With two fellow lieutenants I raced almost daily over the hills, vaulting barriers and sliding sheer drops. Then, in the evenings, we trained our mounts in the delicate arts of dressage, urging them through intricate patterns with invisible shiftings of our hands, legs, and weight.

Our socializing was raucous, and suited to my earlier self. We cavalrymen prided ourselves on drinking harder than any other branch, and our drunks were always sodden with song. Often after retreat in camp we climbed the easy slope to the El Cortez Hotel overlooking San Diego Bay, where the better class of women went to dance to the bands.

From the Sky Room the view floated beneath the music. Coronado Island was ringed with the running lights of a hundred riding ships, while beyond, the biplanes rose and dipped above the shimmering V of the naval station runways. We drank and joked and circled the ballroom floor with women we suddenly adored and never saw again.

When the sin in San Diego was exhausted, we hopped the border to Tijuana, a town devoted to debauch. Bars and brothels sprawled among the souvenir shops, some with a clutch of broken tables and bored girls, others glittering with light and a hundred grinning women. On Sundays we crowded the *corridas*, not to watch the sport but purely for Conchita Cintron.

One of the few female bullfighters in the world, she was splendid in her sequined, skintight *traje* and eighteen years. She fought on foot with bravado, coaxing and caressing the bulls, then leaning back her head, her hair wound sternly, and glowing at the crowd.

But on horse she was a marvel. She floated above the bull

on a mount that seemed an extension of her haughty, sinewed self, responding to her slightest touch—her thoughts, it seemed to us—with gentle sideways steppings or a sudden, potent lunge. She fought her lance and sword with a grace that made us self-conscious of the brutish weight of our sabers and the dumb, utilitarian lumps that were our .45s. Señorita Cintron was cavalier; we were merely cavalry.

By this time, however, the cavalry was changing. Most regiments had lost their horses and been converted to motor vehicles. The Eleventh was one of the few that had kept their mounts, and I, for one, had no desire to surrender mine for a halftrack or a tank. That and polo were the reasons why, in April of 1941, just before my twenty-fourth birthday, I volunteered for transfer to the Philippine Scouts.

I knew nothing of the Philippines—nor of the Pacific, for that matter—but we all had heard that the Twenty-sixth Cavalry, Philippine Scouts, was the country club of the army. The Scouts had a reputation as tough, flamboyant fighters, and the Twenty-sixth for having the best polo team in the service. They were Filipino regulars officered by Americans, and they bore proudly a long tradition stretching back to Black Jack Pershing and America's turn-of-the-century imperialism. Most of the leading cavalry officers of the day had served with the Twenty-sixth and had played on its polo team. I jumped at the chance.

In fact, it was a blind leap. Wholly unaware of the gravity of the situation in the Philippines at that time, I was, like most Americans, not even sure where the islands were. When I mentioned this jokingly to the officer who processed my transfer request, he replied with pointed gravity: "They're damn near Japan."

For years the Japanese had been edging toward the Philippines, which Japan's new war minister, Hideki Tojo, considered "a pistol aimed at the heart of Japan." By 1941, Japan had completed its conquest of Manchuria and occupied the Chinese mainland ports, signed a defense pact with Germany and Italy, and compelled the defeated French to cede their naval bases in Southeast Asia. The Philippines were flanked by Japanese naval power, shadowed by their air force, and within a few days' journey of troop transports.

In late 1940 President Roosevelt had ordered home the families of American servicemen and diplomats; if war broke out, it was feared that the Philippines would be the first and hardest hit. Now the army was accepting only bachelor officers. These were facts that meant nothing to me as I prepared my gear, imagining myself in an exotic post rich with tropical plants and polo ponies, fawning servants and dusky women.

On June 5, I reported to the Presidio in San Francisco, my port of embarkation. The following morning I shipped out aboard the *President Pierce*, a retired liner that had been refitted as a troop transport. The bulging ship held fifteen hundred officers, three thousand enlisted men, and a dozen nurses, and it throbbed the long way to Hawaii with horny high spirits.

I spent the long days on deck wedged in among poker and crap games. This was a new experience for me—and a costly one, for by the time we reached Honolulu I had to hock my pistol in order to enjoy the half-day leave. I was overcome by the tropics. After the dry years in Wichita and Oklahoma, this was an Eden.

I stood at the bar of Trader Vic's, the waterfall rustling behind me, and drank in the colors and fragrance. There were delicate parasols on pastel drinks, and silken prints on the bodies of the women. People of every color and type converged there, milling busily among the hundreds of khaki uniforms. One man in particular, well dressed with a foreign accent, was cordial to us, buying us drink after drink and asking us earnestly about ourselves. Where had we come from? On what ship? How many of us were there, and bound for where?

It was a shadow, I realized, a hint of darkness amid the dazzling glint. Was he a spy? Was his hospitality a trap, were his drinks a weapon, and were his questions not idle but aimed at killing us?

I could not shrug the suspicion, and on my way out, returning to the ship, I reported the man to an MP. For the rest of the night, as the *President Pierce* pulled away from the islands, I felt uneasy, nagged by an indefinable sense that the tropics might be more complex than I had thought, that beneath the exoticism there might, indeed, be danger.

We rounded a point of land and I glanced back across the widening dark sea. There, busy under the night sky, were the lights of Pearl Harbor and its bastion of battleships hulking in neat rows. The sight was reassuring, and as we steamed on toward Manila, eleven days away, I felt easier. There might be danger, but America was a power in the Pacific, a power that no one could challenge with impunity. As for myself, I was not looking for trouble. I was going to play polo.

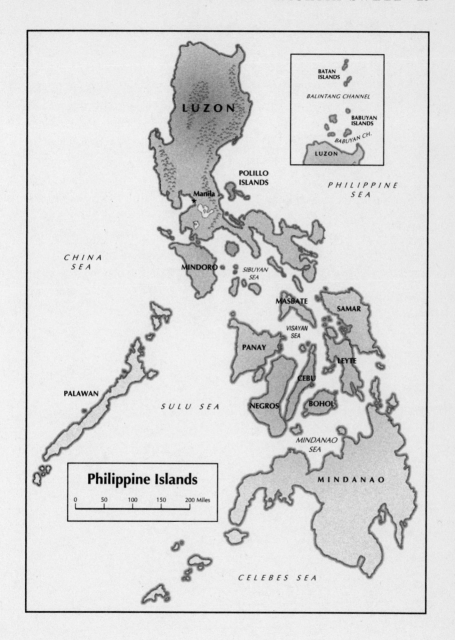

Philippine Islands

PHILIPPINE
SCOUT

1941–1942

MEDAL ON PRECEDING PAGE:
Gold Cross (PHILIPPINE)

Stotsenberg

On June 22, 1941, the *President Pierce* steamed into the Straits of San Bernardino. We had watched impatiently all day as the land drew nearer, and we could scent the sweet smell upon the air. Suddenly there was tufted green everywhere, rising coyly from the azure ocean, a hundred islands dense with coconut palms, limned with white beaches, their coves bobbing with the bancas of fishermen. We shouted to them and waved, and they hallooed back, smiling. Then as we turned into the Philippine Sea, the islands slid by one by one, their names a pagan chant: Samar, Masbate, Romblon, Marinduque, Mindoro, and finally Luzon.

It was night by the time we made the turn into Manila Bay, the peninsula of Bataan on our left, the rocky buttresses of Corregidor guarding the bay's broad mouth. Straight ahead through the warm darkness I could see the lights of Manila. It would be a few more hours until we landed, so I went below deck to sleep.

I awoke at dawn to the ship being shoved by tugs against the pier. I hurried on deck, where hundreds of soldiers were scrambling into their uniforms and stuffing their duffels. The air was heavy with the morning moisture of the rainy season, and the city gleamed beneath it. It was larger than I had expected, and much more modern. There was bustle everywhere, and the characters who swarmed around the docks seemed collected from every part of the world.

High-rise buildings, houses, and clustered tenements stretched from the harbor to the jungle slopes beyond. To the

north, vast fish ponds had been carved from the swamps, while
to the east and south, a blue-green ridge of mountains capped
with volcanoes ringed the city. The whole prospect was exotic
and exhilarating, from the jungle slopes with their rising mists,
to the city glittering beneath the fervid June sun, to the bay
busy with ships, and beyond, the knarled thumb of Bataan with
its twin volcano knuckles.

Host officers were waiting for us as we disembarked. Those
of us who were assigned to the Twenty-sixth Cavalry were
loaded onto trucks and driven to the Army-Navy Club a few
blocks from the pier. The club, founded half a century before by
Admiral George Dewey, was a relic of American imperialism.
High-ceilinged lounges were cooled by languid turning fans,
Filipino waiters in white waistcoats served drinks, and huge
windows were pulled back to admit the bay breeze and frame
the blazing sunset into the China Sea. Opposite the club, across
the Luneta, the old Spanish execution site, stood the Manila
Hotel, whose fourth floor served as the quarters of General
Douglas MacArthur, commander of the U.S. Army Forces in
the Far East, and friend and military aide to Philippine president Manuel Quezon.

We had all heard of MacArthur: top of his class at West
Point, World War I hero, the youngest army chief of staff in
history. His father had been military governor of the islands,
which were still an American protectorate, and the general had
been sent in 1935 by President Roosevelt to implement a ten-
year plan for their defense. That plan had progressed sluggishly, slowed by tendentious tides of American isolationism
and Philippine agitation for independence. The result was that
by mid 1941 the islands were woefully underdefended and their
strategic position misunderstood by everyone except the Japanese.

After lunch and an orientation by a colonel of the Twenty-
sixth Cavalry, we reboarded the trucks for the drive to Fort
Stotsenberg. Stotsenberg lay in the foothills of the Zambales
Mountains, seventy-five miles to the northwest of Manila. It was

the major military post protecting Central Luzon, a plain the size of England that stretched between two mountain ranges from Lingayen Gulf in the north down to Manila Bay. In 1941 it was the headquarters of the Twenty-sixth Cavalry and the site of Clark Field, a concatenation of biplanes and aging bombers.

The officers' quarters, which formed one side of the parade ground, were airy, one-story bungalows built on stilts above the humid earth. The walls were large screens that could be shuttered against the typhoons that swept the area, while the roofs slanted low beyond them for shade, and to shed heat and the heavy rains. Opposite were the barracks of the troopers, some seven hundred fifty men, and the stables. At the west end of the parade ground stood the bungalow that served as post headquarters. The east end of the parade ground was reserved as the polo field.

Our life at the fort was that of the old colonial army. We had servants who lived in the back of the house and acted as our cooks and cleaners, and each officer was assigned an orderly who attended to his horse. Our commanding general enforced the imperial image strictly. We were required to wear the old-fashioned, high-collared white mess jacket in the evenings, and we had to shower and change uniforms twice a day. I was surprised to find that most of the officers wore beards. It was, they explained, a vow they had made when their wives and families were repatriated—not to shave until they were reunited.

It was not until I reached Stotsenberg that I realized how close the war might be. Conversation inevitably turned to the Japanese, and the radio daily carried reports of their seizures of Indochinese bases. There was continual, lively debate over the best strategy for dealing with the threat. The dominant feeling was that the Japanese would not risk an invasion of the Philippines, and that America would never permit it. I was inclined to agree, though I argued that only a strong defense would deter adventurism, and that clearly this was not present in Luzon.

Still, war remained no more than a vague, intrusive presence, a feeling rather than an idea, which we did our best to ignore. Each evening after dinner the officers' club filled up with laughter and singing, and later, when the bar had closed, we strolled beneath the giant acacias, chatting quietly about our own affairs, while the dama-de-noche cloyed gardenia scent and the stars shone clear and cold like diamonds upon the night sky.

But that war was coming closer was clear—to MacArthur and his superiors, if not to us. Our regiment was under an intense training schedule, and I was thrown immediately into it. On the morning after my arrival I reported to the stables and was assigned my charger: Bryn Awryn, a chestnut gelding, fifteen and a half hands high, with a small white blaze on his forehead. He was a powerful, well-schooled mount, and I recognized in him at once an able polo pony.

I was assigned as a platoon leader of Troop G, Second Squadron, commanded by Captain John Fowler, a quiet, reserved career officer in his mid twenties. Troop G consisted of a sergeant, a corporal, and twenty-five privates, all Filipinos. My duties were to train them in mounted and dismounted drill and in combat tactics, and I found working with them a delight.

Though Congress had recently authorized a strengthening of the regiment and new recruits were arriving daily, the average length of service in the Twenty-sixth was thirteen years. This meant that the men were disciplined and highly skilled, and even the recruits responded to their officers with unhesitating obedience. The Twenty-sixth was the elite regiment; everyone knew it, and we all were anxious and proud to serve in it.

Our mornings were busy with mounted drill and maneuvers. There was a rigid physical conditioning program for both men and animals, and accelerated training in rapid deployment. This meant hours of practice loading the men and mounts onto trucks, driving long distances, disembarking, and galloping into action supported by our machine-gun crews.

We trained with blank ammunition at first, to accustom the animals to the noise, and then with live rounds. We also practiced the charge, thundering across the muggy Luzon plains, whooping and firing our .45s. No American cavalry unit had charged on horses since the Pancho Villa expedition in Mexico forty years before. But the charge was the ultimate weapon of cavalry, and we worked at it until we could unleash it on an instant at full fury.

We were by far the best-trained and most professional combat unit among the Philippine defense forces, yet that a *mounted* unit should be the backbone was an index of the impoverishment of our strategy. Cavalry might be useful in the rugged foothills that flanked Luzon's central plain, but its flat, open expanses were an invitation to tanks and artillery. It was a lesson that had been carved from the flesh of men and mounts in France in World War I. Yet in the Philippines, cavalry remained the elite, held in place by tradition and untested by modern war.

Every afternoon, the officers would conference at the fort to discuss the day's performance. We would critique ourselves and make adjustments and plans for the next morning's training. Then we would adjourn to classes in Tagalog, the principal native dialect.

I chafed at this. I had never been an avid student, and the hours of repetition and mouthing syllables that sounded gibberish to me were almost unbearable. Still, it was anticipated that most of our action would occur in the countryside, and some of its inhabitants, particularly the tiny, reclusive Negrito tribesmen, spoke no English.

Occasionally we were briefed on the wider military situation, which I found encouraging though not sanguine. Our own forces in the Philippines comprised some thirty thousand regular troops, American and Filipino, and MacArthur had been authorized to raise a native militia of eighty thousand. These men, however, had had no military training and were scarcely equipped. Most had never seen a rifle and few possessed even uniforms. Yet our adversary, if there were to be a war, would be the Imperial Japanese Army, five million strong, a veteran force of four years of fighting on the Asian mainland.

Preparations to defend the islands had accelerated during the previous year, but the fear was that the effort had begun too late. MacArthur planned to defend the entire archipelago, over seven thousand islands, with the main defenses to be located on Luzon. Here, he felt, the Japanese were most likely to strike, landing at Lingayen Gulf in the north and sweeping down the central plain toward Manila. Their objective would be to seize Manila Bay, the most important harbor in the Southwest Pacific. If such an assault were to come, MacArthur told Washington, he was sure it would not be launched before April 1942.

To familiarize us with the terrain, we were flown in B-17 bombers up the central plain to the gulf and south over Manila, Manila Bay, and Bataan. Bataan was, I could see from the air, a formidable place, buttressed by two volcanoes, its narrow mouth constricted by the southern slopes of the Zambales Mountains.

Even more formidable, however, were the twin mountain ranges framing the plain. They were steep and dense and choked with jungle—impassable, it seemed to me, as I gazed down at them through the Plexiglas nose of the bomber. Between them the plain was a broad funnel issuing onto Manila. The logic of an invasion was obvious, as MacArthur understood: land at Lingayen, drive down the plain to Manila, and seize the bay from within.

But it was unthinkable, I told myself, as we circled back across the bay toward Manila, whose whitewashed buildings and red rooftops shone under the morning sun. It was impossible to imagine this place gripped by war, the plain with its villages and rice paddies trampled by tens of thousands of troops, Manila under fire. Surely the world could not change so violently. Japan would not attempt it; America would not allow it.

On our weekends, which were free, we drove down to Manila. Three hundred years of Spanish influence and forty years of American had made it an eclectic, exciting metropolis. Broad boulevards were lined with palm trees and handsome villas. Next to these were sprawling Chinese districts, and in their shadow the neat neighborhoods of American homes. The streets were always busy, the activity driven by the youth of thousands of soldiers, along with the Filipinos' native elan.

Being cavalrymen we sought out the sin, and there was no shortage of it. Gambling houses abounded, crowded with Asians hollering over mah-jongg, jueteng, and pan, slapping tiles and cards and money onto the smoky tables. There were bars of every kind and class, and bordellos warmed the side streets with their welcoming red lights.

Our favorite haunt was the La Playa, a bar and restaurant run by a syndicate of American gamblers from Shanghai. Its ample back room was devoted to Las Vegas–style gambling, and the craps, blackjack, and roulette tables were always crowded with Americans and Filipinos. One evening in October, after shooting craps for several unfruitful hours, I strolled out into the bar for a drink.

My squadron commander, Major Jim Blanning, was chatting at the bar with several Filipinos in stylish white tropical suits and white oxfords with spats. Instinctively I headed for the dance floor, but no sooner had I reached it than I heard Blanning and the Filipinos arguing. Suddenly one of them hefted his glass and smashed it into Blanning's face. The glass shattered, and the shards splayed across his head and shoulders.

I was the nearest American and so I leapt in, grabbed the Filipino, and swung at his jaw. He dropped with a grunt. I seized Blanning's shirtfront, which was soaked with blood, and shoved him toward a group of Americans at the end of the bar. As I turned again toward the white suits, I caught the flash of a soda-water bottle slicing through the air. It crashed against my head, sending me sprawling across a table.

I pushed myself up, shook my head to clear it, and pressed a palm to my temple. It came away smeared with blood. By now the bar was in an uproar, Americans and Filipinos squaring off against one another.

Buttressed by the melee I hoisted a chair over my head and strode purposefully back toward the bar. As I did so, however, one of the white suits produced a revolver and pointed it at my chest. I halted, the chair poised above me, and glanced over my shoulder for support. The bar had fallen suddenly silent, and everyone was staring at the revolver. I too regarded it, carefully lowered the chair, and with something like a smile, backed away from the bar.

There was blood running down inside my collar now, and my eyes were glazing over. At that moment one of the owners appeared from the game room and in a booming voice ordered the white suits to leave or face the police. They did so, and I was taken to the men's room, where I was startled to see in the mirror blood pouring from a gash above my left ear. While they daubed at me with rum I asked about Jim Blanning and was told that he had been taken to the hospital.

"The glass just missed his eye," someone said.

"Gee," I heard myself reply, "that's swell," and I passed out.

I had the good fortune to be friends with a young officer from a wealthy New York family who owned a brand-new red Buick convertible. That car virtually assured us success with the ladies of the Manila clubs. It was through his Buick that I met Olga, a Russian dancer from Shanghai who was performing at one of the highbrow establishments.

Olga was small, beautiful, and mysterious. She spoke English with a honey-thick accent, and her apartment in the graceful old Malate district was a sanctum to me. I was overcome with her black eyes and snowy skin and the deep exoticism she breathed. We spent late nights together among the bars and the red plush cushions of her parlor. She cooed and swathed me in satin and incense and coaxed me to tell her all about myself. The Kansas boy in me withered, and I wafted with her among the heady scent of the East.

A few weeks after I met her, I was summoned to the office

of G-2, the intelligence section, at Stotsenberg. There, a narrow-faced captain informed me over rimless specs that Olga was believed to be a spy for the Japanese. I was warned to be careful and to stay away from her. I managed it for the next two weekends, but I knew I had to see her one more time.

I climbed into my friend's red Buick and motored to Manila, got out on the edge of Malate, and made my way by back alleys to Olga's. There were MPs posted at her door. I strolled by them, affecting indifference, but it hurt my pride and it left me feeling vulnerable and boyish.

This was not a lark, I scolded myself. I was an officer in a foreign post that was ringed by enemies whose agents were everywhere, having infiltrated even my own life. In Olga, the war, which had been so abstract, had suddenly become intimate, and I had blinded myself to the danger. As I made my way through the warren of back streets, overhung by wet wash and thick with the clamor of the poor, I swore to myself to forget Olga, but never the lesson she had taught me.

Polo season was upon us, and I allowed that to occupy my mind. Training began in September, with our first match scheduled for December. I put Bryn Awryn through his paces, and he did not disappoint me. He was clever and aggressive, and he quickly acquired the indispensable polo pony trait of turning on a dime. Soon I was playing Three and enjoying myself too much to think of Olga, or the war that her sultriness had portended.

Occasionally, however, it intervened. In November I was sent as officer courier with an urgent dispatch to army headquarters in North Luzon. Though the dispatch was secret and sealed, I learned that it ordered all forces in the province on standby alert. Almost every day reconnaissance aircraft were appearing overhead, and though officially they remained unidentified, we knew they were Japanese. In recent weeks two battalions of tanks had arrived from Texas and New Mexico to reinforce our regiment, and more fighters and bombers were being sent to Clark Field.

On the evening of December 1, I was sipping drinks with

the intelligence officer who had warned me about Olga, celebrating my promotion to first lieutenant.

"Are you religious?" the intelligence man asked suddenly.

"No, sir, not particularly," I replied. "Why?"

"Well," he drawled, as he got up to fetch another drink, "you'd better give your soul to God, Lieutenant, because your ass belongs to the Japanese."

TNT

For two months we had been practicing mightily for our opening match against the Manila Polo Club. The cool weather had arrived, presaging the dry season, and it was delightful to work the ponies in the brisk dawn air and evening shadows. Every spare minute beyond our duties was spent on the playing field, which ran between the rows of barracks from regimental headquarters to the parade ground. As we trained, the reports of Japanese overflights became so frequent that we scarcely took notice of them.

Our minds were concentrated on the match, which was scheduled for Sunday, December 7. The Manila Polo Club team had a worldwide reputation, and we worked diligently to ensure that, at the least, we would not be humiliated. The match was to be played on our grounds, before the entire regiment, with Lieutenant General Jonathan Wainwright as umpire. Wainwright, a tall, gaunt man in his forties, was commander of the North Luzon force and was himself an old cavalryman and polo player. We were not a great team, but a good one, consisting of myself and another officer of the Twenty-sixth, and two officers from the tank battalions, former cavalrymen who had been mechanized.

Sunday came crisply clear, wonderful weather for polo. The Manila team arrived in elegant sedans. They were wealthy Filipino businessmen, accompanied by their wives and children. As was the custom, we provided them with mounts, and we watched while they exercised, familiarizing themselves with the ponies, showing a near-professional skill and coordination. We would have to muscle them, we decided, if we were to stay in the game.

Bryn Awryn was in fine form, and seemed to sense the competition. Normally he was well mannered, but that morning he was alert as if for war. Wainwright took his place on the reviewing stand, a tall, grave man surrounded by a dozen generals and colonels. We formed line opposite the Manila team, and the referee threw in the ball. It was 2:00 P.M. Manila time: ten hours from dawn in Hawaii.

The Manila players were splendid. They handled the ball with the sure instinct of men who have played long together. We were far less able, missing cues and leaving openings that the other team pounded on. They scored several times in the first chukker, and we struggled to keep up. By the end of the second, they were far ahead, though we were not yet out of the game.

The third and fourth chukkers were hard fought. We pushed our ponies as far as we could, riding their shoulders down and under the opponents', scooping out the ball, spinning round and racing for the goal. We were soaked with sweat and straining, dust cladding to our white breeches and high boots, while hundreds of Filipino soldiers whooped and moaned, and cheered us when we scored.

General Wainwright kept the score, his face lean and imperturbable, more like a scholar monitoring a debate than a sportsman spectator. By the final whistle we had lost, but not outrageously. We shook hands with the Manila club men and turned our panting mounts over to the orderlies. After showering and changing into white dress uniforms we assembled at the commanding officers' quarters for a postmatch party.

The party was a raucous affair, ripe with liquor and the

slender Filipino girls who seemed always magically to appear. General Wainwright presided with a lean asceticism softened only vaguely by the bourbon. The rest of us drank and sang far into the dark, and somewhere around midnight I and another officer made off with two girls to the rice paddies. The next few hours were cool and comfortable with alcohol and the women. The day, meanwhile, had eased off across the ocean, bringing dawn to Pearl Harbor, and with it the Japanese fleet.

I was in my bunk at reveille next morning, though I could not recall having gotten there. Bleary and nursing a vicious hangover, I did not comprehend the tumult around me. As I made my way to the mess, soldiers were scurrying everywhere, dragging duffels, pulling on their pants, shouting so that my head rang carousel tunes. At the mess hall door I met the chaplain.

"What's going on, Reverend?" I asked.

"Don't you know?" he said. "Pearl Harbor's been hit. We're at war."

We all had expected it, but for so long that the expectation had become comfortable to us. Now the word shook me to my senses. America had been attacked; the Japanese were our enemy; I was a soldier at war.

My duffel was not even packed, so I dashed back to my quarters, joining the general commotion. There was an emptiness in the pit of my stomach, but my appetite had disappeared. I threw a few things together and hurried up the street to regimental headquarters. There General Wainwright was huddling with our CO while the officers assembled. Wainwright strode out as we stood to attention, and the CO began issuing orders.

Our troop, G, was to move to the village of Bongabong, some one hundred twenty miles to the northeast in the Sierra Madre foothills. There we were to relieve Captain Joe Barker's B Troop, which was to return to Stotsenberg. It was almost noon before we had the horses loaded onto the trailers and our truck convoy was ready to move. As we cleared the fort and turned onto the road toward Dao, the first wave of Japanese bombers roared in.

We ducked as they dived toward us, but their target was Clark Field, and they swooped in over our trucks and sped on. Then came the thudding explosions, flinging fireballs into the air and with them the smell of gasoline and sulphur. One after another the B-17s, which were being fueled and loaded with bombs, burst apart, flinging debris across the airfield, igniting the depots and hangars. The racket set our horses rustling in their trailers, and as we rolled away, we watched in silence while our air force was destroyed in roiling rows of flame.

It was sunset when we reached Bongabong. Captain John Fowler set up a command post in the town hall and began dispersing the troop. We expected an invasion at any moment, and though it was more likely to come from the west, there were two bays on the eastern slope of the Sierras that had to be defended. Accordingly, Fowler dispatched Lieutenant Cliff Hardwick with his platoon to Dingalen Bay to the southeast, then ordered my platoon to Baler Bay to the northeast. I was to take command of the local constabulary, organize a defense, and delay any invasion force for as long as possible.

It was a forlorn hope; I knew it as I set out. I had with me twenty-seven mounted Filipino troopers, two machine guns, and a staff car with a radio. I also took a dozen cases of TNT to blow the mountain bridges as we withdrew. The road to the coast twisted up a defile in the Sierras, and for the last fifty miles it was scarcely more than a jungle track, very steep, with bridges so narrow and frail that the trucks could only creep across one at a time.

We drove into the night, reaching the village of Baler after 3:00 A.M. We had been on the move for fifteen hours, and both men and horses were hungry, anxious, and out of sorts. I ordered the animals off-loaded and established a camp behind the town. At daybreak I sent the trucks back to Bongabong and set up my command post on the road above Baler to protect against being cut off by a paratroop drop. Then I went about organizing the defense of the bay.

It was not a promising prospect. Baler was a broad curve of coast some twenty miles long, with a sandy beach and flatland running back ten or fifteen miles to the jungle foothills. A few villages were scattered among the coconut groves that bent thick before the ocean breeze.

This was what I had been trained for, and now I reacted mechanically, the apprehension I had felt dissolving before the details of organizing a defense. I sent squads to reconnoiter the coastline and took the rest of my troopers into town to contact the constabulary and place them under my command. They were a sorry force of some twenty policemen, fearful, as we were, that at any moment the Japanese Army would descend upon them. I divided them up among my remaining squads, dispersing some to observation posts around the bay and sending others back over the mountains to mine the road and bridges leading in.

The next few days were frantic with preparation, which set the local villagers on edge. They were poor people who had nothing to do with this new war, and little knowledge of the events that had brought it upon them. They had no weapons and only the frail shelter of bamboo huts built on stilts, and we urged them to evacuate while there was still time. Few did, even the women and children choosing to remain in their homes to tend their copra groves and rice paddies.

Meanwhile, I kept radioing reports several times a day to Captain Fowler at Bongabong, but save for a few reconnaissance overflights there was nothing to report. My command post, under tall trees above the banks of a mountain stream, was busy with couriers, constabulary, and villagers with urgent questions and requests. I improvised a desk and file system for my reports and made up a bed upon the cases of TNT, as the ground was far too damp to sleep on. It was a hectic time, but after a week we were as ready as it was possible to be. Then the Japanese came.

☆ ☆ ☆

It was late morning on December 17. I was working in my command post when I heard the sudden thrum of engines over the mountains. I ran outside and caught the glint of sunlight off the wings of a dozen fighter planes, Zeros arching in over the northern end of the bay and angling toward us. They came in low above the treetops, the black bulges of 500-pound bombs beneath their wings. My observation post at the far end opened up with rifles and its machine gun and the villagers scattered. In a moment the Zeros were on us.

Bullets began ripping through the huts and scything off the tops of the coconut trees. Women were screaming, some carrying babies as they darted for cover. I ordered the horses moved farther back into the mountains and yelled for my troopers to take cover.

The Zeros circled and came in higher this time, dropping their bombs. The concussions were deafening, throwing up black sprays of sand and ruptured trees, blasting huts to pieces, shoving people to the ground. The machine gun on my staff car began chattering, and the troopers fired their rifles. It was not much, but something, at least, with which to respond to the unequal assault.

By now the Japanese planes were circling and diving at random, bombing and strafing. The whole bay convulsed with fire and explosions and thick clouds of smoke. In a moment I caught sight of a woman running hysterically toward me, clutching an infant. I and two or three of my troopers dashed toward her, but she was completely out of her mind. She yelled and wept and would not let us touch her or the baby. Scarcely more than a newborn, it was soaked with blood that streamed out over her arms and breast. It had been hit by shrapnel and killed instantly, but she would not let it go, nor let us near her.

The sight of her, hysterical among the bomb blasts, gripping that bloody child, horrified me far more than the attack itself, and fused in me a strange sensation of pity and hatred. It was not right, it was not fair, and I wanted revenge.

I ran to the staff car, grabbed the handles of the machine gun, and started firing and yelling. The Zeros buzzed past, their stubby wings spreading like hawks, the sun insignias blood red. Bullets thudded to the left and right of the car as I fired back, screaming curses at them.

The attack lasted for fifteen or twenty minutes, and then the Zeros knifed away over the mountains. I took the toll: Several civilians including the baby had been killed, and several more were wounded. None of my men had been hit, and the horses all were safe. I was wrought up and soaked with sweat, too charged with anger and adrenaline to calm down. I ordered my troopers on full alert, convinced the attack had been the prelude to a paratroop drop and an invasion. Any minute I expected to see the sky speckle with chutes and the landing crafts scudding toward shore.

An hour passed, and then another, and it did not come. By nightfall we began to relax; perhaps it had been a diversion. I sent word to all the posts to remain alert to any sign of movement, and I returned to my headquarters. The place had been badly torn by bullets, the holes tracing right past the cases of TNT. I gathered up my bedroll and ordered some of the troopers to remove the cases farther up the streambed. From that night on, I decided, I would sleep on the ground.

A few nights later, after midnight, I made a surprise visit to my observation posts. The men, I knew, were tired and were becoming careless on guard. At one post I found a trooper sleeping on duty, and I kicked him awake.

"You know that this could cost us all our lives!" I shouted at him.

The young Filipino private struggled to straighten himself and clear his eyes.

"Forgive me, Lieutenant," he pattered out. "I haven't slept in two days."

"None of us has, soldier. That's no excuse."

"It won't happen again, sir, please."

I faced a difficult decision. It was war, and the offense meant court-martial and probably death. I knew the boy; he had not been with the regiment for long. My instinct was to forget the incident. We were all exhausted, and the attack had drained us. Yet I had a responsibility to the other men. There were only twenty-seven of us, expected to delay an invasion. No one could afford to be lax, especially me. It was my first command decision in combat, compelling me to choose between compassion and discipline.

Reluctantly I had the man arrested. The next morning, when the ammunition trucks came by to drop off our supplies, I sent him back to Bongabong to be charged. He loaded miserably onto the cases of cartridges and TNT, as much ashamed as he was fearful, and the trucks started back up the torturous road into the mountains.

The realization that I was probably sending him to his death nagged at me; but I was a commander, and where the safety of my men was concerned I had no choice. Now that the bombs were falling, the enemy was not only the Japanese but also those among ourselves who failed in our duty. I hoped that the court-martial might spare him, but I knew that I could not.

The war itself decided the issue. I learned a few days later that as the convoy made its way to the rear, the trucks were strafed and the one on which the private was riding was blown to bits. It was my first glimpse of the randomness of war's violence. The death it meted out was not personal, not aimed at anyone, and not particularly the consequence of anyone's action. But it was far too early in the war for me to understand this, and the young guard's death continued to haunt me as we clung onto our bay and waited to be wiped out.

We remained at Baler through Christmas, and though we were strafed a few more times, there was no invasion. My men had settled down into a routine of watchfulness and defense against the raids. They even managed to bring down two Japanese spotter planes with rifle and machine-gun fire. But apart from that the days and nights began to blend into one long vigil of anticipating attack.

My initial anxiety had resolved itself into a concern for the morale of my men. Separated from the regiment, they felt alone and vulnerable on the bay. If the Japanese did come, we would not be able to resist for long. I was sure that most of us, including myself, would be killed or captured, and capture, we knew from the horror stories of torture and neglect that we had heard, might be the worse option. Then, suddenly, my own morale was shaken.

On the morning of Christmas Eve I was bathing in the stream above my command post when I noticed a livid sore on my genitals. I remembered the night of the polo party, and a shock went through me. I threw my clothes on and hurried back to radio a request to Captain Fowler for a doctor to come at once to inspect my platoon. All that night I fretted over visions of myself decaying to a syphilitic ruin while the Japanese chased me across the mountains, or of going mad in some prison camp.

When the doctor, a young Filipino lieutenant, arrived next morning I collared him into my staff car and drove up into the mountains.

"Lieutenant," I said gravely when we had pulled over, "I have a problem and I don't want it to go any farther than us two."

My tone, along with the expression on my face, evidently struck him, and he swore he would keep whatever it was to himself. I told him I was sure I had syphilis.

He glanced at me severely, and then asked me to show him the sore. He examined it, and began to laugh.

My fear suddenly turned to anger and shame. "What the hell is so funny?" I demanded.

"What you have there, Lieutenant," the doctor declared, "is an infected mosquito bite."

With this sudden, welcome reprieve, I began to see the humor of it myself. I thanked him and drove him back to Baler to inspect the troopers.

☆ ☆ ☆

Christmas Day 1941 passed quietly. Then, the following morning, I received a radio signal from Captain Fowler: *Withdraw immediately to Bongabong*. I gathered my troopers and commandeered every vehicle in the area. The horses were being loaded while I radioed Fowler for permission to blow the bridges on my way across the mountains. When no reply came by the time we were ready to leave, I grabbed the provincial engineer at Baler and instructed him to destroy the bridges on my signal by telephone.

We arrived in Bongabong that evening and found the rest of the troop assembled and preparing to move south. The Japanese had invaded, Fowler told me, at Lingayen Gulf as MacArthur had predicted, and were driving toward Manila.

Meanwhile, he added, the main body of the Twenty-sixth had been fighting desperately for five days to delay them, buying time for the rest of our forces to organize lines of defense. The price, Fowler said, had been heavy: The regiment had lost more than a quarter of its officers and men, and over half of its horses. The Twenty-sixth Cavalry as I had known it at Fort Stotsenberg just three weeks before had nearly ceased to exist.

Bataan

Fighting was general across Luzon. The Japanese had steamed into Lingayen Gulf on December 22, sixty-nine transport ships carrying Lieutenant General Masaharu Homma's Fourteenth Army. The two Philippine divisions guarding the gulf were poorly equipped and able to offer little resistance to the massive onslaught of planes, tanks, artillery, and troops.

General MacArthur's intention had been to defend the

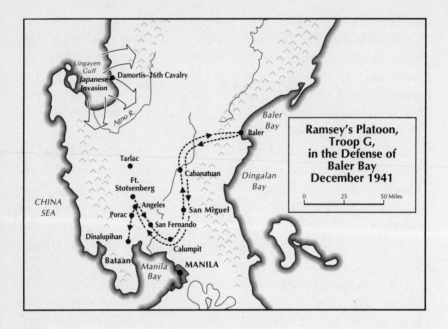

whole of Luzon, but it was soon clear that this was impossible. Except for a few P-40s, our air force of 277 planes had been wiped out, and our troops were scattered all over the island. Consequently, on December 24, MacArthur removed his headquarters to the fortress rock of Corregidor, and ordered all troops to fall back into a series of defensive lines across the central plain.

In the meantime, General Wainwright marshalled the four divisions of his corps, reinforced by the Twenty-sixth Cavalry, to lead a delaying action that would enable an orderly withdrawal. We now hurried to join this action, off-loading the horses at Bongabong and pushing across country to Cabanatuan, the provincial capital, where we were to rejoin the regiment.

Cabanatuan was an important supply depot where we hoped to rest and reprovision. But the day before our setting out it had been bombed, and now as we approached it we could see the fires for miles across the rice paddies. Oil drums were exploding and ammunition crates were thundering their contents into the night sky. The flashes pulsed beneath a black cloud-bank that covered the horizon, blotting out the moon. Thickening the sulphur and oil stench was the smell of burning rice and charred meat. A million pounds of provisions destined for our forces had been destroyed, and we pushed on without rest or food while the cinders of our own supplies rained down upon us.

All through the night and the next day we were followed by Japanese spotter planes, which buzzed above us just out of range of our machine guns. Two or three times they were followed by Zeros that sent us scattering into the brush for cover as they bombed and strafed.

After seventy-two hours of forced march, we staggered into the village of San Isidro. There we found the remnants of the Twenty-sixth main body streaming in. It was literally a skeleton of the regiment I had joined six months before. The men were haggard and showed signs of malnutrition. The horses that were left could scarcely walk, and the few remaining vehicles limped along behind them, riddled with bullet holes.

They had fought five major battles in as many days against vastly superior numbers and equipment. At Binalonan, some four hundred fifty troopers had delayed a Japanese tank column for over two hours, enabling General Wainwright's corps to establish a line along the Agno River. With no antitank weapons the troopers had halted the Japanese armor with fanatical feats of heroism, throwing themselves on the tanks, dropping grenades down the hatches, and firing into the gunports. Then, as they fell back from one defensive line to the next, they gave ground grudgingly, and at a terrible cost.

The first man I spotted was an officer I knew from Stotsenberg, a young lieutenant named Steve Graves. I hardly recognized him. He was frighteningly thin, and his eyes were sunk into his head like those of a dead man. But he was not unique; nearly all the men were prostrate with exhaustion and shock.

When I reported to regimental headquarters, several officers at once shouted at me: "Did you destroy the road to Baler?"

I was so tired and shaken by the sight of the retreating troops that I shouted back at them: "Why the hell didn't you respond to my signal for permission to blow it?"

Colonel Clinton Pierce, the regimental CO, jerked his thumb wearily toward the men dropping down into bivouac outside. "We were pretty busy," he said in a flat, dry tone. "We took a hell of a beating."

I knew Pierce as a hardened combat soldier, a veteran of some thirty years' service who had worked his way up through the ranks. At Stotsenberg he had been thickset, almost chubby, and had had a ponderous, commanding voice. Now, worn thin and exhausted, he could barely speak. His appearance and his remark sobered me.

I apologized and explained that the road could still be destroyed if I could get through to the provincial engineer in Baler. The only way to do that was to drive back to the foothills of the Sierras beyond Bongabong where there was a phone line to the bay. Colonel Pierce told me to take a staff car and driver and set out at once.

The road back to Bongabong was crowded with exhausted troops, American and Filipino, shuffling south. To the north the Japanese were pressing relentlessly, driven by General Homma's timetable. Homma had been given strict orders by the high command to complete his conquest of the Philippines within fifty days of the landing. Troops from his force were urgently needed to seize the neighboring islands and prepare for an invasion of Australia. Failure to move swiftly could disrupt the entire Japanese plan for the campaign in the Pacific.

Homma had expected that MacArthur would pull back into Manila and make his stand there, leaving the plain of Luzon undefended. Instead, MacArthur declared Manila an open city, and the Allied forces threw out one defensive line after another across Luzon, compelling Homma to stop repeatedly and deploy his army—sometimes for hours, sometimes for days—before pushing on. Homma was falling dangerously behind schedule and he knew it, and the fact made him all the more relentless.

Our regimental intelligence officer was able to give me a general idea of the position of the Japanese troops, but the situation was changing rapidly and I could not be sure where to expect them as we hurried north. As we passed beyond Cabanataan, moving northeast, we could hear artillery fire; the Japanese were driving on the town, and the last organized units of our forces were evacuating it. Since they had already fired Cabanatuan, I knew we were virtually surrounded. It would be a matter of hours, perhaps less, until the area we were in was entirely cut off.

I took the mountain road to Katanan, from where I could put through the call to Baler. The village was nearly deserted but the telephone line was still open. I got through to the provincial engineer in Baler, identified myself, and gave him the order to blow the road and bridges. He assured me he would comply at once.

There was no more time to lose. Dusk was gathering, and from all sides we could see fires and the strobing light of artillery. We dashed back to Bongabong and turned south on the road to Cabanatuan. Now, except for a few stragglers, there were no Allied troops in the area. We were in the no-man's-land between the two armies, liable at any minute to be swept up by the Japanese advance.

Cabanatuan was still smouldering as we skirted it, but by now it was also swarming with Japanese troops moving to cut the north-south road. Had we arrived just a few minutes later, we would have been trapped. As it was, we darted past the town and reached San Isidro to find the regiment preparing to move southward again.

A second Japanese force had landed, this time at Lamon Bay, southwest of Manila, and was moving east to separate our forces in north and central Luzon from those in the south. MacArthur understood that the fall of Luzon was now only a matter of time, and he ordered a withdrawal of all Allied troops into Bataan. Supplies were being rushed onto the peninsula in preparation for a siege, and tens of thousands of soldiers and civilians were pouring through its narrow neck and crowding round the jungle slopes of its hulking, mute volcanoes. Bataan would be our last line of defense, our last hope for survival.

After only a few hours' rest, the Twenty-sixth was mounted again and moving. Two days of forced marches brought us to Porac, one of a pair of towns guarding the entrances to Bataan. The other, Guagua, lay at the head of the long line of coastal swamps stretching south toward Manila. Between these two towns the entire Allied army would have to siphon onto Bataan, there to dig in and prepare for the Japanese assault. Until that could be done, the line between Porac and Guagua would have to be held at any cost.

On New Year's Day 1942, what was left of the Twenty-sixth Cavalry was attached to the Twenty-first Philippine Division and ordered into this line. There were only enough horses left to form three mounted troops; the other men were transferred to motorized units. I still had Bryn Awryn, and was assigned as commander of a platoon in G Troop that was dispatched to patrol the foothills beyond Porac, the extreme left flank of the line. Should the Japanese try to turn the flank, our job would be to delay them long enough to allow reserves to reinforce us. With two dozen troopers and mounts weary from weeks of fighting and marching on little sleep and less food, it was a task as unlikely as it was vital.

For three days the Japanese probed the line, searching for a soft spot, being repulsed with heavy losses everywhere. Their position was becoming nearly as acute as our own; the weeks of fighting had weakened them as well, and malaria, dysentery, and beriberi were taking their toll. General Homma, whose best division had now been taken away by the high command, grew impatient. On January 4, he ordered a massive assault against the center of our line, determined to break through and sweep us into the sea.

The blow fell on the Twenty-first Division, which crumpled back across the bridges of the Layac River. Then a Japanese flank attack at the far end of the line began to roll it up toward us. Again the Twenty-sixth found itself in a desperate rearguard fight, protecting the withdrawal of the entire force across the Layac, where it took up a new defensive line. Ours was the last regiment to cross the bridges. As we did so, General Wainwright was waiting to give the order to destroy them.

The Layac line was even more precarious than the previous one, but it was just as necessary to hold since the main force in Bataan was still digging in. Again our troop was thrown onto the left flank and ordered to prevent a turning move. We rode all night through the swamps that bordered the river until our backs were against the jungle slopes of Mount Natib, the volcano forming the center of our main line of defense.

As dawn lifted on January 7, we faced a broad plain rolling down to the banks of the Layac. There was very little natural cover, either for ourselves or our horses. Immediately to our rear were the guns of the Twenty-third Field Artillery, which began flinging shells far over our heads and across the river.

Almost at once the Japanese batteries replied, and we found ourselves caught in the middle of a thunderous artillery exchange. Though we had dug in during the night, there was no place to hide. Shells began whistling and whining toward us, bursting all around with deafening concussions, shredding the air with shrapnel. I gave orders for the horses to be dispersed, but within moments half a dozen had been hit, their sides pierced by red-hot shards, sending them screeching and galloping over the open ground.

For an hour it continued, then two, then three. The shells split the air and shook the ground, and I began to feel a maddening fear that it would never stop. I learned quickly to listen for the high-pitched wailing shriek that warned of an explosion. Then I ducked behind the only tree in the vicinity and hid my head until it was over.

More horses were being hit, so I sent for Lieutenant Clay Mickleson, one of our veterinary surgeons, to tend to them. Lieutenant Cliff Hardwick, who had defended Dingalen Bay, was on my flank, and he too needed Mickleson. Over the next few hours we held hasty conferences while the shells rained all around us, every few moments diving for the cover of the tree.

At one point a sudden, ear-stunning shriek sent us sprawling, Mickleson on the bottom, myself in the middle, and Hardwick on top of me. The shell burst a few yards beyond us, battering the tree trunk and spewing shrapnel through the branches. One shard struck a branch above us and sliced straight down, striking Hardwick on the seat of his pants. He yelped and jumped up, spinning in circles and fanning his backside. The shrapnel had burnt through the material and seared his flesh, though with more damage to his pride than his posterior.

The barrage continued unremitting for eight hours. When at dusk it finally slackened off, my head was ringing and all my senses were numb. I was shell-shocked, scarcely able to think, nearly deaf from the continual concussions, my whole body feeling thick and bloated with sound. We had had two men killed and several wounded, and twenty-one of the horses were dead. Bryn Awryn had come through, but he was badly shaken. We mounted the animals that were left and pulled back through the remnants of the artillery battalion.

There was little left of it. Four of its five guns were gone, twisted into smoking scrap, while the ammunition train of the fifth had been hit, blasting itself to pieces. The whole field looked as if it had been excavated by mad gravediggers; there were craters and bodies and bits of equipment everywhere. The Twenty-third had been annihilated.

Through the night we attempted to regain contact with the infantry division on our right, our horses stumbling along the jungle paths. At 4:00 A.M. Captain Joe Barker, commanding a motorized squadron, radioed that the road to our rear had been cut. To verify this, Colonel Pierce ordered me to take a patrol back down the road to reconnoiter.

I set out with half a dozen troopers through the thick

darkness. Ahead of us a few loose Filipino ponies darted skittishly over the road, materializing from time to time through the dark and disappearing again. They would edge toward us uncertainly, their eyes big with suspicion and, as we felt our way forward, dash away again.

My map showed a bridge a few meters farther on, and we approached it warily. Under the faint moonlight I could just discern the road rising toward its bamboo posts. We moved forward, sending the ponies scurrying onto the bridge, where suddenly they seemed to freeze.

From both sides the jungle flared with tracer bullets, catching the ponies in a crossfire. The bullets thudded into them, ripping open bellies and severing necks, and in a moment the bridge was kicking with carcasses. I swung my patrol around and galloped back up the road. Had it not been for the ponies we would have been wiped out in that ambush on the bridge.

We now knew we were surrounded, and finding a way of reaching our lines was a matter of life and death. The men had not eaten for three days, and the horses had had only the leaves they could snatch as they shuffled along the jungle trails. We began moving across country, dismounting and leading the horses up the slopes of Mount Natib. All that day and through the night we fought for a passage toward our troops to the east, descending into ravines and struggling up the far sides, turned back time and again by gorges so steep it was impossible for men and animals to pass.

Here and there we found Negritos who guided us, dark, diminutive figures who felt their way instinctively through jungle so thick we had to hack our way with bolo knives. Every scrap of food we found we gave to our mounts, for to a cavalryman his horse is survival. Still, it was only a matter of a day or two before they, and we, gave out.

At dawn on January 9, our advance patrol climbed out of a ravine and stumbled upon one of our regimental scout cars. A few kilometers farther on through the jungle Captain Barker's motorized squadron was camped. To our relief they had a field kitchen with hot food and forage for the animals.

Barker told us that he was headed across country for Mauban, the western anchor of our main battle line, where our regiment had been ordered to support the First Philippine Division of Wainwright's I Corps. Our delaying tactics had worked, he told us; the line was now in place, and Wainwright expected an attack at any moment. Our job again would be to protect the flank, patrolling the coastal road between Mauban and the naval base at Olongopo, now occupied by the Japanese.

I checked my map, which showed a rugged, bulging coast, and tried to fix the details in my mind. Between the end of our line and the Japanese troops ran a road, devoid of villages save for one. I made a mental note of the name: Morong.

The Charge

B y mid January 1942, Bataan was a bastion—over a hundred thousand troops and civilians crowded onto a peninsula four hundred miles square. With us was ammunition, food, and forage for our animals sufficient to last no more than forty days. But every day brought new assurances that reinforcements were on the way. There was, we were told, a convoy of ships a hundred miles long steaming to our relief; all we had to do was hold on until they arrived. The fact that no such convoy existed—nor was even possible, given the destruction of our navy at Pearl Harbor—was kept from us.

In his command headquarters in the Malinta tunnel carved from the rock of Corregidor, General MacArthur was directing the final, desperate defense of Bataan, while flooding Washington with requests for relief. He asked for carriers, planes, submarines, and supply ships—something, anything, so that his troops might have reason to take heart. If the Philippines were lost, he cabled Roosevelt, he could "unhesitatingly predict that the war [would] be indefinitely prolonged and its final outcome jeopardized."

On Bataan, meanwhile, the commander's absence began to be felt. Though the Filipino soldiers clung to their devotion to MacArthur, the Americans more and more began deriding him. As ammunition and food ran out, and as the weeks passed with none of the promised relief, they made up derisive songs and jokes about the general, whom they called "Dugout Doug." *We're the battling bastards of Bataan*, one lyric went, *No mama, no papa, no uncle Sam/No aunts, no uncles, no nephews, no nieces/No rifles, no planes, or artillery pieces/And nobody gives a damn.*

On January 10, 1942, at the urging of his field commanders, General MacArthur paid his first visit to besieged Bataan. Upbeat and reassuring, he expressed deep emotion at the condition and determination of his troops. It was unthinkable that Washington would desert them, he said, and to the Filipino soldiers he reasserted America's sacred commitment to the islands.

He spent the day touring the main defensive line, conferring with Wainwright and his junior officers, and stopping all along the line to speak to the soldiers, to whom he habitually referred as "my boys." Upon his return to Corregidor he found cables from Washington assuring him that help was on the way in the form of convoys of aircraft carriers, freighters, and troop ships. This news he jubilantly communicated to the garrison on Bataan, concluding that "the exact time of the arrival of reinforcements is unknown," but that they must hold on at all costs.

To the officers in the field he sent a separate message, reminding us of our duty, and our obligation to preserve "that demeanor of confidence, self-reliance, and assurance which is the birthright of all cultured gentlemen and the special trademark of the army officer."

We arrived near Bagac on the evening of January 10, the day of MacArthur's visit. Our force consisted of Joe Barker's five armored cars and two hundred horsemen under Major Jim Blanning, who still bore upon his face the scars of the Manila bar fight. Staff officers from General Fidel Segundo, commander of the First Regular Division, Philippine Army, directed us into a bivouac area and told us that General Wainwright wanted continual patrolling along the coast to the north. There were reports that the Japanese had landed a force of infantry and tanks at Olongopo and were planning a flanking move toward Mauban.

We hurried to provision our horses, then settled into bivouac. The army was already on half rations, with no fresh meat, fruit, or vegetables. Each of us was given a tin of fish, some canned fruit, and a few handfuls of rice. The rainy season had passed, and it was now terribly hot and dry. But we had been moving almost continuously for more than a week, and we were grateful to get a night's sleep.

For the next five days, G Troop scoured the countryside up to Olongopo looking for the Japanese. Our rations were shrinking daily, and both men and horses were exhausted and growing leaner. By January 15 the animals were scarcely able to lift their feet over the vines that clogged the trails, and the troopers slumbered in their saddles.

I had been on reconnaissance with my platoon for two days, threading the steamy jungle trails, pausing only long enough to swallow a fistful of rice and let the horses forage. Bryn Awryn bore the hardship bravely, and I winced as I watched his flanks subsiding and his head and haunches beginning to droop.

There was no activity to our front, and so we made our way back to G Troop headquarters. Captain Fowler greeted me as I dismounted. "We'd almost given you up for lost," he said. "Welcome back." Then he told me to have the horses cared for at once, since the troop was being sent to the rear for rest. It was welcome news.

I ordered my platoon sergeant to see to the animals and to pass the word to the men that we were being relieved. Replacing us were the remnants of E and F troops, combined into a single, undermanned unit. They had already arrived, their horses tethered in lean rows among the scrub, the troopers, their uniforms in rags, prostrate upon the ground. I made my way among them to their headquarters, a tent fly stretched among the trees, to confer with their commander, Captain John Wheeler.

Wheeler was a year or two older than myself, a mild, fair-haired young officer with an abstracted, almost ascetic manner. He was quiet and diffident, and I had never known him to raise his voice, yet now he was bending over some old oil company maps, sweating and swearing freely. "Jesus Christ," he moaned to me, "these maps aren't worth a damn. I now know where to buy Goodyear tires and Camel cigarettes everywhere between here and Subic Bay, but I'm damned if I can tell where a trail or river or a bridge is anywhere. For Christ sake, Ed, can you brief me on the terrain around here?"

While I gulped down a cup of rice I made corrections on his maps and pointed out the location of a Philippine constabulary unit I had encountered on the slopes of Mount Natib. "It's wild country," I told him, "thick jungle, not many trails, just a few scattered huts. The Japs haven't pushed south yet, but it's only a matter of time—maybe a day or two, maybe less."

I could see that Wheeler was concerned by his unfamiliarity with the terrain. Our reconnaissance mission on the flank of the army was critical, and he needed as much intelligence as he could get. I was desperately tired and anxious to pull back with the troop and rest, but despite this I somehow heard myself offering to remain behind to help.

"I've been in a hell of a lot of combat, and I haven't gotten any medals yet," I explained as cavalierly as I could. Wheeler jumped at the offer and hurried to get Captain Fowler's permission. Fowler agreed and detailed me to assist Wheeler. Then he mounted G Troop and set off on the slow, shambling ride to the rear.

Captain Wheeler put me in charge of the first platoon of E Troop, twenty-seven worn and weary Filipino scouts. I bivouacked with them that night, and next morning I supervised the feeding and watering of the animals before my own breakfast of rice gruel and coffee. At midday General Wainwright rumbled into camp in an old sedan. Always gaunt, he had by now become almost ghostly as he shared our shrinking rations.

Wainwright clearly was angry. He had come to see General Segundo, to reprimand him for having withdrawn the First Philippine Division from the village of Morong. Morong, he declared, offered a good defensive position along the only river that lay between us and the Japanese. It was a line we could not afford to abandon, he insisted, and what was more, it would connect with the Second Division defenses to the east.

Wainwright wanted Morong reoccupied at once, and he ordered Segundo to move his division forward. Meanwhile, an advance guard was to hurry to Morong to reconnoiter and to secure the town until the division came up.

Captain Wheeler and I were standing nearby while this conversation took place, and Wainwright caught me out of the corner of his eye.

"Ramsey, isn't it?" he barked at me.

"Yes, sir."

"You played in the polo match at Stotsenberg?"

I said that I had.

"You take the advance guard," he said. "Move out!"

I had broken the soldier's first rule of never volunteering, and now I was paying for it. I saluted wearily and was about to start off when Wheeler spoke up.

"General," he put in, "Lieutenant Ramsey's been on a long reconnaissance, and he just volunteered to stay behind since I don't know the terrain. Is it okay if I send someone else?"

Wainwright shot an angry glance. "Never mind!" he barked. "Ramsey, move out!"

Wheeler walked me back to the troop. "Ed, I'm really sorry

you got stuck with this," he said, "but there's nothing I can do about it now."

He ordered the troop to mount and put my first platoon in the lead. Wheeler rode with the second platoon, followed in turn by the third. I now knew the coastal road by heart, and despised it. It was scarcely more than a jungle track, deeply rutted and thick with dry-season dust, a gray powder that irritated the eyes, clogged the nostrils, and coated the throat. The underbrush tangled up closely on either side, so dense that one could not see three feet within it. It was a dark, dangerous place, virtually an invitation to an ambush.

I ordered my men to form column of twos and to spread out in a staggered formation along the road to present less of a target. Four troopers were detailed to take the point some thirty yards ahead. After half a dozen kilometers, we reached the eastern edge of Morong.

There were three trails branching left off the road through Morong toward the sea. I signaled column left at the middle one, deployed the platoon in column of squads of eight men each, and gave the command to raise pistols. We watched as the point riders entered the town. There was silence as they made their way among the thatched huts. I ordered the troop forward.

Morong looked deserted. The huts stood empty on their bamboo stilts, the pens beneath them long stripped of livestock by the retreating Allied army. The village center was the Catholic church, its only stone structure, and it too was closed up against the advancing Japanese. Beyond lay thick groves of coconut palms inclining through a swamp toward the sea, while to our right, crossed by a single wooden bridge, was the narrow Batolan River, the line that Wainwright wanted to occupy.

We moved carefully toward the village center, the horses maneuvering head-high among the woven huts, the men alert for movement. I watched the point guard turn in at the church square and disappear from sight, and then there was an explosion.

Rifles and automatic weapons burst out from the center and

northern end of the village, echoing among the huts and sending jungle birds screaming. In a moment the point men came galloping back, one of the privates streaming blood across his horse's neck and flanks. An advance guard of the Japanese army had crossed the river and was passing near the church just as we had entered the village from the side.

Now I could see scores of Japanese infantry in brown fatigues firing from the village center, and behind them hundreds more wading the river and crowding toward the Batolan bridge. In a few minutes more the main body would be flooding across to seize Morong.

Over the rattling gunfire I ordered my troopers to deploy as foragers, and I raised my pistol. A charge would be our only hope to break up the body of Japanese troops and to survive against their superior numbers. For centuries the shock of a mounted charge had proved irresistible; now the circumstances and all my training made it instinctual.

I brought my arm down and yelled to my men to charge. Bent nearly prone across the horses' necks, we flung ourselves at the Japanese advance, pistols firing full into their startled faces. A few returned our fire, but most fled in confusion, some wading back into the river, others running madly for the swamps. To them we must have seemed a vision from another century, wild-eyed horses pounding headlong; cheering, whooping men firing from the saddles.

The charge broke clear through the advance unit and carried on to the swamp, where we dismounted and grabbed our rifles from the scabbards. I threw out a skirmish line of one squad along the river to keep the main column from crossing, and led the rest back into Morong to search for snipers.*

It was hectic, dangerous work. Dozens of Japanese had hidden themselves in the huts and the underbrush of the coconut grove. My platoon, now between two arms of the enemy, was

*Ramsey's charge at Morong, January 16, 1942, was the last mounted cavalry charge in United States military history.

receiving fire from both sides. I knew that Wheeler was on the road behind us and that we had to hold out until he arrived.

We had grenades but we could not use them on the flimsy huts without danger to ourselves, so we began moving from hut to hut, raking the walls with gunfire. By now the Japanese across the river were lobbing mortar shells into the village, the explosions bursting among horses that had broken loose from the troopers. The whole scene was a nightmare of thudding, heaving confusion. In the midst of it I stood shouting and waving my pistol, trying to direct the action like a maestro in a concert hall that has caught fire.

As I rounded a corner of the church, I saw a riderless horse standing rigid a few feet away, a trooper beyond it firing into a hut. At that moment a mortar shell dropped in front of us, the animal taking the full force of the explosion. It reared up on its hind legs with a horrible scream, and I watched its belly peel open, the steaming contents slithering out, and then the horse crumbled onto its haunches in a hypnotic slow motion.

Somehow, in the midst of all that madness, the unreal apparition of the horse fascinated me, freezing my attention. It was not until the trooper, now wounded, began firing again that I returned to myself.

At that moment a burst of rifle fire came from the direction of the road, and I saw Captain Wheeler's second and third platoons fighting their way into the village. Wheeler sent one platoon to reinforce my men at the river, while the other joined in the battle among the huts. The air around the church was alive with metal, whizzing bullets, and whirring shrapnel, while the firing at the river was swelling to a full-pitched battle.

Troopers were falling around me, from mortars and the hidden snipers, even as I shouted directions at them over the noise. Suddenly I spotted an American officer taking cover against the church, and my adrenaline and anger boiled over.

"Hey, you yellow son of a bitch!" I screamed at him. "Get over here and fight!"

The officer seemed more stunned by me than the firing, and

he hastily disappeared behind the church. I was about to yell after him when I was distracted by an explosion of gunfire behind me. Wheeler's men were driving the Japanese back across the river, and I could see them sliding down the bank and wading shoulder-deep, some being hit, throwing up their arms and disappearing under the dirty brown current. I started back toward the church and found a figure standing right behind me. It was the young private of the point guard, covered with blood from three bullet wounds.

"What the hell are you doing here?" I shouted at him. "Get to the rear!"

He was weaving and fighting to focus his eyes. "Sir," he said, his voice thick like a drunkard's, "I cannot go back. I am on guard."

We held Morong until late afternoon, when Segundo's First Division came up and secured it. At last I was able to gather my men and take accounts. One of my troopers had been killed and six were wounded. Of the Japanese, dozens lay dead and wounded all over the village and across the open fields toward the river.

Captain Wheeler came toward me, his clothing matted with sweat and dust. I was still wrought up from the fight, and did not understand when Wheeler frowned at me.

"Ramsey," he said, "you've got blood on your leg."

I glanced down and saw the broadening brown stain where a piece of shrapnel had punctured my left knee. I nearly laughed, from exhaustion and irony.

"Look who's talking," I pointed at Wheeler. "What do you call that?"

There was a hole clear through his calf, oozing blood from the uppers of his knee-high riding boot.

Neither of us was hurt badly enough to go to the rear, and so we supervised the evacuation of the wounded. Among the Japanese was a young infantryman who was lying near the church, half buried by the bodies of his comrades killed in the charge. I knew that Wainwright needed prisoners to interrogate, and so Wheeler and I struggled to save this man. While we ministered to him, giving him water from our canteens, he begged us to kill him with a bayonet. He was terrified and in great pain.

Instead I ordered him and two other wounded Japanese put on stretchers and taken to the rear, giving the Filipino sergeant in charge strict instructions to keep them alive for questioning. The sergeant, however, was a local man, who had seen his own village destroyed. Once out of our sight, he killed all three prisoners.

With the First Philippine Division in place we were ordered to the rear to regroup and receive medical treatment. Because the road was under artillery fire, we had to withdraw across the rice paddies along the coast. Bryn Awryn and some of the other horses had been tethered in a grove close by the river, but they could not be recovered due to the heavy sniper fire, so most of us had to walk. It was a long, weary way, but we were proud of our action and the discipline and courage the troop had displayed.

After my knee wound was dressed, I returned to our bivouac for some desperately needed rest. Besides the wound, I had suffered another injury, this one to my pride: The front of my riding breeches was soaked, and I realized to my dismay that it was not with sweat. At some point during the battle I had wet myself, but the fear and frenzy of the fighting had anesthetized me both to that and to the shrapnel.

I changed my breeches and dropped down to sleep. I had lost my bedroll at Morong, and Lieutenant Cliff Hardwick kindly offered me his. It was a selfless gesture, typical of the tall, courtly young Texan, for though the days were suffocating, the nights were wet and chill. Hardwick stretched out on the ground beside me and pulled from his pocket a cable he had received from his father in Texas. It read simply: *Give em hell, son.* I handed it back with a nod, thanked him for the bedroll, wrapped myself up, and was asleep in an instant.

Before I awoke next morning, Cliff Hardwick was dead. He had ridden early into Morong to recover our horses. As he was leading them out, a sniper shot him through the head, killing him instantly. His Filipino sergeant, still taking fire, managed to rescue the horses, but Hardwick's body had to be left behind.

The news hit me with a force I could not have expected. It shocked me, tormented me, and I could not get it out of my mind. Why had Hardwick, who had not even fought in the battle, been killed, while I, having been in the thick of it, survived? It made no sense. I had seen him the night before; he had lent me his blankets and slept on the ground for my sake. Then, in the morning, in an instant, he was gone. I brooded over it all day, until I felt I might be going mad.

I went to the regimental chaplain to talk about it. I knew I had to hear myself voice the questions that the battle, my survival, and Cliff Hardwick's death had raised. He heard me out patiently, sympathetically, but with nothing concrete to offer. It was, I knew, a question I would somehow have to resolve for myself.

Our situation in Bataan, I realized, was so unequal in its forces, so unlikely of success, that my chances of survival were virtually nonexistent. It was like the charge at Morong: The odds were ridiculously uneven, and I was likely to be killed. If somehow I survived, there would be no explanation, just as there had been none for Hardwick.

But I could not shake the sense that, for me, there was a deeper mystery. We had been promised relief but none was coming, and all of us in Bataan shared a sense of betrayal. We were fighting as hard as we could just to stay alive, and with each of us who died that fight became more desperate. I had struggled to ward off the sense of hopelessness that many men were succumbing to, but the weeks of fighting, the battle at Morong, and Hardwick's sudden death had stripped my defenses and left me vulnerable to brooding.

It was the old perplex of my father's example. He had felt betrayed, desperate, locked in a losing struggle, and his brooding had destroyed him. I was determined that I would not follow in his wake. I would not brood about dying, for brooding itself meant death. I would do my duty and not look for explanations. The danger was within me as well as outside. And if I could not control the external threat, the other was entirely my own war to win or lose.

Jaundice

We remained at Mauban for several days, waiting for the Japanese assault. I felt myself growing weaker, and slowly my eyes and skin began turning yellow. It was jaundice, I realized, no doubt caused by the shrapnel wound and compounded by our diet, which by now had been reduced to nothing but rice.

I was sent to General Hospital #2, near the town of Mariveles on the southern tip of Bataan, a ramshackle affair of tents and flies stretched beneath the lauan trees. I could hear and smell the place long before I saw it. There were rows of men on metal bedsteads hung with mosquito nets, suffering from every kind of sickness and wound. Their screams were terrible, and the stench hung thick upon the air, almost visible in the morning light.

I was helped from the truck and lain between two American officers. One had been shot through the kneecap, the bullet tearing up the nerves so that he howled continually in pain. Even the heavy doses of morphine no longer had an effect, and now he was bound to his bed by belts to prevent him from bashing out his own brains against the iron frame. He begged every doctor and orderly who passed to kill him or to take off his leg. And the screaming and cursing never stopped until he passed out from exhaustion and pain.

The other officer was the reverse. A bullet had passed clear through his head from one temple to the other just below his eyes, missing his brain by a fraction of an inch. He lay stoically silent, not speaking, hardly moving, a curious center of calm within the tumultuous ward. Then one night a python fell from the limb over his bed, crushing the mosquito netting against him with its black bulk. The officer screamed and leapt up, thrashing at the snake and the tangled mosquito netting, then ran naked and howling down the row of bunks until he collapsed. He was taken away, and I never saw him again.

His bunk was filled next day by a phantom: "One-Man Army" Wermuth. An infantry captain, Arthur Wermuth was already a legend in Bataan. Taking only a tommy gun, he would crawl alone through the Japanese lines at night and shoot up command posts and depots.

He was a long, lean man in his thirties who lay impatiently in his bunk as if annoyed with his bullet wound, a look of nervous determination in his eyes. When he decided he was well enough he left, not waiting for the doctor's permission. A few days later he was back with another wound from yet another solo raid.

I regarded Wermuth with a kind of wonder. He was anxious to return to the fighting, eager to kill, and he was accumulating medals as quickly as wounds. We all were in awe of him, but to me he seemed obsessively isolated and alone. That he was brave, that he was daring, no one could doubt. But I thought there was a madness in the way he had transformed the war into his private fight. And as he lay in the bunk beside me impatiently willing himself to heal, I could not help but wonder what there was in his character or his past that drove him to take such risks, and whether the Japanese were not the only enemy he was fighting.

I had not been in the hospital long when I had a visitor. John Wheeler, too, had developed jaundice from his leg wound, and now that he had recovered, was on his way back to the regiment.

"I thought you should know," he remarked to me, "that they've put you in for the Silver Star."

"Who?" I asked.

Wheeler smiled. "You remember that officer you yelled at in front of the church? The one you called a yellow son of a bitch? That was Wainwright's chief of staff. He wasn't shirking, he'd just come up to report on the action. Well, he's the one who recommended you."

I had to shake my head at the irony. "I suppose I'm the first soldier who ever got a medal for chewing out a staff officer," I said.

"I never told you, by the way," Wheeler added, "but I got shot because of you. When you yelled at that guy, I thought you were talking to me, calling me yellow. I got so mad I ran all over the place trying to get myself shot at just to prove you wrong." He laughed. "Now look who's yellow."

He asked if there was anything he could do for me at the regiment.

"Just look after my mount," I answered.

He gave a frown and glanced away. "Oh, I guess you haven't heard."

"Heard what?"

"Quartermaster confiscated all the horses. Must have happened just after you left. Butchered them for meat for the troops. You know how it was."

"All of them?"

"All of them. They were going to die anyway, I mean, there was no fodder left, and the men were starving."

"Of course," I agreed. Wheeler, too, was a cavalryman, and there was no need to say more. He went on with a little shrug, trying to sound offhand.

"I can't imagine they got much meat from them, they were all so scrawny. Still, it's a sad end, though fitting in a way, don't you think?"

I remembered Bryn Awryn and the days I had spent schooling him in polo. He had carried me through the game and through the opening weeks of the war. Wheeler was right, it was a sad end, but I would not let myself feel it. So many men had died in so short a time, were still dying and were yet to die. Some, like Cliff Hardwick, would be sacrificed randomly; others, like Wermuth, would practically invite it.

In the midst of such tragedy one horse more or less made no difference, I told myself. I dared not mourn an animal when wounded men lay all around me. Besides, the cavalry was finished long ago. The army knew it; only we resisted in our pointless pride. Now the horses were gone and we were all alike. Good, I grunted to myself after Wheeler had left, it was just as well. I would walk, or ride in an armored car. It could not last much longer, and then what difference would any of it make?

I glanced down at my sallow arms and legs. I was jaundiced alright, I reflected, in spirit as well as body. It was amazing how quickly and how thoroughly the war had invaded me, annexing my perceptions, twisting my point of view. Just a few months ago such thoughts would have been repulsive to me. Now I shrugged off the deaths of men and horses. How long I could sustain such psychic indifference I could not tell. It was a defense against despair, and for the moment, at least, like the defense of Bataan itself, it was as necessary as it was surely doomed.

By the end of February the jaundice was receding, but so was my morale. The days of inactivity in the hospital combined with the heat and the unbroken screams and moans of the wounded depressed me, and I became anxious to return to my regiment. I badgered the doctors until they discharged me, and I climbed into the back of an old army 4 × 4 truck headed for the main battle line.

By now the line had been forced back onto the lowlands behind Mount Natib. This meant that our entire force, some seventy-eight thousand men, had been squeezed onto the thumbnail of Bataan, which was dominated by the volcano jungle slopes of Mount Mariveles. What was worse, the Japanese had landed more troops near the southern tip of Bataan on a five-fingered outcrop of rocky promontories, provoking a vicious series of battles that came to be known as the Battles of the Points.

The Japanese Navy, meanwhile, was enforcing a blockade of Bataan. By the time I returned to my regiment in the first week of March, we had scarcely a month's worth left of the miserable ration of rice and tinned fish on which we had lived and fought for so many weeks. The regiment was being held in reserve behind the main battle line, and what was left of Troop G had been assigned as security for I Corps headquarters under Captain Joe Barker.

I had never been close to Joseph Rhett Barker II; indeed, I had never particularly cared for his aristocratic Alabama manner and West Point hauteur. But there was little of that left now. Barker too was emaciated; it was a brotherhood we all shared, an inescapable fraternity of malnutrition, exhaustion, and doom.

"How do you feel, Ed?" he asked me when I reported to him.

"Pretty good, sir."

He gave a disdainful frown at the "sir."

"We're all in it now," he shrugged. He put out his hand and I shook it.

In *for* it now, crossed my mind, but I said nothing.

Escape

O n March 12, President Roosevelt ordered General Mac-
Arthur to Australia to assume supreme command of
America's Pacific forces. President Quezon followed shortly after, flying to join MacArthur and then continuing on to Washington, where he established the Philippine government-in-exile.

For weeks MacArthur had resisted the idea of leaving the
Philippines, and only Roosevelt's direct order had impelled him
to go. Though he did so with the conviction that he would return
immediately with a relief expedition, leaving his men on Bataan
and Corregidor was the most deeply troubling act of his long
career.

His chief concern was the effect that his departure might
have on the morale of his troops, who had held out so stubbornly
against such terrible odds. And, in fact, news of MacArthur's
departure did affect the army profoundly. Some hailed it as a
prelude to a counterinvasion, clinging to the old stories about
the hundred-mile-long convoy. But others, worn out from weeks
of fighting, hunger, and sickness, saw it as abandonment. Mac-
Arthur had saved himself, they grumbled, and left them behind
to die.

From Australia MacArthur explained his departure to the
troops and to the Filipino people. He had been ordered to
Australia to organize America's offensive against Japan, he told
them, a main object of which was the liberation of the Philippines. "I came through," he concluded, "and I shall return."

MacArthur was widely criticized for the personal nature of
his pledge. Washington chastised him for placing his own intentions over the national purpose, while the press chided him for
megalomania. But MacArthur knew better.

America had failed to defend the Philippines, and the promised relief had never appeared. A trust had been violated, a confidence betrayed. In its place MacArthur offered the Filipino people a personal pledge, and they accepted it unquestioningly. "I shall return" was more to them than a promise; it bespoke a convenant—a prophecy of a second coming.

MacArthur left General Wainwright in command of the Bataan defenses with orders to hold out until his return. Wainwright's first move was to withdraw the Twenty-Sixth Cavalry behind the main battle line, as a reserve to fill any gap created by the attacks that we knew were coming. The line now ran across Bataan from Bagac on the China Sea to Orion on Manila Bay, a frail, forlorn defense peopled by ragged, starving men. Among them were thousands of sailors, airmen, and police, Americans and Filipinos, many of whom had never fired a rifle in combat before.

The Japanese, on their side, made no move, resting their battered troops and awaiting reinforcements. General Homma's timetable was now an embarrassing artifact of the Pacific campaign. The fifty days he had been allotted to conquer the Philippines had stretched to a hundred. Now troops were being sent to him from successes in Singapore, the Netherlands' Indies, and Hong Kong for one massive, final assault. Our patrols beyond the battle line drew curt, curious fire and returned with reports of fresh, well-equipped enemy soldiers arriving every day.

In early March, General Wainwright visited our headquarters on inspection. He could not have been encouraged by what he saw. Our ration was down to a few hundred calories a day, mostly rice, scarcely enough to sustain a sedentary life. Wainwright himself was as skeletal as ourselves. He joined us for mess, but all we could offer was the usual four ounces of rice, though the cook had found somewhere a little can of corn, which he grandly produced as dessert.

Wainwright was frank. We had, he told us, no more than

thirty days' worth of supplies remaining if we kept to our starvation regime. The few submarines that had managed to run the blockade were of little help, their own slender bellies carrying no more than half a day's ration for the garrison. The Japanese offensive was bound to come anytime, he went on, and when it did he was counting on the Twenty-sixth to plug the gaps, rushing to support either the I Corps to the west, or the Second to the east.

We promised that we would not let him down, but there was little doubt in anyone's mind what would happen when the Japanese assaulted. Four-fifths of our men were suffering from malaria, three-quarters from dysentery, and a third from beri-beri. We were mortally wounded before the battle had begun; our resistance could not be based on stamina but on sheer stubbornness. We had stuck it out this long, far longer than anyone—especially the Japanese—had expected. As far as we knew in our isolation on Bataan, we *were* the Allied war effort in the Pacific, and we would not give up without a final fight.

It came in April. On the 3rd, General Homma sent a polite request to our commanders that we follow the example of Singapore and Hong Kong and accept an honorable defeat. When he received no reply, he ordered the assault. It opened on the Second Corps, with the most massive artillery and air strikes of the world war thus far. From our position in the rear we could hear the bombs and bombardment, which thundered from Orion to the foothills of Mount Mariveles. Then the eastern flank of our line was hit, the cacophony stretching right across Bataan like giant orchestras tuning.

After two desperate days of it, the Second Corps collapsed and began streaming back toward Limay, Limao, and the town of Mariveles, bending I Corps back to protect its naked flank. Report after frantic report rushed to us of penetrations all along the front. On April 6, Wainwright threw us forward into the center of the shredding line, with instructions to counterattack. No sooner had we started, however, than word reached us that the Japanese had broken through on our right, and all roads to the Second Corps had been cut.

The whole center had collapsed, and the eastern flank was in danger of being turned. Wainwright ordered us to circle back around Mount Mariveles and then cut across country northeastward to the coastal town of Limay. It was an index of how desperate the situation was becoming, for Limay was nearly ten kilometers south of Orion, once the eastern anchor of our line.

We loaded into buses and trucks and threaded our way along the trails that traced the Mariveles jungles to the coast. The coastal road was littered with the evidence of our army's retreat. Equipment had been blasted and abandoned, and troops were pulling sullenly back toward Mariveles at the bottom of Bataan.

We had no air force left, and the skies were crisscrossed with Japanese planes. At every clearing they sliced down at us, bombing and strafing with a lethal efficiency. When we reached Limay early on the morning of April 7, we were directed to a bivouac near the ruins of a hacienda, but no sooner had we dropped down for a few hours' sleep than the Zeros spotted us and we had to scatter back into the jungle.

Our orders were to report to General Clifford Bluemel of the Thirty-first Division, which was reeling under the continued Japanese attacks. Where the general himself was, however, was by now unclear. At 7:00 A.M. we started out in the direction of his headquarters, somewhere between Limay and Orion. On the dry coastal trail our convoy raised a dust cloud that sifted up over the trees, pinpointing our movements. The Zeros swooped to it instinctively. They dived and strafed for hours, bullets decapitating the trees and ripping up the jungle canopy with the dull rent of soggy bed sheets. At last our ammunition truck was hit, spewing fire and shards hundreds of feet into the air. The explosion sent us all headlong for cover, and it was some time before we were able to regroup and clear the road to continue.

We found General Bluemel moving back along the trail

toward us, accompanied by one or two exhausted officers. He explained that his division as well the Forty-fifth and Fifty-seventh Infantry, Philippine Scouts, had broken and were falling back through the jungle all around. He had lost his headquarters staff in the fighting, so he commandeered our regimental staff and ordered our Second Squadron forward to hold the Japanese advance as long as we could.

We did not have to move far to find them, and we opened a fierce firefight to force them to deploy. We held for ten minutes, then fifteen, then thirty, giving Bluemel's men time to withdraw. Then, as the Japanese began to turn our flank, we pulled back, still firing, for a few kilometers.

Here the trail we had followed mounted an escarpment and intersected another along the top of a bluff. The drop was sheer, falling several hundred feet to a river. Atop the bluff the trail crossed a clearing some hundred yards wide and deep in dust. As soon as we set foot upon it, Zeros darted for the dust cloud, and in a moment the whole bluff was heaving with explosions.

There was nothing we could do. Hundreds of men were crowded into the clearing, helpless under the bombs. Some fled for the jungle, while those of us closest to the bluff had no choice but to dive over the edge. It was terrifying; dozens of us hung there, grasping at vines and shrubs, flattened against the cliff face as plane after plane roared in, bombing and strafing. The concussions were endless, convulsing the ground, blasting our ears, and raining down on us debris of equipment and flesh.

At one point I pulled myself up to the lip and peered over. Through the flailing earth and smoke I saw several soldiers make a dash for cover. Just as they did, a 500-pound bomb dropped among them. The whole group was hurtled into the air, and I watched as the mucous bulk of one man's body was smeared against a tree.

I was horrified and shaken by shellshock; it seemed that it would go on forever, this brutish killing and maiming, and that there was nothing I or anyone could do to stop it. I fought mad impulses to let go and fall from the cliff or heave myself over the edge and run screaming across the open ground.

The attack lasted for five hours, until dusk put a silence to it. When at last the ground stopped pounding I unclenched myself and crawled up over the edge. The carnage was horrible. Most of our staff and rear guard had been wiped out, men and vehicles ground into the earth or flung among the trees.

The wounded were everywhere, moaning mournfully or screaming curses. Some had had limbs torn off, others groped at gashes that exposed splintered bones or the florid sacks of organs. One man sat with his back against a tree staring stupidly at the open pit of his stomach from which the intestines coiled out upon his thighs. I called to my men to assemble, my voice sounding unnaturally loud in the sudden absence of the bombs. When they had all pulled themselves up over the cliff I formed them into line and started them farther down the trail.

"What about them?" one of my troopers asked, pointing at the wounded.

"There's nothing we can do," I snapped at him. "We've got to get under cover." But as we left them behind in the clearing, their moaning growing dimmer, I felt a surge of pity and shame that only anger could fight down.

That night General Bluemel deployed the shattered remnant of our regiment along a ridge line farther to the rear, and ordered us again to hold until his command could regroup. We had now not slept for over two days, nor had we eaten in three, but we labored all the night long to build cover against the planes and the artillery attacks we knew would come with daylight. When they did, they were as terrifying as the day before.

All morning and into the afternoon we were shelled and bombed, and when at last it stopped it was only to allow the advance of the Japanese infantry. From our dugouts we could see them working their way up the ridge, feeling cautiously over the shattered ground.

It was a respite, and we seized on it. Food had been sent

forward—tinned salmon, one can to every five men. And so while the Japanese inched toward us, threatening at any moment to overwhelm and annihilate us all, we measured out the precious salmon and savored it.

Then suddenly there was a report of enemy behind us, tanks moving up the coastal road. Within the hour they were lobbing shells toward us, from both our right and rear, and again we were pinned down, unable either to move or respond. Under the fire our engineers managed to build a roadblock out of some crippled cannon that halted the tanks on our flank. The Japanese then deployed infantry to try to get behind us, and another firefight erupted. We were now surrounded on three sides, but we managed to hold until midafternoon when Major Jim Blanning, our squadron commander, received orders for us to withdraw.

There was only one escape: a narrow jungle track carving south and west toward Mariveles. As we filed down it, shoving abandoned trucks and half-tracks across to stall the Japanese, we came upon a cache of food, hundreds of cans of salmon. Major Blanning ordered each of us to stuff our pockets and move on.

A few kilometers farther we found Captain Joe Barker, who had gone ahead to scout, working his way back toward us. The trail ahead, he told us, had been cut by the Japanese. Blanning ordered us into the jungle. For the next six hours we hacked a path through undergrowth so thick that one man could not see another. Platoons became separated, and then squads. After midnight we reached a ridge and worked our way down to the river below, where we bivouacked. By now only the remnants of Troop G and one platoon of E/F Troop were left, altogether about sixty men. We were surrounded, cut off, and lost. We were not so much soldiers now as fugitives, seeking lines that we doubted existed, trying to rejoin a fight that we suspected was already over.

Dawn next day, April 9, 1942, broke silent. It was a weird though welcome calm, the first morning since the attacks began that daylight did not bring artillery and bombing. Major Blanning ordered me to take a squad downriver to scout for a trail, but we had not gone far through the jungle, crawling on our hands and knees, before we heard the tread of troops. The Japanese were crossing the river not a hundred meters beyond, masses of infantry and vehicles pushing south toward the town of Mariveles.

There was simply no place left to go. We knew now that the Japanese were behind, in front, and to our left. The bank on the far side of the river was too steep to climb, and so our only choice was to wade upstream in search of a trail leading up Mount Mariveles. From the slopes we might at least be able to observe the countryside and determine whether there was any escape.

One by one we slipped into the muddy water, keeping close to the banks, and started upstream. We were so debilitated that it was necessary to halt every twenty minutes, pulling ourselves up onto the bank to collapse panting among the rocks. All day we encountered Philippine Army stragglers cut off, like us, by the previous day's battles. Some joined us, but others, dazed and demoralized, simply staggered on.

That night we bivouacked again on the riverbank and risked lighting fires to cook our few remaining handfuls of rice. It was the first hot food we had had in five days, and with the canned salmon it was a godsend.

Joe Barker and I divided our ration and cooked it among some rocks by the river. For the past few days we had made the march together, falling into step with each other and sharing desultory conversation. All formality had dissolved between us as our condition worsened, and I had come to admire his stoicism and courage.

"No artillery today," he said, pinching some rice and fish between his fingertips and fitting them into his mouth. His face was haggard and hollow, and his beard hung in dirty tangles. His uniform, like mine, was in rags and stained with sweat from the unbroken weeks of marching, fighting, and hiding. As he scrupulously gathered up the bits of food from the bottom of his tin mug, I noticed that his fingers had become so thin that he now wore his big West Point ring on his thumb.

"You thinking it means what I'm thinking?" I asked him.

He shrugged. "I don't see how it could be anything else. We'll find out soon enough."

"What'll you do?"

"Don't suppose I'd last long in a prison camp. How 'bout you?"

"Me neither. I guess I'll take my chances."

Barker nodded. "If it comes to it, I guess I will too. Try for the southern islands, then maybe New Guinea and Australia."

"What do you think are the chances?"

He smiled wanly. "Slim to none. Surrendering doesn't appeal to me, though."

It was a sentiment I appreciated instinctively. "You want to try for it together?" I suggested.

He thought it over a minute and put out his bony hand to me. "You're on," he said.

The next morning came thick with jungle mist. Again there was the eerie absence of artillery as we slid down into the stream. Around noon our point men came splashing back to report a trail ascending the far side toward a ridge. We hurried forward, crossed the river, and started the steep climb.

The mist rose with us, cloying to the blue-green vegetation, then curling up toward the cone of Mount Mariveles. We heaved ourselves up by roots and vines, our slick boots sliding at every step, sweating, gasping, slipping to our knees. Everyone's lungs ached, everyone's stomach was empty. The effort to climb was more than we could bear, yet we had no purpose now except to reach the ridge line.

Just below the ridge we saw two figures descending. We halted and watched them come toward us, Filipinos in tattered civilian clothes. When they reached Major Blanning they saluted. They were, they told him, military police from Mariveles.

"Why are you in civilian?" Blanning demanded.

"Because, sir," one of them replied, tears coming suddenly to his eyes, "Bataan has surrendered."

We all understood that it was true: The silence of the past two days could have had no other meaning. Still, it was a blow, blunted only by our exhaustion. To have fought so hard, to have lost so many and so much only to surrender ripped at our pride, the only source of strength we had left. *Bataan has surrendered*. It had a hollow sound, as stark as it was inevitable.

On April 8, General Edward King, commander of the Luzon force, had sent his chief of staff to Wainwright at the fortress of Corregidor. "You know, of course, what the situation is," Wainwright was told. "You know what the outcome will be."

"I do," he replied. "God help you all over there."

At midnight, General King decided to surrender.

In four months of fighting, some six thousand Americans and thirty thousand Filipinos had been killed or wounded. Now forty-two thousand men were surrendered to General Homma. In signing the surrender King asked for assurances that his men would be accorded fair and humane treatment as prisoners of war. "We Japanese are not barbarians," Homma's representative replied.

Our situation on the jungle slopes was now both perilous and vague. Though our forces had surrendered, no order to do so had reached us. Major Blanning explained that, technically, we were missing in action, lost behind enemy lines. He therefore gave all of us the option of either going into Mariveles to surrender or breaking up into groups of twos and threes and trying to escape.

"Talk it over," Blanning said. "But make it fast."

Joe Barker and I held a quick conference.

"What do you say, Ed?" he asked me. "You still game for an escape?"

"What's the alternative?" I answered. "At least it's a chance. If we move fast, we just might make it."

"No matter what happens, we stick together," Barker said.

"Agreed," I answered, and we shook on it.

Blanning called us back together and asked for our decisions. No one chose surrender. Accordingly, he divided our few remaining supplies equally among us, one can of fish and two handfuls of rice for each two men. We chose our companions and said good-bye.

It was a difficult moment. The past few weeks of fighting and privation had welded us together. So far as we knew, we were all that remained of the Twenty-sixth Cavalry, and the enemy had not managed to destroy us. Now, voluntarily and with slim hope, we would scatter in an effort to flee the Philippines and get back into the war. We shook hands, patted shoulders, and wished one another luck. "See you in Australia," we said.

The Orchid

J oe Barker and I climbed on up the ridge toward the summit of Mount Mariveles, wrapped in the rising jungle mist four thousand feet above us. We carried only our rations and a .45 Colt automatic each. We were too weak from hunger and fatigue to arm ourselves more heavily, and besides, we had to move as quickly as possible.

We picked and fought our way through the slimy undergrowth, gaining elevation slowly. After an hour of climbing we stopped short. There was movement in the jungle ahead, someone coming toward us.

Barker and I drew our pistols and watched as a lone figure emerged. It was a young American infantry private, cut off from his regiment and lost among the hills. Small and frail in his emaciation, he wore a uniform in such rags that his bony arms and calves were naked, covered with dirt and abrasions. He looked scarcely more than twenty, and his pale eyes had a bewildered look. He said that his name was Gene Strickland. When we told him of the surrender, he asked if he could come with us.

As the three of us climbed higher, the jungle thinned to lean scrub and the air grew chill. We had only our khaki uniforms, tattered and soaked with sweat, and we started to shiver. At sunset we decided to make camp below the summit and wait for dawn.

That night around a little fire we divided the last of our rations with Strickland, and then took turns standing guard and keeping the fire going. It was all the consolation we had in that alien, hostile place; our only protection against the night cold and whatever creatures inhabited the shingles of the volcanic slopes.

Strickland told us that he had been with the Thirty-first Infantry Regiment at Limay on the extreme right flank of the line when the Japanese had assaulted.

"We were already starved," he said as he licked the rice grains from his dirty palm. "Some of the fellas couldn't even hold a rifle. They hit us with everything—tanks, artillery, planes. We never had a chance."

I asked how long he had been wandering in the jungle.

"Two, three days," he said, wiping his mouth with the back of a slender forearm. "A few of us were trying to get back to Mariveles, but we got separated. We thought that if we could get over to Corregidor the navy might get us out." He gave a little laugh. "We figured that if they could get MacArthur out, why not us? Pretty stupid, huh?"

"Why's that?" Barker asked.

"Well, I guess they don't send PT boats to fetch privates, do they, sir? I mean, I guess that's the difference between us."

☆　☆　☆

Water was precious to us; we had no purification tablets and we were sure the mountain streams were contaminated from the days of fighting and death. The next morning we drank as much as we dared from our canteens, determined to make our supply last as long as possible, and started for the top. The last few hundred feet were over loose rock, and in the thinning air we gasped and stumbled our way up. By midmorning we had reached the top, an irregular gaping mouth lipped with scrub and a few spare trees.

Below us stretched the jungle for miles in every direction. To the east we could see Manila Bay and the rocky island of Corregidor, where Wainwright was now desperately trying to hold out with a garrison of fifteen thousand. From far below in the crater's floor a few wisps of fire smoke snaked up, Negritos, almost certainly, shying from the vast, imponderable violence all around them.

For three hours we worked around the crater rim that crested in places to a sharp inverted V, handling our way along by the few spiny branches. The effort and the altitude were more than we could bear, and on the far side we collapsed and lay panting beneath the rim, unable to go any farther.

"We've got to get down," Barker said, straining to stand.

Strickland was prostrate, his breath coming in rasping gulps. "Which way, sir?"

"Toward the road. If we can get across, we might make it."

I pulled up to my hands and knees and straightened myself. As I was struggling to stand, my eye caught something below me, a shape, a color, just inside the crater rim. I stared at it stupidly, trying to make the image come clear in my exhausted mind.

It was an orchid, depending from a limb just a few feet beyond my reach. I had seen orchids before, in flower shops in Wichita and on the corsages of the college girls, but this one was different, a delicate, pale green in color. It was the only living thing amid the desolation of that place, and its petals pulsed seductively on the air.

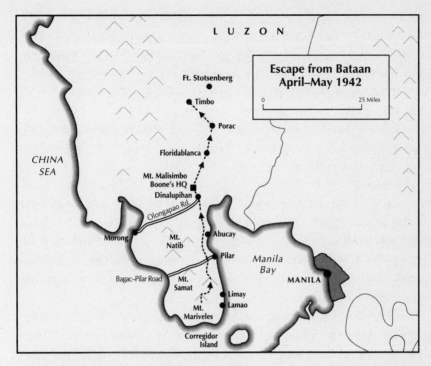

It struck me as strange, exotic, a taste I had not known through all this terrible time, a recollection of why I had come here, a reminiscence of what I had expected to find. The reality had become brutal and had shaken me to my core, yet this sudden vision seemed to restore me.

I called Barker's attention to it, and he too stared at it in wonder. Perhaps it was our weeks of enforced fasting, perhaps the sheer desperation of our condition, but for a long time we stood in silence, unable to take our eyes off it.

At last we moved on, descending. Our goal was to reach the Bagac-Pilar Road, cross it, and get out of Bataan. As it was the main east-west connection across the peninsula, we knew it would be thick with Japanese heading for the coastal roads to complete their occupation. We could not know until we reached it how, or even whether, it could be crossed. But crossing it was the key to our escape from Bataan, and to our survival.

For the next two days we threaded through the jungle, keeping to the mountain ridges, stumbling, falling, growing weaker from lack of food. At last we reached Mount Samat, at the northern base of which ran the road.

The traverse of Samat was tense and drained our last reserves. We knew we were entering an area where enemy troops were concentrating, and we struggled to keep our minds alert to signs of movement. Samat was lower than Mariveles, but its jungle was denser and more dank, slowing our progress even more.

By now Strickland was dangerously weak and in desperate need of food and water. We had crossed dozens of small streams, and though they had looked clear we had hesitated to drink from them. Now we had no choice; our canteens were empty and we were badly dehydrated. At the next stream we knelt and drank, washed ourselves, and filled the canteens.

It was a wonderful relief, but it was cut short by the sound of men moving in the jungle before us. The voices seemed very close, and it was a long, tense moment before we could tell that they were speaking Tagalog, not Japanese. Cautiously we started toward them, keeping out of sight until we saw that they were wearing Philippine Army uniforms.

There were half a dozen of them, stragglers cut off by the Japanese advance. They were glad to see us, and more important, they had food, a few extra handfuls of rice that they shared with us. They had not heard of the surrender and were surprised and sorrowful to learn of it. For them, for the time at least, their country was captive and the war was over.

The stragglers said that there were more such groups in the mountains, and they told us where we might find them and where the Japanese were concentrating. The information was almost as welcome as the food, for now we could push on with a little more confidence.

By dusk we reached the farther side of Samat, encountering on the way a few more Filipinos, who shared their scant rations with us. As the sun set we eased down the slopes toward the road, keeping close under the cover. We could hear the rumble of engines and the shuffling route step of troops. And then, finally, the road was revealed to us, with its unbroken stream of Japanese infantry and artillery stirring the gray dust eastward toward Pilar.

"Oh, God . . ." Strickland groaned.

"Shhh . . ."

We watched for an hour, but there was no end to it. Crawling on hands and knees, the three of us moved farther back up the slope.

"We'll have to wait until dark," Barker said. "Then maybe we can find an opening."

"You don't think we can get across, do you, sir?" Strickland asked.

"What alternative do we have?" I answered him. "We either cross or we stay here and wait to get captured, or starve."

Night came without a moon, fortunate for us. But with the night we began to feel the effect of the unpurified water we had drunk: diarrhea, with all the ripe promise of dysentery. Our bowels began to move spasmodically, dehydrating us further, debilitating both our bodies and our morale. We were now not only anxious and weak, we were disgusting to ourselves.

At 10:00 we crawled down to the edge of the road, scouting left and right until we found a place with cover on both sides. There we lay on our bellies in the jungle fringe, timing the intervals between Japanese units as the boots and wheels passed not a dozen feet from our faces.

"Trucks, then infantry, then a few seconds before artillery," Barker whispered. "That the way you make it, Ed?"

I nodded. "After the next infantry column we go."

"Right."

Half a dozen trucks went by, followed by a company of infantry. If the pattern held true, there should be a break of several seconds. Barker got to his knees.

"This is it," he said, and he slipped from the brush out onto the road.

"Come on," I said to Strickland, and I followed him, crouching across after Barker. For a few naked seconds we were exposed, then under cover again on the far side. We dropped down almost on top of one another and lay still, breathing hard.

It was midnight, pitch black, and we had no idea what was in the jungle before us. We dared not move before daylight, so for nearly six hours we lay without a word or gesture to one another, afraid even to sleep for fear that a cough or a snore would give us away. Nor was there anything we could do about our bowels.

Dawn showed us how fortunate we were. The jungle ahead of us had been torn and shredded by shrapnel, and through it, not a hundred yards away, we could see an entire company of Japanese infantry camped, still asleep.

We began edging northward, keeping low, circling the Japanese camp. In a few kilometers we came out into open country, rice paddies overgrown and abandoned since the invasion. Wading among them, up to his thighs in water, was a Filipino farmer, coaxing his crop to life again. When he saw us he came running, waving his arms and shouting in Tagalog.

Barker and I had both suffered the mandatory Tagalog lessons at Fort Stotsenberg, but now they served us well. The farmer made it clear that he was loyal, and we explained our need for food, water, and help to escape. With anxious glances over his shoulder he led us to his village across the paddies, where we climbed the bamboo ladder into his hut.

It was the first shelter we had had in weeks, and the fire, the food, and the farmer's kindness refreshed us. He killed the last of his chickens to feed us, and while we ate we tried to thank him. But he waved it off, determined to tell us something of great importance that made his whole face frown.

In broken phrases, repeated over and over so that we could understand, he told us that the road we had crossed was used not only for the movement of troops. For days, thousands of American and Filipino prisoners of war had been marched along it at gunpoint. Many were little more than skeletons, scarcely able to stand, yet the Japanese prodded them on, day and night, without rest. When one collapsed, he was immediately bayoneted. Others who stopped to drink from the filthy roadside puddles were shot, and civilians who came to give the prisoners food or water were also killed.

It was a death march, the brutality and suffering of which had shocked the local people and given rise to the first stirrings of resistance. Already, the farmer told us, small groups were forming in the countryside, and he offered to take us to one of them in the mountains above Dinalupihan at the entrance to Bataan.

"You think it's possible?" Barker asked me after we had bedded down in the farmer's hut that night. "About the prisoners, I mean."

"He says he saw it himself. If most of the army surrendered they'd have to get them out of Bataan if they're going to move on Corregidor. Forced marches, starving men . . . it's possible."

"Sounds like we made the right decision, then."

"We'll see," I said.

Barker raised himself on an elbow. "You know, Ed, I never much liked you. Before, I mean. I thought you were an arrogant son of a bitch."

"That makes us even," I answered. We both laughed quietly. Strickland was asleep.

"What about him?" Barker asked.

"He's in bad shape. We've got to get him out."

"You think that resistance group could help?"

"Looks like it's all we've got going for us," I said.

He nodded and lay back. "I don't think that anymore, by the way," he said.

"What?"

"That you're an arrogant son of a bitch."

"Good," I said. "Glad to hear that even a West Point gentleman can be wrong."

☆ ☆ ☆

The next day, the farmer and two or three of his friends guided us out of Bataan to the rugged country that lay at the foot of Mount Malasimbo. As Barker and I took turns helping Strickland, we passed over some of the battlefields at which we had fought in the past four months. Everywhere blasted trees and equipment lay in silent chaos, and corpses, long stripped by the animals, were slowly being swallowed by the jungle. The sights were mournful, and we hurried past them as quickly as we could.

We reached the outskirts of Dinalupihan in early evening and turned west toward the tangled bulk of Malasimbo. As we neared the barrio that was our destination, we could hear children's voices laughing and singing, a wonderfully unexpected and welcome sound. At the village four men greeted us, three Filipinos and one, to our surprise, an American enlisted man. He saluted and introduced himself as John Boone, a corporal of the Thirty-first Infantry Regiment. I guessed that he was forty and was amazed to learn that he was in his late twenties. Malnutrition and illness had taken a fearful toll on him, but nonetheless he made disdainful jokes about it, flashing a mischievous, irrepressible grin.

He explained that he, like us, had chosen not to surrender, but instead of escape he had decided to stay behind and help organize a guerilla resistance. His spies had told him of our arrival, and he had hot food ready for us as well as some local medicines, including a herbal treatment for our dysentery.

That evening while we ate, Boone told us about the guerilla army being organized by Colonel Claude Thorpe, a cavalryman from Fort Stotsenberg who had been sent out of Bataan by MacArthur to establish a resistance movement.

"It's strictly voluntary," Boone said, "but Thorpe is authorized to enlist any Filipinos and Americans who want to join into a guerilla force that'll carry on the war behind Jap lines."

"Where is he now?" Barker asked.

"He has a camp in the hills above Fort Stotsenberg. The

Japs control the lowlands and the roads, so everything's done from the hills."

It had not occurred to Barker and me to remain in the Philippines; up to now we had thought only of escape. Also there was Strickland. Worn out from the malnutrition and dysentery, he had lost an alarming amount of weight.

"I don't think he could make it," I said.

"It might be his best chance," Boone replied. "Near Thorpe's camp there's a plantation owned by some Americans— family named Fassoth. They've got food and medical supplies and they're taking in escaped soldiers. If you want, I can give you guides to take you there."

"How far is it to the Fassoths?" Barker asked.

"Two days' march," Boone replied. "It's rough country, and there's lots of Japs."

Barker turned to me. "What do you think?"

I shrugged. "If Strickland's going to have any chance of escaping he'll need medical treatment. Besides, Thorpe may be able to help us get out. It's worth the risk."

Barker agreed. We asked Boone how soon we could start.

"Soon as you feel up to it," he said.

We rested for a few days at Boone's camp and then set out for the Fassoth plantation in the hills above the village of Floridablanca. The irony was not lost on me. Just ten months before, I had made the journey from the plush and pampering of the Manila Army-Navy Club to the polo ponies of Fort Stotsenberg. Now I was a half-starved fugitive from a defeated army—surrounded, cut off, hoping only for survival, seeking only to escape. How quickly the war had stood the world on its head. That it would be righted again I had no doubt, but how long and how much suffering it would take, none of us could begin to imagine.

Pandora

B oone's guides led us north through the Zambales foothills, keeping out of sight of the lowland villages and roads. Barker and I had recovered some strength at Boone's camp, but Strickland continued to weaken. He shuffled along, leaning on a bamboo stick, pausing every few dozen yards to catch his breath. He had lost even more weight, the food and water sliding through him in sloughs of bloody dysentery. We reassured him that he would soon have medical attention, and though he pushed himself as gamely as he could, it was more than three days before we reached the Fassoths' camp.

Bill Fassoth and his brother, Martin, were American sugar planters who had lived in Luzon for most of their lives. When news of the death march had reached them, they and their families opened their homes to escapees, knowing that discovery would mean their own deaths.

Before long, hundreds of desperately sick men began finding their way to the Fassoth plantation, and Bill and Martin set about constructing a refuge for them in the security of the mountains above. They stocked it with food and clothing as well as medicines purchased on the black market in Manila. The sick, meanwhile, were cared for by Fassoth's Filipino workers and their families, also at the risk of their lives.

It was from Bill Fassoth that we learned the full scope of the suffering of those who had surrendered. Hundreds of Americans and thousands of Filipino soldiers had been killed on the forced marches from Bataan to the POW camps in central Luzon. Those who had escaped and fled to Fassoth's told of the callousness of the Japanese. Men weak from starvation and disease were driven forward with clubs and bayonets. Those who fell out of ranks from exhaustion were shot, beaten to death, bayoneted, or beheaded. The agony of malnutrition, thirst, dysentery, the broiling heat, and the savagery of the guards drove men to despair, madness, and suicide. From the lips of those few who had managed to flee had come a tale too terrible to imagine, too tragic to describe.

We listened in silence, scarcely able to absorb the meaning of what we were hearing but grateful for our own decision not to surrender. This was not warfare in any sense that we understood it, but sheer, pointless brutality. The news only made us more determined to get back into the war, and as far as we were concerned that still meant escaping the Philippines. Fassoth told us that Colonel Thorpe had established a base on Mount Pinatubo deeper in the wild, high country to the north, from which he was organizing his nascent guerilla movement. Barker and I decided to leave Strickland at Fassoth's camp to recover, while we reported to Thorpe. Strickland, however, was frantic at the idea of being left behind.

"I can make it," he insisted. "I just need a little help." He pulled himself up the bamboo pole to his feet and straightened unsteadily.

Barker laid a hand on his frail shoulder. "Look, Gene, there's no need for you to go. These people will take care of you until we get back."

He shook his head determinedly. "I want to stick with you two, sir."

"Joe's right," I told him. "It's necessary for us to see Thorpe, but you don't have to."

Strickland fixed me with his pale, sunken eyes. "Didn't we make it this far?" he said. "You're not going to go off and leave me like MacArthur did?"

Through his weak and pleading voice came a rebuke that Barker and I both absorbed. We were officers, and he relied on us. Though we doubted he could make it, we agreed to take him along.

Fassoth provided us with supplies and two Negrito guides to lead us through the Zambales foothills to Thorpe. Half carrying Strickland between us, Barker and I fell into line behind them, and we started north.

The tiny Negritos had an instinctive knowledge of the jungles and mountain slopes, and we had difficulty keeping up with them. We were still skeletal, but they were all sinew, their dry black skin stretched taut over the muscles of their scrawny legs, which seemed never to tire. Under the pace and heat, Strickland's remaining strength was quickly sapped. By the time we reached barrio Timbo, Thorpe's advance base in the hills above the village of Porac, he was again prostrate. We lay him in a hut, shivering with malaria, half delirious from exhaustion.

"I told you I'd make it," he whispered, giving a faint smile.

Barker patted his arm. "You rest now."

Strickland nodded. "You didn't leave me, sir," he said. "I appreciate it."

Colonel Thorpe was at Mount Pinatubo to the north, organizing his base camp, and so we sent a message to him and settled in to wait with Strickland. He lingered through that night and the next day, unable to eat or to talk coherently, sinking deeper into the lassitude of fatigue and dysentery. On the following morning, April 23, he died. He was twenty-one years old.

It was four more days before we had a reply from Colonel Thorpe. I was grateful for the respite, for I had developed a tropical ulcer on my foot that had become infected. An ugly, livid thing that oozed pus and stubbornly refused to heal, it made walking a torment.

While we waited, the people of Timbo were wonderfully kind to us. There were over a hundred of them, Filipino soldiers and their families who had fled from Fort Stotsenberg to the safety of the mountains. Stotsenberg was now garrisoned by a division of Japanese infantry, and Japanese air force units were using Clark Field. Though it was only four hours' hike from

Stotsenberg, Timbo was remote, protected by heavy jungle, deep chasms, and rivers that swelled to flood in the rainy season.

The refugees took pity on us at once, shared their food and medicines with us, and even entertained us during the evenings. They also brought to us two more American officers who had escaped from Bataan, Colonel Martin Moses and Colonel Arthur Noble of the Eleventh Infantry Division. Moses and Noble planned to organize resistance in the mountains of northern Luzon, where they had served before the long withdrawal into Bataan.

The night of their arrival coincided with a wake for one of the elderly villagers. A village wake was a grand affair, filled with guitar music and singing and volumes of *tuba* and *bossy*, the local liquors. The villagers had even managed to bring an aging upright piano for the occasion, dragging it on sleds pulled by carabao, the local water buffalo, up the steep jungle trails.

According to custom, the women ranged on one side of the village square and the men on the other, sipping at their drinks and talking among themselves. At last Colonel Noble, still emaciated from his weeks in the jungle, made his way to the piano. He eased himself onto the makeshift bench, pulled the sleeves back from his skeletal forearms, and launched, at first haltingly, then jauntily, into a raucous ragtime tune.

It was more than I, the Wichita swell, could resist. Despite the ulcer on my foot I hobbled over to the nearest girl, took her by the waist, and began dancing. In a moment Joe Barker had dropped his courtly reserve, grabbed a girl of his own, and followed suit. The villagers clapped and cheered us on, and before long everyone was dancing in the little square while Noble pounded the ancient upright into life.

That night of dancing restored to me the boyhood I thought I had lost in the bloody chaos of the previous few months. I was only twenty-four and as alien from my old self as it was possible to be, yet I slipped back into the music and the familiar motion with an ease that surprised and settled me. But it had a deeper meaning as well.

Up until this time I had thought of the Philippines only as a post; now I began to see it as a place, and a people. We had failed in our defense of them, leaving them in the hands of their enemies. They ought to have owed us nothing; instead they were sharing what little they had with us and risking their lives to help us. As an American soldier the war had been over for me since the surrender of Bataan, and my duty now was to escape. Yet that night I began to reflect that perhaps I still owed the Filipino people something. The war might be over for me, but it was not over for them. I might escape, but they could not. They still had a war to fight, and I began to wonder whether I should volunteer to join it.

Barker shared my feelings, and during our days at Timbo we discussed what we should do. The question centered on our status as officers of a surrendered army.

"Technically we were never ordered to surrender," Barker reasoned, "and so we still have a duty to go on fighting. Since there's no organized resistance, the guerillas are our only alternative."

I pointed out that such arguments would do us little good if we were captured. Soldiers who continued fighting after a surrender were no longer considered combatants but war rebels, and were subject to summary execution if apprehended.

"Besides," I said, playing devil's advocate, "what do we know about guerilla warfare?"

Barker gave a little, resigned frown. "I guess I was absent the day they taught that at the Point."

"Well, we didn't study it at OMA either," I said. "But we're cavalrymen and we understand shock, surprise, and mobility, and I guess that's what guerilla fighting is all about. If anybody's qualified to organize a guerilla force, it'd be cavalrymen."

We talked the decision out at great length, weighing the question of our duty to escape against Thorpe's need for our help. Thorpe was our superior officer, and though we knew he would not order us to join him, we had a duty to provide him with whatever assistance we could. Whether or not that assistance was sanctioned under international law or the rules of war was not for us to decide. And what was more, we were cavalry-men, and it was not in our tradition to turn our backs on a fight.

By the time Thorpe's messenger arrived inviting us to visit him on Pinatubo, we had reached our decision.

"It's settled, then?" Barker asked me.

"It's settled," I said. "We're volunteering for the guerillas."

"Whatever that means."

"The other part still goes, though," I added.

"What's that?"

"We stick together."

"Agreed," Barker said.

My foot was healing, but it was still impossible for me to make the climb to Thorpe's camp, so Barker went up alone while I remained at Timbo. He had not been gone many days before partisans in the lowlands reported that the Japanese were planning raids in the Timbo area, looking for Thorpe. As I still could not move quickly, I relocated with some of Thorpe's men to a camp higher up in the river valley. When the rumors of the pending raids persisted, it was necessary to move even farther.

A carabao was brought, dragging an improvised sled onto which I was loaded with a few provisions, and we set off for a Negrito dwelling high on the mountain slopes. It was dank, inaccessible country, the remotest area I had yet been to. The sense of isolation was compounded by the nearness of the rainy season, with ponderous clouds bulking low over the ridges, rendering even more oppressive the heat and humidity.

Until the danger had passed I was to stay with a Negrito family known to be loyal. My host was a small, reclusive man called Pandora who lived with his wife and two young children in a makeshift hut set against a cliff face high above the river. The hut was nothing more than a square of split bamboo with spindly posts supporting a palm-leaf roof, and it was barely large enough for the four of them to lie down in.

Pandora and his family were naked except for loincloths of

string and rag. He spoke a little Tagalog, and I knew none of his language. When Thorpe's men left to return to their homes and wait out the Japanese raids, I felt an isolation more intense than I had ever known. For the most part Pandora ignored me, going about his ancient business of making tools and weapons. His wife, too, remained distant, regarding me from time to time with a suspicious curiosity and keeping the children carefully away from me.

Occasionally as he wound his arrowheads, biting off the bamboo thongs with his sharp little teeth, I caught Pandora glancing at my .45. Pistols were rare among the Negritos, and I reflected that mine was more than enough motive for him to murder me. I was now so isolated that no one would ever know; Pandora and his family could simply move on, and my body, dropped into a ravine, might never be found.

When darkness fell we all retreated into the hut. The children were soon asleep, curled up under their mother's breasts, and Pandora sat imperturbably chewing on a reed. I tried to make conversation, asking him the names of the thunder and lightning that grunted and glowed in the distance. He rolled the reed around in his mouth and repeated the syllables for me. Then, peremptorily, he leaned down over his wife and went to sleep.

The breeze was freshening and there was the scent of rain on the air. I folded myself into a corner of the floor, my knees pressed against Pandora's legs, my head against his wife's, and tried to sleep. In a minute she was coughing, a dry tubercular cough that continued all night, and then the mosquitos began to attack. I had tried diligently to avoid malaria, but now I had no net, and I spent the night fretting and swatting at myself.

Had I really volunteered for this? I grumbled to myself. I had wanted to play polo, live a country-club life, wear a white dinner jacket, and have servants. That had been the poetic side of me, the dreamer. But the dreams had turned into nightmares, and I had sunk to a level prehistoric in its crudeness and exposure. I was going to be a guerilla, and I did not even know what that meant. Fighting behind Japanese lines, no weapons, no organization, no army—it was madness. I would be captured and shot, or worse, and I had no one to blame but myself.

I kept it up all night, growing angrier, and as the mosquitos buzzed and tore at me and the Negritos twined me in their legs, the children squirming between us, I cursed myself for violating the soldier's first rule: Never volunteer. By dawn I was utterly exhausted and glad to see the sun.

That morning Pandora went down into Timbo and returned in a few hours. He told me that Thorpe's headquarters had been raided and that he was leaving to guide two of the colonel's men through the high country to try to find him. A few hours after he left, his wife and children also disappeared. At first I was glad to see them go, but as night came on and they did not return, I found myself becoming overwhelmed by loneliness. It was an uneasiness due not only to my isolation and the absence of companions but also to an irresistible sense that something was wrong within me.

I tried to sleep, but I felt my temperature gradually rising until I was burning up. Then suddenly it plummeted, and I was shivering uncontrollably with cold. It was malaria, and all night long I rode the roller coaster of its alternating fever and chills.

I had carried with me a supply of sulfanilamide for infection, along with twenty or thirty quinine tablets. I had no idea how much quinine I was supposed to take, but when I could stand the sweating and freezing no longer, I gulped down thirteen pills at once.

The dose nearly killed me, and by morning I was delirious. I lay on the bamboo floor thrashing and sweating, a chaos of unconnected thoughts raging through my mind. There was Wichita and dancing, the Philippines, fishermen waving to the boat, and corpses hanging from trees. And there were sounds, a cacophony of explosions and moans, the screams of horses, dance band music, and men pleading to be killed.

Then, from farther down the valley, I heard gunshots, and I went completely mad. I ran screaming from the hut toward the sheer cliff behind, frantic with the need to climb it, to get up and out of my horrible isolation and fever.

Again and again I threw myself at the cliff, pulling myself up with my fingers and boots until I fell off flat onto my back on the ground. I lay there half conscious, unable to get up, overcome by my own helplessness and depression. At last I managed to crawl back to the hut, where I fell facedown on the bamboo slats.

It was the end. The months of anxiety, the loneliness, illness, and isolation all had become too much for me. The verse from the Fiddler's Green poem I had learned as a cadet came to mind, about the cavalryman's duty when he is down and the hostiles are coming for his scalp. If ever a trooper was in that condition, I now was.

I took my pistol from the holster, slipped off the safety catch, and pressed the muzzle to my temple. My finger was on the trigger, and I began to squeeze.

But my mind would not let me. Somewhere deep down within myself my misery was turning to anger. The longer I hesitated, the angrier I became. I had not done this to myself, a voice in my mind was saying, it had been done to me, done by the enemy, the Japanese. They were responsible, and they ought to be made to pay. Them—not me.

That anger saved me, for I decided that since I would probably die anyway, I ought to recover my strength, go back down the mountain, and take a few of them with me. I put the pistol away and lay back on the bamboo.

The sky above the grass roof rumbled and the rain began to fall, splashing through the thatch onto my face, easing the fever. Lightning flicked the ridges all around me, and the thunder burst right overhead. I searched my mind for the two words Pandora had taught me in his language. *Kidlot* was lightning, I remembered, and the other one, thunder . . . was *dool* . . . something, like the sound, repeated, *dool-dool*. *Kidlot*, *dool-dool*, I kept repeating, *kidlot*, *dool-dool*, until I fell asleep.

☆ ☆ ☆

I lay in the hut for several more days, unable to move, fighting the fever and chills. I used a bamboo tube to urinate, and when the dysentery welled up I dragged myself a few feet into the underbrush. Then, on a clear morning in early May with clouds towering over the ridges and the jungle scrubbed clean by the night rain, Pandora returned. I was relieved and happy to see him as he made his way up the riverbank, his big knobbly knees and skinny legs taking the slope in easy strides. Across his back were slung strips of meat and supplies from Timbo, and folded under the string of his loincloth was a letter from Joe Barker.

Barker wrote that he and Thorpe had escaped the Japanese raids, but that it would be a week or more before they could return to the district. Meanwhile, he added, he had joined Thorpe's group and had been assigned the task of organizing the guerillas in central Luzon with Timbo as his headquarters.

"I tried to volunteer you too," he wrote, "but Thorpe wouldn't hear of it. He wants to speak to you personally."

Pandora watched me while I read, frowning at the wretchedness of my condition. He set about cooking the meat for me and boiling rice. Then while I ate, he built a lean-to under the cliff where, he made me understand, I would be more comfortable. When I had finished, he half-carried me to it and lay me inside. From then on, he or his wife came up two or three times a day to cook my meals and care for me until I was strong enough to go back to Timbo.

It was May 9, 1942, my twenty-fifth birthday, when I started back down the mountain. The first news I received on reaching Timbo was that Corregidor had surrendered three days before, and General Wainwright and the garrison had been taken prisoner. The Japanese had expected to take the Philippines in fifty days; we had held out for six months.

Though I knew it was inevitable, it was strangely disheartening news. However, I set about the work of organizing a guerilla base at Timbo for Barker's return. For America the war in the Philippines was now truly over, but for me a new war was just beginning.

WAR

REBEL

1942–1943

MEDAL ON PRECEDING PAGE:
Bronze Star Medal (AMERICAN)

Faces

May 15, 1942, marked the birth of the East Central Luzon Guerilla Area force. Rather than wait for Thorpe to arrive and accept my enlistment, on that day I selected a site some two kilometers up the river valley from Timbo and, with some of the Timbo refugees, began constructing a base. We would need huts for our headquarters and for our staff, as well as barracks for the recruits. With some of the local men I laid out a rough plan of the camp and divided up the work force.

I was at the campsite helping the men to clear the jungle for huts when an athletic young Filipino walked up to me.

"Lieutenant Ramsey," he began in excellent English, "please, sir, may I go with you?"

I asked where.

"Wherever you go," he replied.

I had to laugh. "You make me sound like Jesus Christ," I said. "What's your name?"

"Processo Cadizon, sir." He told me that he had a wife and baby son, but that he was a patriot and would leave them to help fight the Japanese.

"You have any military training?"

"No, sir, but my father was a Philippine Scout, and I was raised at Fort Stotsenberg."

"Well, Cadizon," I said, "you're a sergeant now."

He gave me a broad, delighted smile and asked what his duties would be.

I put him in charge of organizing work crews and transporting supplies to our new headquarters. Other men began joining us. Alejandro Santos, a newspaper reporter, and Fausto Alberto, a policeman, had come to Timbo together from Manila. They had brought with them a mimeograph machine with which they set about printing leaflets attacking the Japanese and rallying their countrymen to resist, and so I enlisted them as our propaganda section.

Living at Timbo with his family was a young Filipino Scout sergeant named Claro Camacho. Camacho was a short, tough career soldier who combined a gregarious, outgoing personality with a fierce military discipline and loyalty. I recognized in him a valuable asset and appointed him as my personal aide. He immediately set about organizing the military side of our operation, recruiting and training our headquarters troops.

By the time Colonel Thorpe returned to the Timbo area on May 24, our base was nearly built. Thorpe sent for me, and I made the short trek up the river to meet with him. He was surrounded by an entourage of men and women, his headquarters staff and their companions who traveled everywhere with him. To my surprise, Joe Barker was not among them.

Thorpe explained that Barker had come down with an ulcerated foot and would be along in a few more days. The colonel was no longer as I remembered him from Fort Stotsenberg before the war. Then he had been a stout man with a shock of graying brown hair and an authoritarian manner. Now he was thin and rather frail, worn out from months in the jungle. His hair had gone completely white, and his manner was now merely gruff.

"Ramsey, I've convinced Barker to stay behind and help organize guerilla warfare," he began without ceremony. "Now that Corregidor has fallen, it's more important than ever. I hope you'll join us."

I replied that Barker and I had agreed to stick together, and so I would stay. "Besides," I added, "I've just about finished building our headquarters."

Thorpe gave a surprised lift of an eyebrow, and then went on. He explained that his command would be called the Luzon

Guerilla Force and that it would be divided into four parts, each the responsibility of an American officer: Northern Luzon would be under the command of Captain Ralph Praeger; west central Luzon under Captain Ralph McGuire; southern Luzon to be commanded by Captain Jack Spies; and east central Luzon, the entire plain from Lingayen Gulf to Manila and including Bataan, would be Joe Barker's command. I was to be his deputy. Thorpe added that since Mount Pinatubo was no longer safe, he was reestablishing his own headquarters nearby, in the mountains west of Timbo.

"You seem to know what you're doing," he concluded.

"Not really, sir," I replied.

"Well," Thorpe said, "get on with it."

A few days after my meeting with Colonel Thorpe, Joe Barker returned. We now were commanders of a nascent guerilla force with responsibility for the vast central plain of Luzon, Bataan, and the city of Manila, and we had not the slightest idea how to go about organizing them. We began timidly, making contact with civic leaders in the nearby town of Porac who were known to be loyal and anti-Japanese. Five of these we commissioned as officers in the East Central Luzon Guerilla Area force and charged them with recruiting local people into cadres. To each cadre we assigned a soldier from our headquarters who was to provide basic military training.

From the first, Barker and I had to improvise tactics. Under Thorpe's instructions we followed the structural formulae of the Communist guerillas who were already operating in central Luzon. Called the Hukbalahap, or Huks, these guerillas were the military wing of the Philippine Communist party, and they had had years of experience in clandestine organizing. By the time Bataan fell, they were already mobilized and moving swiftly from one battlefield to the next, scavenging weapons and supplies.

Their tactics were derived from the writings of Mao Tse-tung, who at that time was supreme commander of the guerilla army in China. Through contacts within the Huks, Barker and I managed to obtain a copy of Mao's book on guerilla warfare, and we passed it back and forth, studying it in our spare time and discussing its lessons over meals and on the march.

The essential principle framed by Mao was that a guerilla army could not compete with a regular army in the field. Instead it must be made of irregulars: peasants and villagers highly trained and organized. For us it was a wholly new approach to warfare, in many cases the reverse of everything we had been taught.

"Pretty good stuff," Barker remarked one night when we were lying on straw mats on the floor of our hut, a candle burning between us. "This business about the guerilla commander being like a fisherman casting his net wide and drawing it in tight again . . . the fellow's a poet."

"He's a damn commie," I grunted.

"But he knows what he's talking about," Barker countered.

"All the worse for the rest of us," I said.

"Well, he could be a Jap for all I care, so long as we can use what he says. What do you make of this business about fighting a war of contradictions?"

I rolled onto my side to face him. "The way I see it," I said, "what 'Comrade' Mao is saying is that we have to turn our weaknesses into strengths. We have to stay on the defensive but assume the initiative, take advantage of the terrain and the fact that the Japs are fighting in a foreign country among a hostile population. We have to stay flexible but organized and avoid pitched battles. Most of all, we have to build our credibility and get the people on our side. We fight only when we have the advantage, but we don't take on the enemy directly."

Barker raised an index finger professorially. "Exactly. We attack only when we know we can win; otherwise, we stay low and concentrate on organizing, gathering intelligence, and sabotage."

"It's all his political stuff I don't swallow," I said. "Our job isn't to start a revolution, it's to prepare for MacArthur's invasion. We're military men, not politicians."

"That's what Mao calls the purely military viewpoint," Barker said with mock admonition. "It's heresy."

"For a professional soldier, it's dogma," I grumbled. "Though God knows there's precious few of them around."

Barker opened the book to the page he had been studying. "Listen to this," he said, and he began reading in his lilting Alabama accent: " 'The regular officers assigned to the guerilla forces should shoulder this sacred task conscientiously, and they should not think their status lowered because they fight fewer big battles and for the time being do not appear as national heroes. Any such thinking is wrong. Guerilla warfare does not bring as quick results or as great renown as regular warfare, but *a long road tests a horse's strength, and a long task proves a man's heart.*' " He glanced up triumphantly. "He goes instinctively for the equine metaphor. Maybe Mao's a cavalryman."

I rolled over onto my back. "And maybe he's just a horse's ass," I said.

Barker blew out the candle. I settled myself on the mat, and as I slipped into sleep I could not help but wonder what sort of a war this was in which a West Point graduate and Southern gentleman, dressed in a uniform of rags and lying in a jungle hut, read from the works of a Chinese Communist revolutionary about tactics, logistics, and the philosophy of the human heart.

With the exception of its political dimension, Mao's approach did fit well with our instructions from General MacArthur, relayed to us by Thorpe. MacArthur wanted us to organize the population, gather intelligence on the enemy, and keep ourselves in readiness to support the return of American forces. Thorpe told us that MacArthur set great store by our work, and that until the invasion we were to be his presence under the occupation, the living symbols of his promise to return.

The initial organizing went more quickly than we expected. The great majority of the people, we discovered, were actively anti-Japanese and anxious to cooperate with us. Soon we were forming cadres all over the Porac area, and Barker and I were continually on the move, traveling from village to village to address the local leaders and swear in new units.

Our army was, as Mao had said, an irregular one. In every village we sought out men with military or police training, and these we commissioned as officers. There were few of them, however, and often we substituted with local government officials or people who had had some higher education.

Our ranks were made up of men and women anxious to do something to hurt the Japanese, and to these we gave such military training as we could. But there were few weapons to train with and even less equipment. None of our soldiers had uniforms, but instead trained and drilled in their homespun native clothing, many in shredded trousers and torn shirts, most of them barefoot. It was a peasant army in the truest sense, sustained by patriotism and a determination to resist.

Among the principal obstacles we faced were a lack of communications equipment, the terrain, and, with the coming of the typhoon season in late June, the weather. Messages between us and Thorpe and among our cadres had to be sent by messenger, a dangerous and slow process for all of us, for there were roadblocks everywhere, and the Japanese patrolled the foothills, searching for rebels.

Everywhere we traveled we went on foot, keeping as far as possible from the roads and towns. Barker and I had fought in the jungles in Bataan, but we never expected to live in them, and we were a long time accustoming ourselves to the insects, snakes, suffocating heat, and the endless blue-green gloom through which we moved. In the dry season the temperature would reach 120 degrees during the day, and when the rains came we soaked and slogged through mud that sucked off our shoes and downpours so heavy that it took an effort to walk upright.

More insidious than these, however, were the Huks. Our intention had been to consider them as allies, and to work in tandem with their leadership. To this end, Colonel Thorpe had met with their Supreme Military Committee, one of whose leaders was the well-known Communist organizer Luis Taruc, to sign a protocol by which the Huks agreed to place themselves under Thorpe's command.

Almost immediately, however, Taruc published this protocol to prove that he was cooperating with the American war effort, and accompanied it with letters ostensibly from Thorpe, Barker, and myself directing the people to surrender their arms to the Huks. Barker and I were reluctant to believe the reports of this deception until we saw the letters ourselves, bearing bad forgeries of our signatures.

From that point, tensions between our forces and those of the Huks became acute. Quite apart from their intention to seize the Philippine government, the Huks, based at Mount Arayat in central Luzon, now found themselves surrounded by our people. They thus perceived us to be as much a threat to them as the Japanese, and they warred on us equally. And so we soon had thrust upon us a war not with two fronts but with two faces: one the stolid face of the Imperial Japanese Army; the other, much closer and more cunning, that of a guerilla force like ourselves.

Barker and I knew that it was essential to our movement that we create cadres in Manila. Organizing the capital would give us prestige and would place our agents at the very heart of the Japanese occupation authority. We therefore decided to send our propaganda officers, Alejandro Santos and Fausto Alberto, back to Manila to organize the resistance groups that already existed there and integrate them into our command.

It was dangerous work, but within a few weeks Santos and Alberto reported back to us that a network was forming across the city, including many civilians who were employed by the Japanese administration. These courageous men and women soon began funneling to us invaluable information about Japanese strengths, organization, and intentions both within the Philippines and beyond.

By September our little headquarters above Timbo was busy with information and activity. We were accumulating reams of intelligence that we sent by runners to the southern islands, from where it was smuggled by boat to MacArthur's headquarters in Australia. Since we had no radio we were never sure how much of our intelligence got through, but we kept the stream flowing through a small army of couriers who were as selfless as they were brave.

They were usually young men and women from the villages who volunteered to make the seventy-mile trek to Manila. They carried our reports woven into the false bottoms of wicker baskets, or else written invisibly in lemon juice on the backs of personal letters.

Some of these people we scarcely knew; they were little more than faces that appeared at our headquarters eager for some work to do for their country. We thanked them, gave them messages on troop strengths or ship movements, and saw them off. They went understanding full well that if they were caught they would be tortured for information and then executed. Many we never saw again.

As our work expanded, so did our exposure, and the Japanese came to know more and more about us. Conversely, as our Manila network grew and penetrated more deeply their high command, we learned more about them. Responsibility for capturing us and destroying our cadres fell upon the kempei-tai, the military police, commanded by Colonel Akira Nagahama. Nagahama, a graduate of the Japanese Military Academy and the Imperial War College, was as brilliant as he was ruthless, and he devoted himself to the extermination of our movement with an almost religious fervor.

Our agents in Nagahama's headquarters informed us that a wanted list had been created, headed by Thorpe and including the names of virtually all the other American officers involved in the resistance. Colonels Moses and Noble, whom I had met at Timbo, were on it, as well as Captains Praeger, McGuire, and

Cadet Edwin P. Ramsey at Oklahoma Military Academy. "A versatile and colorful character, his adroitness in leading his dancing partner is matched only by the skill he manifests in leading his platoon" (OMA YEARBOOK, 1937).

Ramsey (EXTREME RIGHT) *on the OMA polo team. A combination of recklessness and discipline, polo was an ideal training ground for cavalrymen.*

Nadine Ramsey in the cockpit of her P-38. She was one of only eight women qualified to fly fighter planes during World War II.

Fort Stotsenberg, Luzon, the Philippines, home of the Twenty-sixth Cavalry, Philippine Scouts.

Clark Field at Fort Stotsenberg. The principal U.S. air base in Luzon, in December 1941 it became the first target of Japanese dive bombers.

Ramsey as Philippine Scout, mounted on his charger Bryn Awryn.

General Jonathan Wainwright (LEFT) *and General Douglas MacArthur. Wainwright took command of the Luzon defenses after MacArthur was ordered to Australia. A cavalryman himself, Wainwright relied heavily on the Twenty-sixth Cavalry in his defense of Bataan.* (UPI/BETTMANN NEWSPHOTOS)

Victorious Japanese samurai celebrate the fall of Bataan, April 9, 1942. (UPI/BETTMANN NEWSPHOTOS)

Japanese Premier Hideki Tojo in Manila following the surrender of the Philippines. He had planned to capture the Philippines in fifty days, but his arrival was delayed for nearly six months by the stubborn resistance in Bataan and Corregidor. (UPI/BETTMANN NEWSPHOTOS)

Images of a Death March: (ABOVE) *Starving survivors of Bataan, their hands bound behind their backs, are given a few minutes' rest on their march to POW camps in central Luzon.* (BELOW) *Captured Filipino soldiers carry prostrate comrades in improvised slings, knowing that those who fall behind will be killed. The brutality of the death march sparked the first stirrings of resistance in Luzon.* (UPI/BETTMANN NEWSPHOTOS)

Members of the Negrito tribe of the mountains of Luzon were early volunteers in the resistance. With an instinctive knowledge of the jungle, they helped guide and conceal Ramsey and his officers throughout the war.

Luis Taruc, commander of the Communist Huk guerillas in Luzon. After Taruc denounced him as a Japanese spy and ordered his execution, Ramsey declared all-out war on the Huks.

Pacifico Cabral, pictured here with his wife, was one of the first volunteers in Ramsey's East Central Luzon Guerilla Area force (ECLGA). Young, energetic, and fiercely loyal, Cabral became one of Ramsey's personal bodyguards.

Spies. Joe Barker and I were also listed, and prices were put on our heads.

There was little that Barker and I could do to minimize the danger. We each had bodyguards whom we trusted with our lives. Barker's was a former bantamweight boxer nicknamed Tarzan, and mine were Processo Cadizon and Claro Camacho. Neither of us traveled without these men, nor could anyone approach us except past their bolo knives and submachine guns. Our work, however, required us to move continuously, and to meet with hundreds of strangers. Such exposure was inherently dangerous, and we walked a razor's edge between the conflicting needs for security and trust.

Another precaution on which Barker and I agreed was celibacy. We had heard reports of guerilla officers compromised by their relations with local women, either directly through treachery or because of a jealous boyfriend or husband. Neither of us had touched a woman since the war began, but ruefully we pledged to each other that we would not become involved so long as we remained in the guerilla forces. It was not an easy promise to make, but we knew it was essential, both for our own safety and for the sake of the integrity and discipline of our command.

"I won't if you won't," Barker said to me, putting out his hand.

I shook it dolefully. "It's going to be a long war," I replied.

Through the fall our efforts were slowed by the typhoon rains that swept across Luzon. We had no vehicles and had to go everywhere on foot, but soon the trails were sunk in mud and the mountain streams had swollen into torrents that made even short trips dangerous. I was still weak from dysentery, so Joe Barker did much of the traveling during this time. One stormy morning he set off with his bodyguard for a nearby village to gather money and supplies. It was only a few hours' hike, and I was surprised when he had not returned by nightfall.

The rain had stopped, and I was sitting by the entrance to our hut with Cadizon and Camacho, looking out for Joe, when

we heard shouting from down the trail. It was Joe's voice calling
for a light.

Cadizon grabbed a torch and ran toward him. In a moment
he was back, half carrying Joe into the hut. He was a mess, and
my first thought was that he had been shot. His clothes were
caked with filth, his face and beard a matted mask of mud and
blood. I brought a coconut oil lamp closer to him and was
shocked to see his teeth protruding through a gash in his lower
lip.

The three of us stripped off his filthy clothes and washed
his face as carefully as we could. I then grasped his lip and eased
it over his teeth and daubed the whole area with gin to disinfect
it. I dug out a needle and gut from our medical supplies, gave
Joe a long draft of gin, and razored his beard away.

"What're you doing?" Joe mumbled through the mess.

"I'm going to stitch you up."

"Have you ever done this before?" he asked.

"Once," I told him, threading a short darning needle. "I had
to sew back the lip of a horse that was hit by shrapnel."

Barker snorted. "I used to be a cavalryman," he said. "Now
I'm a horse."

While Cadizon held the oil lamp and Camacho cradled Joe's
head, I poked the needle through the ragged edges of the gash,
slipped the gut tight, and snipped the end off. The flesh came
together with surprising ease, and I stitched again and again
until the entire gash was closed.

I dusted the lip inside and out with sulfanilamide and poured
more gin down Barker's throat. His face had gone a peculiar
gray green. When I asked him what had happened, he explained
that on the way back he had become separated from Tarzan,
gotten lost in the jungle, and fallen off a cliff, landing headfirst
among a rubble of rocks. His back was aching, but there were
no bones broken. It was clear that he would be taking no more
trips for a while.

We had arranged a meeting with the mayor of Porac and
another in the village of Santa Rita, and so the following day I

set out for these, taking Processo Cadizon with me. As I was
leaving Santa Rita I was handed a note from a colonel of General
Wainwright's staff of whom I had heard in Bataan. He wrote
that he and half a dozen other Americans were hiding out at a
hacienda in the nearby barrio of Natividad, and he asked that I
visit him. I was weak from the trip and suffering from malaria
and dysentery, so I arranged for a carabao sled to take me to
the meeting.

I found the colonel living in a large, well-built house owned
by a wealthy family of Filipino planters. He and the other
Americans—officers and enlisted men—had all escaped from
Bataan and had been adopted by the family. They no longer had
the emaciated aspect of the past months, but were filling out
under the care of their hosts and their three unmarried daughters.

I could barely walk, so Cadizon helped me from the sled and
up the steps into the spacious *sala*. The Americans crowded
around me, shaking my hand. Their uniforms had been mended
and pressed, their skin was scrubbed, and their plump faces
beamed at me. In my worn khakis and cadaverous slump, I felt
suddenly soiled and spare.

As we sipped tea and nibbled at the sweets the daughters
pressed upon us, my compatriots questioned me about my
activities. Explaining our organization and plans, I offered to
take them back to Timbo to meet with Thorpe and join the
guerillas. There was a distinct pause.

"I knew Thorpe before the war," the colonel said. "Good
man. Do give him my regards when you see him."

Clearly they were not interested in guerilla warfare but had
decided to wait out the war in the comfort of the hacienda. I
could feel the warm wellings of the dysentery, and so, fearful of
embarrassing myself and our hosts, I said good-bye. Outside I
again lay on the bamboo sled slung behind the black bulk of the
carabao, and the Americans waved and wished me luck as we
started back toward Porac.

For a moment as I bumped and jostled along I felt a

righteous resentment at their comfort. They would wait out the war as guests of the planters, enjoying the attentions of the ladies, while I faced a future of hiding in the jungles and dodging the Japanese. But then my resentment turned upon myself. Had they not taken the practical decision, and had I not allowed myself, yet again, to be swayed by romantic notions? I was no guerilla commander darting through the jungles: I was an invalid cavalryman without a horse; a law student at Oklahoma, a paperboy from Wichita. Why did I keep volunteering myself for thankless causes? When would I ever learn?

It was growing dark as we arrived at a *barrio* south of Porac. The dogs were barking, a certain sign of trouble, and we stopped short. At a nearby farmhouse, light still flickered in the windows, so I sent Cadizon to inquire. The farmer was terrified. A squadron of Huks had entered the village a few moments before, he told us, and had announced their intention to spend the night.

By this time our conflict with the Huks had escalated to a dangerous degree, and so I took this chance encounter as an opportunity to meet with their leaders and reason out a settlement. Cadizon helped me to my feet, I straightened my uniform as best I could, and together we started off on foot across the village. There were no lights and no moon. The Huks had not yet posted guards, and so we were not challenged as we made our way to the hut where we could see their officers squatting around a lantern and their rice bowls.

I climbed the ladder and poked my head up through the opening in the floor. A young, square-faced lieutenant was seated at a table haranguing the others. When he caught sight of my white face floating above the bamboo floor, his mouth snapped shut and he sat staring stupidly. The others turned, and there was a stunned silence in the room.

I smiled, lifted myself into the room, and asked to speak with the senior officer. The lieutenant demanded to know who I was, and Cadizon explained. Their surprise turned to amazement.

"Stay where you are," the lieutenant pattered out in Tagalog. "I will get my superior."

He was down the ladder in an instant. I stood among the other men, fighting the numbness I felt creeping over me. I knew I could not show weakness among these people, yet the days of travel had worn me to the point of collapse. Cadizon watched me out of the corner of his eye and warily scanned the Huks, who still sat staring in silence.

From outside came the lieutenant's voice calling me to come down. I eased myself down the ladder with Cadizon close behind and confronted the lieutenant. Without warning, he barked an order and a dozen men appeared from the darkness, jerking their rifles at me and bolting cartridges into the chambers. I looked at them a moment in disbelief, and passed out.

When I regained consciousness an hour later, I was lying on the floor of a hut with my head in Cadizon's lap. At first I was terrified by the thought that I was paralyzed, for I could not move my arms or legs. Then, gradually, the sensation returned, and I cautiously opened my eyes. A coconut oil lamp burned in one corner, casting a dirty amber glow about the room. A guard had been posted at the door, but his back was to us. I squeezed Cadizon's arm to let him know I was awake, but I made no further move.

Outside an argument was raging. Voices shouted back and forth in quick and strident Pampango, the local dialect, of which I could not understand a word. The fight became so animated that the guard slipped down the ladder to get a better look, and I asked Cadizon in a whisper what was going on.

"The lieutenant says you are a German spy," he whispered back. "He says Taruc has denounced you and given order for your capture and execution. But one of his men says he knew you in the Twenty-sixth Cavalry, and he says that it is not true."

I told Cadizon that we must get away, and that with his help I thought I could make it. There was a small back entrance to the hut. Cadizon dragged me to it and lowered me to the ground, dropping down after me. Then, lifting me onto his back, he carried me to a sugarcane field at the edge of the clearing and we slipped in.

The cane was higher than our heads, and it whipped and slashed at us as we hurried through. Every few dozen yards I had to stop and hang onto Cadizon to keep from blacking out. Suddenly we heard shouts from the village, and we knew that our escape had been discovered.

Cadizon gripped me under the arms and uged me forward. I was swaying between nausea and collapse, and my legs would not respond. We could hear the cane being thrashed behind us as the Huks waded in. In that crazy labyrinth thick with spiking leaves and darkness, we saw no way out. We could not tell if we were going straight or in circles, outdistancing the Huks or heading back toward them.

Shouts came from all around us now, along with the sounds of men shoving the cane aside. Cadizon whispered in my ear: "There, look!" Ahead the cane thinned out, and we could make out the banks of a stream. We hurried forward, dropping to our knees at the edge and sliding down into the water. The stream swirled with the recent rains, and we were dragged and tossed wildly along, trying to swim or stand. At last we were thrown against the bank at a bend, and we managed to pull ourselves free. We crawled up onto the earth and hid ourselves in the jungle until we felt sure that we were safe.

My collapse among the Huks at Porac, I began to understand, had been a mild stroke, and all the way back to the Timbo district I experienced fits of paralysis and unconsciousness. I was anxious to get back to our headquarters, and to the friends and provisions there. Also, I wanted to warn Barker and our people about the Huks, on whom it was clear we now needed to wage all-out war.

Cadizon left me with some farmers from our network and went on ahead to fetch a carabao to take me in to Timbo. When he returned, however, it was with the worst possible news. During our absence, Timbo had been raided by the Japanese.

The village had been burnt and the families scattered. Thorpe and Barker had escaped, but no one knew where they were.

It was a blow, and my morale plummeted. With Timbo gone we would have to take refuge at one of our outposts. The nearest was a training camp we had established on Mount Negron, southwest of Porac. It was a wild, inaccessible place, a jungle clearing now sunk in a sea of thick cogon grass that bristled up seven and eight feet high and made travel all but impossible. The camp was run by a Filipino major named Francisco Ocampo whom I had recruited at Timbo, and again I sent Cadizon on ahead to notify him of our arrival.

When Cadizon returned, he brought a carabao sled for me and a squad of Ocampo's soldiers to guide us. They had with them a prisoner, a wiry Negrito whom they had caught stealing guns. He was led between two soldiers by ropes tied around his neck, and his black face was twisted and tormented by the ceaseless tugging.

I was dragged on the carabao sled to the jungle slopes, where the sled was discarded and I was hefted onto the animal's back. Then, as the soldiers slashed a path for us, the carabao lumbered forward, its loose skin shifting sluggishly from its shoulders to its croup, threatening with every step to slide me off.

It was afternoon before we reached Ocampo's base, a pair of huts built back to back in the heart of the cogon wilderness. The major welcomed me and ordered his men to make me comfortable in one of the shacks. The Negrito prisoner was placed in the other under guard.

I told Ocampo that my immediate concern was to contact Joe Barker, and he offered to send men at once with Cadizon to search for him. He set up an outpost down the trail to warn us of Japanese patrols, dividing his men into squads and dispersing them across the hills. Meanwhile, Ocampo went down to the lowlands for supplies, leaving one of his lieutenants behind to supervise the guard and prisoner and look after me.

That night the lieutenant cooked rice and fish over the little firebox in our hut and, after serving me, went next door to feed the prisoner. After dinner I fell into a deep sleep, the first I had had in days, and was disturbed only vaguely when the lieutenant got up to check on the prisoner. Through the thin dividing wall of grass I could hear him talking quietly with the guard, and heard the restless shuffling of the little Negrito on the bamboo floor.

At about 1:00 A.M. the lieutenant rose again and went next door. I heard him make his way to the hut, but this time there was no whispered exchange. Instead, a rifle shot exploded close to my head, the blast ripping through the grass divider.

I was torn, terrified and trembling, from my sleep. My nerves, wrought up from the day's events and the illness, now throbbed to breaking. The explosion had loosed my bowels, and I lay alone in the hut, sweating and shaking uncontrollably. I shouted several times for the lieutenant, and when I got no reply I knew instinctively what had happened. The prisoner and the guard must have conspired to kill the lieutenant, and next they would be after me.

I expected at any moment that they would burst in and shoot me. I pulled out my .45 and fired three quick shots through the wall, then dragged myself to the entrance and stumbled across the clearing into the cogon grass. I crawled on my belly for a few yards, then rolled onto my back and froze.

It was pitch black and I could not see six inches from my face. I knew that Negritos were excellent night hunters, and I expected the prisoner to be upon me before I realized it. I lay still, listening for any sound, swinging the barrel of the .45 this way and that, barely restraining myself from squeezing the trigger. I would have to get him with my first shot. If nothing else, my smell would draw him.

An hour passed. There were stirrings in the grass all around me, but none came near. My only hope was that the gunfire had alerted the outpost and that the guards would come to my rescue. After four hours the sky lightened, and I could hear voices coming up the trail. I called to them, and in a few minutes the outpost guards were crashing through the grass in search of me.

My instinct had been right; the guard had been a relative of the prisoner and together they had killed the lieutenant. His body was found inside the hut door, shot through the heart. Trails in the cogon grass showed that the killers had then come in search of me, but had given up and fled.

I sent a runner to Major Ocampo to tell him what had happened. When the major returned he was furious; the lieutenant had been a close friend of his, a local man with a wife and eight children. He ordered an immediate search, swearing that the fugitives must be found and brought back alive or dead. Meanwhile, the lieutenant's body was carried down to his family, who greeted it with a display of ritual howling and tears.

It was a week before Ocampo's men found the murderers, following their trail through the cogon grass and jungle. I was hobbling around the little camp with Cadizon's help, trying to get back on my feet, when the patrol returned, parting the curtain of grass. Two of the men carried bamboo trays of the kind that I had seen women use to winnow rice. Major Ocampo was called and the trays were placed on the ground before him. But instead of rice, each bore a severed head. In one I recognized the twisted, tormented face of the little Negrito. Ocampo nodded approvingly and told the men to impale them on bamboo poles as an example.

Later that day I had news from Joe Barker. He was staying at a barrio of Angeles, an important town and railroad depot south of Fort Stotsenberg. Major Ocampo offered to take me to the farm of one of his men in the lowlands, and to bring Barker to meet me. I was glad to accept, and gladder still to be free of the sea of cogon grass in which I had been marooned these long weeks.

I was still weak from my ordeal, but I waited impatiently for Barker to appear. At last he came ambling up the trail, looking even leaner and more worn than when I had last seen him six weeks before.

"I hear you've had adventures," he said, smiling, as he shook my hand.

"You haven't exactly been on vacation yourself," I remarked.

"Life among the guerillas," he shrugged. "We're homeless, I'm afraid. Timbo's gone."

I told him that I knew. "We'll start someplace else."

He nodded. His face had grown thinner and, I thought, older. "You know what Comrade Mao says: Guerillas need a base like a man needs his rear end—a place to sit down when they're tired. But first, since we've got this little break, why don't we take the cure at Fassoth's. They have a doctor there, I understand, an American."

I was in no condition to disagree. We gathered up our few things and started back into the hills. It was October and the typhoon season would soon end. Then, after the streams had shrunk and the trails were dry again, we would scout a new base and rebuild.

Our army now numbered more than twenty-five hundred men and was growing every day. And there was work to do in Manila. Once we were healthy again, Barker and I agreed, I would go there and visit the cadres in person. It was a risky trip, but Santos and Alberto had written us that it was important to the morale of the Manila network.

For my part, I was looking forward to it. Many brave people were there whom we had come to know only through their code names and their reports. Now I was anxious for the opportunity to meet them and to thank them for their sacrifices face-to-face.

Gold

B ill Fassoth's camp had grown considerably since last Joe Barker and I had visited it. Now, in the fall of 1942, nearly a hundred American soldiers were living at the camp full-time, men who had abandoned plans for escape and were waiting out the war. The doctor about whom Joe had heard was a Captain Warshall, and he greeted me with a grimace.

"You're not going anywhere for a few weeks, Lieutenant," he told me after the examination. I tried to protest, but he ordered me to shut up. "You need rest, and I intend to see that you get it."

Barker, too, was in a bad state, but the doctor agreed that he could travel again in a week or two.

"It looks like I'll be going to Manila instead of you," Joe said to me.

Reluctantly I had to agree. I was in no condition to make the long, trying trip. The journey itself would so wear me out that when I got there I would likely be of little use. I was drained physically and emotionally. Never having regained the weight I had lost on Bataan, I was now down to about a hundred and twenty pounds, a good forty below my prewar weight. What was more, the Huk encounter and the Mount Negron shooting had shattered my already frayed nerves.

My stay at Fassoth's was an enforced idleness, and in some ways it was as hard on me as the months of organizing had been. I lay around the camp chatting with the other Americans, trying to interest them in the guerilla movement, but they made it clear they had no wish to join. A few even resented my presence, suggesting pointedly that it might be better for everyone if Barker and I moved on.

"We're not guerillas," some of the men told us. "If we're captured, we'll be treated as prisoners of war. But if they take us with you, we might all be killed."

It drove home to me the unorthodox position I was in, and for the first time since I had joined Thorpe I tried to take stock of my condition. I had now lived and fought in the jungles and rice paddies for ten months. Strictly speaking, I was no longer a soldier but a war rebel; an outlaw more than an officer. But though our legal status as American guerillas was vague, I never doubted that we had the right and the duty to oppose the Japanese occupation.

Indeed, guerilla work had now become second nature to me. I no longer felt strange slipping through the countryside at night, hiding out in the hills, and carrying on secret induction ceremonies in the barrios while Camacho or Cadizon held an oil lamp and I swore strangers to my service with whispered oaths. And if any proof of the necessity of our work was needed, it could be found in the support and kindness of the Filipino people. Thousands of them had already risked their lives for the resistance, and hundreds had been captured, tortured, and put to death.

There had been sacrifices among our own ranks as well. Captain Jack Spies had been killed on his way to take up his command in southern Luzon. We learned that those of our officers who were captured were being held in Fort Santiago in Manila, a prison that was becoming notorious as a torture chamber. Our operatives in Manila occasionally got word to us of their sufferings, and the reports were grim.

Agents working around the prison told of tortures medieval in their crudeness. Suspected guerillas had had lighted matches thrust under their fingernails and white-hot irons applied to their genitals. Women came in for especially cruel treatment, including rape and mutilation. Most insidious of all was what the Japanese called "the water cure." A hose was forced down the victim's throat and water pumped in until the stomach bloated out grotesquely. Then a guard kicked and stamped the prisoner until he talked, or his insides burst.

Colonel Nagahama was sparing nothing to uncover our agents in Manila and to raid our posts in the provinces. Intimidation, threats, and violence were the kempei-tai's chief weapons in the effort to break our movement, but despite severe suffering our cadres remained steadfast, and the Filipino people's loyalty to the resistance continued unbroken.

I was not high on the kempei-tai's death list, but that was of little consolation. More troubling to me was the anguish I knew my mother and sister felt, for I had been officially listed as missing in action. Even though the War Department knew that I was still alive, the fact of my survival had to be kept a classified secret, for my security and that of my comrades in the resistance. I was thus as isolated as it was possible for a soldier to be: behind enemy lines, stripped of my status as an officer, the very fact of my existence held as a military secret.

A vital friend of the resistance in central Luzon was Father Joseph Hurley, the head of the Jesuit order in the Philippines. While I remained at Fassoth's camp, I wrote a long letter to him explaining my situation and entrusting him with my will and letters to my mother and sister to be delivered in the event of my death. All of these documents, he promised, would be kept in his safe at the Jesuit residence in Manila. It was a selfless act, for if the Japanese raided his home and discovered them, it would mean his death.

These were strange gestures for me, and I reflected during the long days of convalescence on how much had changed in my short life, the whole of which was now shaped by wars of varying levels of brutality.

There had been the desperate, forlorn fighting on Bataan, the failure of which MacArthur in Australia and we in Luzon were struggling to redeem. And there was this peculiar guerilla war, whose methods and meaning we were still trying to invent. There was, too, the annoying war with illness, which sapped mental and physical strength that I sorely needed in order to keep up with Barker's dogged organizing.

Shadowing the other conflicts, imbuing them with a more intimate darkness, was the struggle within myself, which emerged with particular violence whenever the other fights had weakened me beyond my power to suppress it. It was the old struggle to stifle brooding, to curb emotion, and to be effective, efficient, and practical.

Fighting on all these fronts at once was draining, but it was also making me a better officer. As I became more spontaneous and more relaxed in command, I relied more and more on my instincts and inventiveness. My perceptions, my responses, my love of risk had been refined by my experiences from casual to calculated. I no longer enjoyed danger for the excitement of it; rather, I saw it now as a necessary part of a larger purpose.

Some of this was the result of Joe Barker's example. He was as cool as it was possible for a committed man to be: His passion warmed his commitment but did not consume it. He did his job methodically, ardently, ignoring circumstance and, so far as I could tell, without any thought of failure. Though only twenty-six, scarcely two years my senior, he seemed to me possessed of a composure deeper than his age. Despite Bataan, defeat simply never formed a part of his calculations. What had to be done was clear, and so he attended to the business of its details.

His attitude sharply contrasted with that of another young officer at Fassoth's camp. A first lieutenant fresh out of college, he had escaped from Bataan, where he had suffered the same privations as the rest of us. He, however, refused to recover. Though there was plenty of food at Fassoth's, along with the active care of a doctor and nurse, this young officer would not eat, would not will himself well again. Instead, he was obsessed with the idea that his government had deserted him and left him helpless before his enemies. And so, while everyone around him was regaining weight and health, he continued to decline until finally, for no reason the doctor could resolve, he died.

It was my first introduction to this strange malaise, and it was a sobering one. It drove home to me once again the truth of which I was already aware, that mind and attitude together shape will, and that when will is lost, defeat follows. It was a lesson Nadine had learned so keenly after the awful plane crash. She had not surrendered; she had fought back and won. I had seen it myself, I had helped her, and for my own part, I reflected, I must do no less.

After a week's rest, Joe Barker set out on a month-long organizing trek prior to his trip to Manila. Before he left we agreed that as soon as I was able to travel I would go to Bataan and integrate John Boone's guerillas into our command. That, together with our efforts in central Luzon and Joe's trip to Manila, would mean the consolidation of half of the territory for which we were responsible. Then it would be necessary to extend our network northward, toward the mountain provinces and Lingayen Gulf.

A few days after Joe left, the camp was thrown onto alert. One of the runners who brought us supplies from the lowlands was captured by the Japanese and tortured until he revealed our location. As soon as word reached us, the senior officers gave orders to break up the camp and disperse. The few possessions the men had accumulated were thrown into duffels and bamboo baskets. Documents were destroyed, and the men splintered off into small groups and headed into the hills. Only Dr. Warshall and Martin Fassoth chose to go with me, guiding me to the hut of a Negrito loyalist higher up in the mountains.

We remained there through the first week of October, and it was an extraordinary time. Our aging, diminutive host had three young wives, and he spent considerable time regaling us with accounts of his sexual exploits and imparting marital wisdom to us. He was hilarious, pattering out anecdotes in broken English, the main feature of which was an elaborate array of swear words.

"You see my goddamn women," he would lisp happily through big gaps in his teeth, "you see they got no sonofabitch-ing shoes? Never give no shoes to no goddamn woman, 'cause she just run away into town on you. Woman don't need no goddamn shoes, need a man like me to make her a big belly." And while he railed good-humoredly about them, his coquettish wives stood giggling behind the hut.

In the evening, however, around his little stone-ringed fire, he would squat on his haunches, his thin loincloth tucked tightly between his thighs, and tell us stories about gold. There was, he assured us solemnly, a mountain far back in the range, many days' trek, with three streams flowing from its top. In each of these streams he had found nuggets, some the size of pebbles, some the size of his clenched fist. It was a bad thing, gold, he said, and he wanted nothing of it; he was content with his wives and hunting. But any man might go up there and scoop the nuggets from the streams, he swore to us, and become rich.

He spoke in such earnest that we believed him, his little yellow eyes flitting from one of us to the other, now painting pictures of fabulous wealth, now of the danger of gold. It made men mad, he said, ruined their lives. His gold was here, the three black women who served and doted on him, and who kept him young with their incessant wigglings. But Fassoth, the doctor, and I decided we would take the risk, and we swore that when the war was over, we would come back and have the Negrito guide us to the mountain.

There was no word of trouble from the camp, and so we started down again. On the trail I stumbled over a log and found blood on my trouser leg. The log, I saw, was smeared thick with it, and the trail was spotted. We moved on more cautiously until we came in sight of the camp. It was a ruin burnt to the ground, the bamboo rubble still smoldering.

We turned and ran; the Japanese might still be in the area. A hundred meters farther on we came across the outpost that had protected the back entrance to the camp. The cooking pots were scattered, the grass was trampled flat for yards around, and blood was spattered everywhere. A few yards off in the grass we found the bodies of the guards, their throats slashed.

We withdrew farther into the mountains, where we wandered for several days until we found Bill Fossoth's men. Bill told us what had happened.

He and the others had hidden out in the foothills until it appeared the danger had passed. One by one the little groups came back, until most of the men had returned to camp. Then one night an outpost guard raised the alarm: It was a Japanese raid, and the men began diving through windows and scattering into the bush. Five were captured, Bill told us, and thirty more were killed.

He and a dozen men had managed to escape, but the Japanese were onto him now, and for the sake of his family he had decided to turn himself in. I could not dissuade him. His courage and his kindness had meant a great deal to me, and as we parted I wished him well. I never saw him again.

By the end of October, I was strong enough for the trip to John Boone's camp in Bataan. My health was better but by no means good. The malaria had receded, and I was controlling the dysentery with weekly injections of a drug called demetine, which our Manila cadres smuggled out to me. I was still badly underweight, however, and subject to spells of weakness and fainting. Joe Barker, meanwhile, wrote to tell me that he was starting out for Manila. We were now both back at guerilla warfare full-time, and the fact was invigorating to me.

Boone's camp was in the hills northwest of Dinalupihan at the entrance to the Bataan peninsula. He greeted me with the same brash grin I'd remembered from our meeting in April, and before I asked, offered to place his guerillas under Barker's and my command. It was a selfless, dutiful gesture, for Boone's group had grown to several hundred men, and they were clearly attached to him. I accepted and then promoted Boone, who was a corporal in the regular army, to captain in the East Central Luzon Guerilla Area forces.

"*Captain* . . ." Boone repeated, savoring the sound of it.

Then he gave me a disbelieving squint. "Can you do that?" he asked. "I mean, with respect, you're a lieutenant, sir."

"I'm deputy commander," I answered. "I'm acting on Joe Barker's authority and Colonel Thorpe's." I reflected a minute and then added, "And General MacArthur's, too."

In the way of this strange war I supposed I *was* acting on MacArthur's authority. There were so few of us in the guerilla command, and we were operating under such unorthodox conditions that each of us would have to take extraordinary measures if we were to have any chance not only to succeed but simply to survive. It was no time to stand on ceremony; an army had to be built from scratch, and that army was MacArthur's. I was a twenty-five-year-old lieutenant speaking for the commanding general, but his name was the most potent weapon I had, and for the sake of realizing his promise to return, I would act on his authority.

"Well, if it's okay by MacArthur," Boone drawled, "it's okay by me."

I planned to stay with Boone for the next few months, supervising his efforts to complete the organization of Bataan. He welcomed the help and told me that he had a favor to ask.

Some months before, his troops had killed a local man who had been collaborating with the Japanese. For security reasons the man's wife had been brought into the camp as a prisoner, and this had posed a tricky problem for Boone. He could not release her since she knew the location of the camp, but the presence of an attractive young woman might cause trouble among the troops.

"It's a tough problem," I admitted. "We haven't been in business long enough to have a policy on prisoners. Up till now we've just been interrogating them and letting them go. But I guess we're going to have to come up with some . . ."

Boone interrupted me. "That's not the problem," he said. "Fact is, since she's been here, we've fallen in love with each other."

"Oh," I said, with some embarrassment. I had been prepared to formulate policy, when in fact his concern was romance.

"We want to live together," Boone went on, "but it'd be bad for morale. But it's driving me nuts that we can't be together. What do you think I should do, Lieutenant?"

I thought it over a long minute. "Why don't you marry her?" I suggested.

"But . . . how?" Boone asked.

"Well, I'm the senior officer in this area," I said. "I'll do it."

I was not sure I had the authority to conduct a marriage, but I could not imagine who else had. Besides, Mao had written that the guerilla commander must act as the sole legitimate authority in the country, and I supposed that included having the power to marry people. In any case, Boone jumped at the idea. It was November and his birthday was coming up, so he proposed that we combine the two celebrations.

When the announcement was made, Boone's headquarters troops set to work at once preparing for the ceremony. A hillside behind the camp was dug out to make room for the reception, and a sprawling shelter of bamboo covered with banana leaves was erected for the wedding. Young ladies were recruited in Dinalupihan for the dancing, and an orchestra was raised among the troops comprising a bull fiddle, two guitars, a violin, and drums.

When the day came, the bride and groom appeared through an archway of palm leaves, he in clean khakis and she in a pretty print dress. I had no breviary, and so I made up the words of the ceremony as I went along. It was quite moving, or at least I was moved as I enunciated the vows and pronounced them man and wife.

The reception was a gleeful affair. There were barbecued chickens and pigs, roasted yams, and an unquenchable quantity of *bossy* and *tuba*. Speeches were made in English, Spanish, Tagalog, and several local dialects, and though I could not understand most of them, the message was clear: long life, prosperity, and peace. Then the orchestra huffed and strummed and squealed to life, and as usual I led the dancing. The Japanese, obligingly, were absent.

The party lasted into the evening. Over the jungle hills the sun set slowly. I strolled down from the camp to a languid stream and sat down to watch the daylight disappear. Everything was green and gold and fading, and for the first time the jungle took on a tranquil, even beautiful aspect.

There was a noise behind me and I looked up. It was a young woman from Dinalupihan with whom I had danced more than once. She came and stood by me shyly, saying nothing. I asked if she was looking for someone.

"You," she managed to say.

I asked what she meant.

"I think you are alone," she began quietly. "It would be a great honor to me if you would take me as your woman." She glanced at me quickly to be sure she had not offended me and then continued on. "I will come and live with you and take care of your needs."

I did not know how to reply. She stood in silence, watching me expectantly. She was lovely, small, and slender, with long black hair and dark eyes. I was fearful of offending her, but I had made a pledge; I had given my word to a friend, and his safety might depend on it.

I thanked her and told her as gently as I could that it was not possible. The way I lived—the danger, the uncertainty— was not something I could ever share with someone so precious. She nodded, and I thought from the expression of her eyes that she understood. She was about to turn and go when I stopped her.

"Please," I heard myself say, "before you go, let me just . . . look at you. . . ."

She smiled and turned back toward me. Unfastening her party dress, she let it drop to the ground. Her body caught the last glow of the sun, and it too shone gold. Only the shadows beneath her breasts retained their native brown.

I looked at her for a long time. There had in all these

months of war been moments of beauty: the orchid, the jungle sunset, and now her. Somehow they were smoothing out the turmoil in my soul, balancing the effects of war. For a moment I wanted to try to explain to her how much her gesture, her beauty, meant to me, but I knew that I could not make her understand; I was not sure I yet understood myself.

Instead I whispered thank you. She smiled, wrapped herself again, and was gone.

It was December before I had word from Joe Barker. He was in Manila, swearing in Santos's and Alberto's cadres, and it was going well. There was bad news, however. Barker had learned from our operatives in Manila that Colonel Thorpe had been captured. He had been taken at his headquarters north of Fort Stotsenberg in a lightning raid. Evidently there had been an informant, for the Japanese had known exactly where to find him. Now he was being held in Fort Santiago with the others, and tortured mercilessly. Barker warned me to be careful.

He added that he supposed he would have to take Thorpe's place in command of the Luzon Guerilla Force, and that I would be in charge of east central Luzon. "I ought to congratulate you," he closed, "since, according to our agents in Manila, you are now number two, behind me, on the kempei-tai's death list."

General Baba

I t had never seriously occurred to Joe Barker and me that we would survive the war. When we escaped from Bataan we had given ourselves at most ninety days to live. Since then we had lived one day at a time, knowing that at any moment we could be killed. The stress of that awareness might have destroyed us had we not plunged completely into our work. To blunt it we kept ourselves busy—indeed, preoccupied—with the job of organizing the resistance.

I allowed myself no time for reflection, concentrating wholly on the business of identifying civic leaders, preparing them as officers, recruiting cadres, and training the troops. Had I stopped to think about the work in wider terms, I might have been overwhelmed by the immensity of it. Joe Barker and I were to organize an underground army with no communications and virtually no resources among a population of three million and under the noses of a hundred fifty thousand Japanese soldiers. We were not, as Mao had suggested, fish in the sea; we were minnows in an ocean infested with sharks.

Isolation was another factor. Totally cut off from the outside world, we had no comprehensive knowledge of the progress of the war. We knew that MacArthur still held out in Australia, but though we sent every scrap of intelligence we accumulated to his headquarters, we rarely received replies. More and more I came to rely on faith—faith in the importance of the resistance, faith in the Filipino people, and faith in MacArthur, whom I had not met and had never even seen.

It was this faith, and a narrow focus on the labor to be accomplished in Luzon, that preserved my equilibrium and absorbed my energy. The work was new, demanding, and dangerous, and I concentrated all my attention upon it. For not only my morale was at stake; my health required that I not let up an instant, for whenever I did I was subject to collapse. I thus relied on the weight and momentum of my work to keep my emotional and physical health intact.

Every so often, however, the truth of our condition imposed itself with brutal force. The news of Colonel Thorpe's capture was one such reminder. Another was the report I received of the death of Captain Ralph McGuire. McGuire had been commander of the west central Luzon guerillas, an energetic, amiable man whom I had known slightly before the war. One of his own men had cut off his head and taken it to the Japanese.

Such treachery, rare as it was, reflected the changes that had taken place within the Japanese command. Resistance was growing throughout Luzon and in the neighboring islands as well, and the Japanese were unable to suppress it. Their unbroken propaganda about a "Greater East Asian co-prosperity sphere" and "Asia for the Asians" had not shaken the Filipino people's determination to be free, nor eroded their loyalty to the American war effort.

Critical to this resolve was MacArthur's promise to return. The Filipino people believed that pledge implicitly, and they welcomed us as his representatives in his absence. For my part, I did not doubt that MacArthur would return, and all of our efforts were geared to that end. But how long it might be before an invasion was possible, I could not know, for I had no idea of the course the war was taking. What was more, with each passing month the Japanese occupation assumed a greater air of permanence, penetrating every aspect of Filipino life and thought.

They were heavy-handed conquerors, appealing at once to visions of wealth as well as to racism and fear. In return for cooperation the Japanese promised fabulous prosperity within a pan-Pacific commonwealth of Asian peoples. This theme formed the centerpiece of their propaganda, and in the face of shortages and rationing the racial aspect was stressed.

Much was made of the Filipinos sharing their Asian identity with the Japanese, though in fact they were invariably treated as inferiors. The Japanese made it clear that destiny had made them masters of Asia, and failure to recognize this resulted in punishment of the most severe kind. A sharp sword-edge divided the promises of prosperity that cooperation brought from the reality of retribution that resistance of any kind invited.

Nonetheless, only a small minority of Filipinos was cowed into neutrality and an even smaller one into collaboration. Even as the occupation took hold and became more vicious and brutal, the volume of intelligence flowing from our movement to Australia increased, and the cadres began to engage in acts of sabotage.

In keeping with our dictum to attack only when sure of success, our cadres concentrated on scattered, punctual acts of violence. Whenever a convoy could be isolated in the hills it was attacked, the guerillas melting into the countryside. Supply dumps and ammunition depots were frequent targets, and vehicles parked in motor pools and airplanes on the tarmac were disabled whenever possible. The constant in all these actions was their low-risk nature. Our cadres were sternly discouraged from undertaking operations that would expose either them or the wider population to Japanese retaliation, though arbitrary reprisals aimed at intimidating the people occurred nonetheless.

For the Japanese the resistance was not only a military problem but also an affront to their pride, an insufferable loss of face. An all-out effort to annihilate the guerillas was launched, and responsibility for its success was given to the chief of the Japanese counterintelligence corps, General Baba.

In January 1943, Baba installed himself at Colonel Nagahama's kempei-tai headquarters in Manila and laid out his program. Its key elements were informants, raids, rewards, and torture. Informants were to be recruited wherever and by whatever means possible. This included threats as well as bribes. Baba also ordered greater use of the Sakdalistas, a militantly pro-Japanese group of Filipinos who had collaborated with the invasion and actively supported the occupation.

The Sakdalistas had set up their own informant network called the Makapili, which reported directly to Baba's headquarters. Although very small in number, the Makapili were insidious, for they were extremely secretive, wore no uniforms, and were indistinguishable from their countrymen in towns and villages.

Raids on our camps were to be carried out on a continuous basis; no moment's peace could be allowed for us to organize or relocate. When necessary, entire villages and even districts would be raided in the hope of sweeping up our cadres. Such raids could be ruthless. Japanese soldiers would descend without warning, burn everything, abuse and threaten the people, and arrest anyone who looked suspicious.

Torture was stepped up and became more systematic and concentrated. Baba knew that fully a fourth of our guerilla army was engaged in intelligence, that our spies had infiltrated the Japanese command, and that even his own headquarters were compromised. Whenever his people captured one of our officers or operatives, word reached us quickly and we began at once to make preparations to move. This meant that the kempei-tai had only a short time, a few days or less, in which to force information about us from their prisoners.

General Baba also put prices on our heads—literally. His headquarters announced that bounty would be paid to anyone who brought in the severed head of a guerilla leader. It was in this way that Ralph McGuire had been killed. The hunt for the rest of us became an obsession with Baba, and though every officer who was taken was immediately replaced, each new capture was for him a personal victory.

The growing pressure did not serve to frighten the Filipino people from us. After New Year's, 1943, John Boone and I traveled throughout Bataan recruiting cadres and appointing new officers. At Morong, where I had led the cavalry charge, we were welcomed by the mayor and the entire population as heroes. In Bagac all the town leaders volunteered to join our army, and in a matter of weeks the entire west coast of Bataan had been organized. From that point on, no ship could enter or leave Manila Bay via the China Sea coast without our knowledge and without reports being sent at once to MacArthur's headquarters.

January was nearly over when we returned to Boone's camp at Dinalupihan. Waiting for us was Mercado, an officer from one of our Manila cadres, and I could tell by his face that he bore bad news. The Japanese had learned of Barker's presence in Manila, Mercado said, and General Baba had ordered a manhunt. Informants were squeezed for any scrap of information, hundreds of people had been hauled in and tortured, whole districts were being raided.

Barker, he said, was based in Tondo, the flood-plain shanty-town of Manila, overrun with refugees and bandits and crowded with squatter shacks. It was so forbidding a neighborhood that even the kempei-tai were reluctant to enter it, and what was more, it was a center of intense anti-Japanese hatred. From his hiding places among its swarming streets, Joe made forays across Manila dressed in the soutane of a Roman Catholic priest. For nearly three months he had been moving ceaselessly among the cadres, giving speeches, swearing in officers, collecting intelligence.

Then, on January 8, Joe Barker's bodyguard, Tarzan, was captured, betrayed by a Makapili spy. The little boxer was tortured steadily for three days until he gave up the where-abouts of Alejandro Santos. On the 11th, Santos and most of his staff were seized in a raid. Under torture one of Santos's staff officers revealed that Tarzan was Joe Barker's bodyguard, and the kempei-tai again turned savagely upon him.

Barker, meanwhile, had fled Manila to a remote hill district northeast of the city. He stopped for the night at the home of one of our operatives, intending to return next morning to Porac. At dawn dozens of heavily armed kempei-tai troops surrounded the house. Joe had no chance. They burst in and arrested him as he slept.

He has taken to Fort Santiago where he joined Thorpe, Santos, and dozens of others in the filthy underground cells. Our agents in the prison reported that he was being tortured continuously, and that stories of his defiance were already spreading across Manila.

For me this was the severest blow so far. It was not only a deep personal loss but an organizational one as well. Fausto Alberto, now the senior officer in Manila, reported that infor-mation gained from the prisoners about the size of our organi-zation had shocked General Baba, and he had ordered the raids kept up. Thousands of people were being arrested, including hundreds of our operatives and senior officers. The Manila network had been dealt a heavy blow.

I wrote back to Alberto, appointing him as acting commander of Manila until I could come to the city and take charge personally. I ordered him to begin making preparations for my visit, but he wrote back quickly to say that it was still far too dangerous for me to enter Manila.

It was an unstable, potentially dangerous period for the resistance. Despite the devastation, the leadership had to reassert itself. Accordingly, on February 1, I wrote and issued a document that I rather grandly titled General Order Number 1. In it I announced that, in view of Captain Barker's capture, I was assuming command of the East Central Luzon Guerilla Area forces, effective as of January 13, the date of his capture. This order I had printed and distributed to our cadres all over Luzon.

I was now the sole commander of the Luzon Guerilla Force, which now numbered over ten thousand men and women, and one of the few American guerilla commanders still at large in Luzon. As such I became the most wanted man on General Baba's death list, a fact confirmed to me within two weeks of my order by our agents at kempei-tai headquarters.

Their report added an interesting detail: From the kempei-tai's interrogation of prisoners, a composite drawing of myself had been assembled that Colonel Nagahama now kept displayed on his desk. Our agents assured me that it was a good likeness. Meanwhile, the price on my head had been doubled, to a quarter of a million pesos, some $100,000.

The pressure to capture me and to dismantle our organization was now on in full-force. In addition to their strikes on Manila, kempei-tai raids were being carried out all across central Luzon. General Baba had also initiated a pacification program intended to dissuade citizens from joining or supporting us. This program was accompanied by a massive wave of interrogations, arbitrary arrests, and torture, most of which were aimed at locating me. Baba also introduced a macabre ritual called "zoning." An informant would be brought into a village by the kempei-tai, his head covered by a sack in which two holes had been cut for the eyes. The whole village would be ordered to assemble, and the hooded man would then silently point out collaborators, who were immediately arrested. The tactic was terrifying to the Filipinos, in its anonymity and often arbitrary denunciations. But throughout it all, despite the bribes, the threats, and the abuse, no one betrayed me.

I could not go into Manila and I had completed my work in Bataan, so I decided to move north, as Barker and I had planned, to organize the northern provinces and integrate the guerilla groups there into my command. I knew little about these groups except that they were loosely under the command of two American officers, Robert Lapham and Charles Putnam, neither of whom I had met.

As I was preparing to start north, two prisoners from Boone's camp escaped. An alarm went up, and as the two darted past the outpost, shots were fired. One of the prisoners was hit several times and killed, but the other got away.

Boone and I gave orders to prepare to move the camp in the event that the escapee betrayed us to the Japanese. While we waited for word from our people in the lowlands warning of a raid, everyone remained in a state of anxiety. Over breakfast one morning, one of Boone's officers assured us solemnly that we would not be raided that day. I asked him jokingly how he knew.

He regarded me with his pale blue eyes. "I am a psychic," he replied.

His name was George Williams, and he was a peculiar character. Part British, part Spanish, and part Filipino, he was strikingly handsome, tall, reserved, and distant. I had sometimes seen him laying out cards and gazing at them intently, but I had not known how seriously he took it. I knew that I did not, and I began to chide him. He fixed me with a rather bored but deadly earnest stare.

"I know things," he said. "I know, for instance, that I will not survive the war."

"That's a fair guess," I remarked.

"It is not a guess."

"But today we'll be safe?"

"Yes," he replied.

"Good," I said, "then maybe I'll get a decent night's sleep."

That night I bedded down in the headquarters hut with Boone, Williams, and some of the other officers. At around three o'clock we were awakened by a high-pitched, urgent shout of "Japanese! Japanese!"

It was a teenage boy who had been staying at our outpost, and now he was racing around the camp waking everyone. We all jumped from our bunks, yanked on our clothes, and grabbed our weapons.

Outside, the night was filled with moonlight. While some of the men threw out a skirmish line around the camp, Boone and I hurried up the hill behind and scanned the countryside. Everything looked quiet. There was no sign of movement in the foothills, and the trail was clear. For another hour we watched and waited, but there was nothing.

We headed back into camp, having decided that the boy had been frightened and raised a false alarm. In the headquarters hut, George Williams was laying out his cards.

"I thought you promised me a good night's sleep," I grumbled at him as I lay down again.

He looked at me in the same dispassionate way, a card poised in one hand. "I said there would be no raid yesterday," he stated. He turned the card over and laid it among the others, studying them carefully. "However, Lieutenant," he suddenly said to me, "if you are interested, we will be raided at dawn."

I pulled the mosquito net around me and growled at him to go to sleep. Then, half under my breath I muttered something about nonsense and superstition, which I hoped he would hear.

That night I had a peculiar, peaceful dream. I saw myself standing on the deck of a ship pulling out of Manila harbor.

There were people waving to me from the dock, faces I vaguely recognized, friends and fellow officers, some dead, some still alive. I was very moved; I knew I was going home, and I waved in return as the ship slid smoothly away from the Philippines. It was the first suggestion I had had since the war began that I might survive.

Then, a few hours later, just as dawn broke, our outpost was indeed attacked. There was a sudden cacophony of rifle and machine-gun fire, and in a moment mortar rounds were chugging into the camp, heaving up huts and blasting palm trees from their roots.

I dropped down the ladder and darted across the clearing for the jungle. As I reached the edge of the camp I spotted George Williams standing stoically above the cliff face that dropped away to the river below the camp. I was about to yell at him to get down when he turned suddenly and threw himself over the cliff.

Our outpost troops held off the Japanese attack and pulled back through the camp, dissolving into the jungle. Later that day Boone's men regrouped at an advance camp higher in the mountains, which Boone would now make his base. George Williams was among them, his face scratched and bruised from his leap, but otherwise unhurt.

"George," I declared, "if I ever see you with a deck of cards in your hands again I'll kill you myself and save the Japanese the trouble."

"That won't be necessary," he replied.

I remained at Boone's camp for two more weeks to help with the reorganization, and then I sent for Cadizon and Camacho to accompany me on the journey north. John Boone walked us as far as the lowlands and wished us luck.

It would be two months before I heard from Boone again. By then I was in the north, and a runner from his headquarters reached me with a letter, bringing the latest news of Bataan. "And by the way," the letter closed, "George Williams went into

Dinalupihan this morning for supplies, walked into an ambush, and was killed."

George had been right; he had not survived the war. The news left me strangely shaken. Yet my encounter with him had provoked in me a premonition, if only unconscious, that *I* might survive, and that premonition too, I could still hope, might also prove correct.

Files

I had three choices: One was to go northeast through the Huk stronghold around Mount Arayat. Another was to travel northwest through the jungles of the Zambales Mountains. The Huks still had a price on my head, and so the first was far too dangerous, while the second would take me through some of the roughest country in Luzon. So I was forced to consider a third option, to hike directly north through Fort Stotsenberg, the main Japanese garrison in central Luzon.

Since this would be my longest trip so far, nearly two hundred miles, I decided on this last, direct route. It was the riskiest of the three, and yet somehow for that very reason seemed the most likely of success, for Stotsenberg was the last place the Japanese would expect their most-wanted man to appear. What was more, I knew the area well, and Cadizon had relatives there.

We started out in early March, hiking for several days along the line of a railroad spur, then turning up a river wash and following it to the outskirts of Stotsenberg. Over ten thousand Japanese troops occupied the area, and the fort was patrolled continuously. We worked our way cautiously up the wash until we reached the little barrio of Sapangbato, where Processo

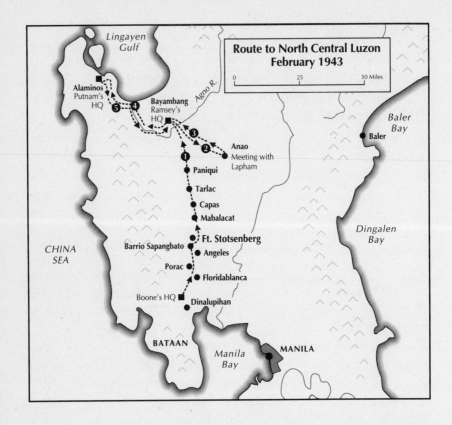

That night we had a generous meal, and Cadizon basked in
his reunion. With the wooden shutters tightly closed, we kept
the lanterns and our voices low. Every few hours we could hear
the tread of boots as a Japanese patrol passed by. They were

Cadizon's family lived. While Camacho and I kept low beneath
the overgrown banks, Cadizon slipped into the village.

He was back after nightfall. There were periodic Japanese
patrols through the barrio, he told us, but it was safe now to go
in. We followed several yards behind him, walking as casually as
we could directly to his family's hut. Cadizon's family was
excited to meet me, and for the first time it began to occur to
me that I was something of a celebrity.

That night we had a generous meal, and Cadizon basked in
his reunion. With the wooden shutters tightly closed, we kept
the lanterns and our voices low. Every few hours we could hear
the tread of boots as a Japanese patrol passed by. They were

tense moments, Cadizon's parents fretting nervously, as much for my safety as that of their son.

In the morning we were awakened by the bugles from Fort Stotsenberg. A ceremonial cannon was fired for the raising of the Japanese flag, and we could hear the soldiers shouting "Banzai!" as they bowed to the emperor and the east.

We waited in the hut all day for dark. Our plan was to move straight across the eastern edge of the fort to Clark Field, cross the runways, and push on through the town of Mabalacat. This too was a danger, since Mabalacat was sometimes controlled by the Huks.

The parting was long and emotional, and then, beneath the clouded crescent moon, we slipped out into the fort. We kept to the perimeter roads, which I recalled from my days of riding maneuvers with the troop. I had forgotten, however, how vast Stotsenberg was, and it took us hours of crouching in gullies and brush until we reached the runways of Clark.

Japanese fighters and light bombers hulked in the darkness not a hundred yards away, guarded by soldiers with bayonets fixed. We could catch a few words in Japanese as they paused to light cigarettes on their rounds. We edged along the runway until they were out of sight, paused to listen for dogs or motors, then darted across. It was now the middle of the night, and we still had not reached the northern boundary of the fort. If we were to get beyond Mabalacat before sunrise, we would have to hurry.

We kept low, nearly running, our backs to the airfield, until I spotted the perimeter road. A Japanese motor patrol was passing, and we dropped to the ground. When the clatter of the engines had died, I crept forward to the road, peered long and hard through the darkness, and signaled to Cadizon and Cama-cho to follow. We were across in seconds, crouching in the underbrush and listening hard. In the distance a motor started up but faded quickly. There was no time to lose, and we pressed on.

It took us nine hours in all to reach Mabalacat. There was not enough night left to skirt the big town, so we went straight through, counting on the last of the dark to hide our faces. On the far side we cut across the rice paddies until we found an abandoned farm shack and ducked into it for the day.

From then on, we traveled only at night. Beyond Mabalacat we found the main line of the railroad, which ran from Lingayen Gulf down to Manila. Rather than move through the rugged hill country farther west, I decided to travel straight up the tracks, quitting them only to detour around the towns where, our people had told us, there were Japanese roadblocks and posts. We kept a loose single file with yards between us so that if one of us were spotted or fired upon, the others might still get away.

We continued on another seventy kilometers to Tarlac City, a provincial capital and Japanese stronghold, circled it, and rejoined the tracks toward Paniqui, where we had cadres. Once there we would be safe, but until then we moved like fugitives, in silence, our senses alert, the safety catches off our submachine guns. It was a wearing trek for all of us. Instinctively I felt the cavalryman's resentment at being forced to walk, and I remembered Bryn Awryn with rueful bitterness.

Captain Manuel Reyes, the guerilla commander of the Tarlac district, came out to meet us, and for the next few days he guided us from town to town to swear in the cadres he had been forming. His cadres, as well as the others in Nueva Ecija and Pangasinan provinces, were under the overall command of Lieutenant Robert Lapham, a young infantry officer who had been sent north by Colonel Thorpe and Joe Barker. I did not know Bob Lapham, and I was not sure how he would react to my presence in his district or my effort to persuade him to place himself under my command.

I sent a message to Lapham notifying him of my arrival and asking for a meeting. Meanwhile, I continued north to the village of Bayambong, Claro Camacho's home. It seemed that half the town was related to him, and we were welcomed

eagerly. Most of the men were active guerillas, including Camacho's brother, Flaviano, and they took it as an honor to be
sworn in by me personally. An exception was Camacho's wife,
who was terrified of the Japanese and nearly fainted at our
appearance.

Camacho hurried her inside her family's little house, where
they proceeded to talk at great length. When at last they
emerged, Camacho's wife was carrying a cardboard suitcase.
She glanced at me with angry tears, and, accompanied by
several of the guerillas, she left the town.

I did not want to intrude on Camacho's affairs and so I said
nothing about it. Later that night, after a raucous celebration
of my visit and Camacho's return, I went for a walk through the
village with his brother, young, bright-faced Flavio. He had the
wide, friendly smile of my friend, but, as his irrepressible good
nature indicated, less of Claro's intensity.

"My brother is very proud to be on your staff," Flavio told
me eagerly.

I said that he was a good soldier.

"He must be very strong for you," Flavio went on more
seriously.

I asked him what he meant.

"This afternoon when you arrived, his wife was very upset.
She was pulling her hair and moaning, afraid the Japanese would
come and kill her and her family. When Claro came she told him
that they must betray you to the kempei-tai. It was the only
way to save themselves, she said."

"Was that why she left?" I asked.

"Yes, sir," Flavio replied with a deep nod. "There was a big
fight, and Claro told her that if she tried such a thing he would
kill her himself. Then he sent her away to live with her relatives.
When she was packing he told her that if she said anything to
anyone, he or his men would find her and kill her."

"I see," I said.

"That is why I say that Claro must be very strong for you,
to send his wife away like that. All of the people here are strong

for the guerillas," he concluded with a grin. He clearly was anxious for approval from me, but the talk of Camacho's wife had sobered me.

It was a measure of the intensity and intimacy of guerilla warfare that the struggle superceded family. The guerillas were fighting not only for family but also for a larger cause—the life of their nation. For men like Camacho, the war was a crusade, and devotion to the resistance had assumed a religious zeal. Yet their struggle was being directed by my orders, the orders of a foreigner.

I, an American, was leading their crusade for liberty and the life of their nation, and it was a heavy responsibility. Yet ultimately I was nothing but a symbol, a paraclete reminding them of the promise of salvation. That promise had been made by the man whom they trusted more than any other and in whose distant shadow I stood: MacArthur. Not until he returned would the Filipino people be liberated, nor would I be liberated, either.

I met with Bob Lapham in the village of Anao midway between his headquarters in the eastern mountains and my base at Camacho's house in Bayambong. Lapham was a handsome young man, tall and very thin with a wide grin and a casual country manner. His men referred to him as "Major" Lapham, and when I kidded him about the promotion he told me that both he and I were, indeed, now majors.

"Thorpe put us both in for a jump of two grades," he explained. "Took a few months for his message to get through to Australia, but MacArthur confirmed it. Congratulations."

He added that Joe Barker had been promoted to lieutenant colonel, and Moses, Noble, and Thorpe himself had also been promoted.

Over lunch we addressed the issue of command. Lapham had received my General Order Number 1, and I asked if he would serve under me as my deputy in the East Central Luzon Guerilla Area forces. We were the same age, twenty-five, our birthdays separated by only two weeks, and we held the same rank.

"What's your file number?" he asked.

"0-368746, I replied. "What's yours?"

"0-379114."

I was the senior officer, but just barely.

"Does this mean I get to call you the Old Man?" he grinned.

It was settled. Lapham would become my deputy, placing his cadres under my authority. If I were captured, he was to assume overall command of the guerilla forces, just as Barker had done when Thorpe was taken, and as I had done on Barker's capture.

Through April and early May of 1943 we traveled the northern provinces of Tarlac, Pangasinan, and Nueva Ecija, recruiting more civic leaders and creating more cadres. Everywhere we went we were welcomed; the northern people were fiercely anti-Japanese and eager to join us. And everyone had the same urgent question: When is MacArthur coming back?

His name was like an invocation to them, a holy word that had special power and meaning. None of them doubted his promise to return, but they were anxious to learn when the invasion would come. We told them honestly that we did not know. We still had no radios and could contact his headquarters only through the long and perilous process of hand-carried messages. But we assured them that when the invasion did come it would come suddenly, and they must be ready to support it. Until then their duty was to gather intelligence so that when MacArthur returned, the liberation would be swift and with little loss of life.

At the end of April, Lapham and I made the long trip by riverboat to Lingayen Gulf to make contact with Charles Putnam's guerilla groups on the coast. We boarded with our bodyguards at Bayambong for the slow, sinuous crawl down the Agno River toward its broad mouth. Our boat was weighted with cargo, a lengthy, shallow barge sheltered by a bamboo latticework within which we hid ourselves. So long as we remained inside we were relatively safe. Commerce had returned to the river, and the Japanese rarely inspected the hulking boats as they crawled past.

The bridges were another matter. Each was patrolled by the Japanese, and as we slid beneath them the soldiers regarded our boat idly. For those tense minutes we lay beneath the bamboo, the safeties off our guns until we were clear of them again. The last and most heavily guarded bridge was near the town of Lingayen. There was a machine-gun post at either end, with sentries pacing the boards. We considered leaving the boat and hiking across country, but decided instead to chance it.

As we neared the bridge we could see the fish ponds curving up the coast, the open sea beyond, and the road to Alaminos, which was our destination. We kept low within the lattice, our Thompsons loaded and ready, while the boatmen called and whistled to one another and the helm kept to the center of the channel. Through the chinks I could see the Japanese machine guns, and I heard an officer barking orders at his men. But there was no challenge, and the big boat shouldered past the pilings and out among the Hundred Islands at the gulf.

We disembarked at night at a tiny barrio deep among the fish ponds. A local guerilla leader came to meet us and guide us overland to Alaminos, the principal town upon the peninsula that formed the extreme western tip of central Luzon. This was the limit of my command, the final piece of the puzzle that Thorpe had given Barker and me to assemble a year before.

The area had been organized by Charles Uziell Putnam, an American mining engineer and reserve artillery captain. Putnam had lived in the Philippines most of his life. He was a big, boisterous man in his forties who spoke in a booming voice and drank long and hard.

Putnam was very popular among the local people, and it was his personality that held the squabbling cadres of the peninsula together. After a lengthy discussion about our organization and goals, Putnam agreed to place his guerillas under my authority, and in view of his influence in the district I appointed him as overall commander for the province of Pangasinan, reporting directly to Lapham.

Putnam insisted that we celebrate the pact by breaking into a store of prewar rum at his headquarters. We had a few drinks and Lapham turned in early. Putnam took two bottles and walked with me out onto the veranda.

"You like this work, Ramsey?" he asked me.

I told him that I was used to it.

"But do you like it?"

"It's my job," I said.

The drink loosened his tongue and thickened it.

"It's not a job," he snorted. He waved one of the bottles toward the coastline that curved blue-green and silver under the moonlight. "We control these people. We hold their lives in our hands. Being a guerilla leader is like being a king, Ramsey. You have absolute power over people."

"We're military men," I reminded him.

He filled his glass again and pointed with it to the far shore of the gulf.

"You see those hills there? That's the territory of the Igorots and Ilongots. You know about them?"

I answered diplomatically that I had heard of them.

"Well, what you've heard is true. They're headhunters, and some of 'em are cannibals. They love Japanese raids, Ramsey; they invite them. You know why? Cause that's the only time they have full bellies. That's not military, and it sure as hell's no job. That's guerilla warfare, and as far as they're concerned I'm no captain, I'm the king." He took a long drink and turned to face me. "And if you value your skin, Ramsey," he said, "you'll be one too."

With the addition of Lapham's and Putnam's forces, my command now numbered over twenty thousand guerillas and embraced the whole of east central Luzon from Lingayen Gulf to

Manila and Bataan. The vast skeleton of our guerilla army was assembled, and Lapham and I at once set out to finish fleshing it.

We paused, however, in the first week of May, to take a few days' rest and to celebrate both our success and my twenty-sixth birthday. Lapham and I, together with Cadizon and Camacho and half a dozen guerillas, were staying at a farmer's house near Anao, a remote village amid the rice paddies north of Paniqui. It was flat, open ground broken only by desultory clumps of mango trees. For the first time in weeks we allowed ourselves to relax, confident of the ability of our intelligence network to protect us, and looking forward to the party that Camacho's people in Bayambong were planning.

Around noon a runner came scrambling into our camp, breathless with news. The Japanese had learned our location, he said, and kempei-tai units were converging on us from the south, west, and north. It was impossible to escape across the open wetlands in daylight, and so we remained at the farmer's house, waiting for nightfall.

In an hour a second runner rushed in to say that one of the Japanese units was less than a kilometer away. Lapham posted his men under the house, and the rest of us took to the doors and windows. After a hasty dividing up of ammunition, we watched as the Japanese soldiers came into view.

The column turned in at a cluster of huts across the rice paddies and the soldiers began dispersing among them. They entered first one house and then another, their senior officer becoming more vociferous as they searched each one. At last he was shouting at the top of his voice, exercising his wrath on a civilian who, evidently, was acting as their guide. In a few minutes more he had reassembled his men and was marching them off in a smart single file back in the direction from which they had come.

We learned later what had happened. The Japanese had become lost on the way and had forced a local man to guide them. He was one of Lapham's guerillas, and assuring them he knew the way, he dutifully led them to the wrong location. There were still two more kempei-tai units in the area, and so as soon as it was dark we set out for my base at Bayambong.

We could not risk taking the roads, and so we headed instead across the wetlands to the town of Moncada and then into the swamps that ring Lake Mangabol. We entered a vast, sunken wasteland choked with reeds and thick with vegetative ooze, with no roads nor even any trails. Two guides led us as we waded in a ragged line, straining to keep sight of one another through the dark, chest-deep in slime, holding our weapons and belongings above our heads.

The place was alive with snakes and the sudden dark shapes of water birds that frighted up at our approach and flapped, complaining, away. Here and there were the few landmarks, fishermen's huts or humpbacked ricks of burri palms. Had it not been for the guides we would have been hopelessly lost within that shapeless sea of weeds. As it was, it took us all night and half the next day before we were free of it.

We reached a barrio of Bayambong at dusk. Our clothing was slick with slime, and we were anxious to be rid of the stench we still carried of the swamp. I was exhausted as I climbed the ladder into the barrio lieutenant's house, but when I reached the top I was startled by a burst of applause.

The house was crowded with guerillas and their families, the walls and ceiling were decorated with bright strips of cloth, and on a table at the center was a cake topped with candles. A banner in English and Tagalog read HAPPY BIRTHDAY MAJOR RAMSEY.

I was stunned. I stood in my swamp-soaked khakis, my pistol belt around my shoulders, the odor rising from me like a mist, moved almost to tears. Everyone was beaming at me, shaking my hand, and patting my back despite my reeking clothes. Some of the women kissed me. Lapham, Camacho, and Cadizon elbowed in beside me, and in a moment they were singing congratulations to me in Tagalog.

It had been more than a year that I had lived and struggled

among these people, and in that time a change had worked itself in me under their unfailing kindness and courage. I remembered the Negrito hut high in the mountains where I had vowed to stay alive solely to revenge myself on the enemy. That vengeance had served its purpose, but it was too negative an impulse to prevail. Gradually it had burned itself out, to be replaced, just as gradually, by a more positive motive. For me that celebration marked not only a birthday but also the birth of a new consciousness, a new purpose for fighting, the beginning of a new war.

I began to realize that I was no longer fighting for revenge: I was fighting now out of loyalty, even out of love. It was a love I had learned from the Filipino people, a love for country—not my own, perhaps, but a country that had adopted me and to which I belonged as surely as to my own.

It was a love that I not only shared with them but that I also felt for them. And I was amazed that as a soldier and a stranger I could be moved to such devotion, and that war, which had seemed to me such a random, brutal mystery, could be made to take on so much meaning.

GUERILLA
COMMANDER

1943

MEDAL ON PRECEDING PAGE:
Distinguished Service Star (PHILIPPINE)

Mona

In camp one night in a *barrio* of Bayambong, Bob Lapham told me a remarkable story.

After the surrender of Bataan, a group of prominent Filipinos formed a clandestine network to help the prisoners and escapees. Among the leaders was the New York *Herald Tribune*'s Manila correspondent, Tony Escoda, and his wife, Josefa. The Escoda Group, as it came to be known, was composed mostly of young Filipino women from Manila's social circle. This conspiracy of debutantes risked their lives to channel money and supplies to the men in the camps as well as to the fugitives and guerillas in the hills. Many were captured, tortured brutally, and killed. And though the Escodas themselves were caught, taken to the old Chinese cemetery in Manila, and beheaded, the group continued its work.

In late 1942 Bob Lapham had become dangerously ill with malaria and dysentery. His people sent word to the Escoda Group that he urgently needed medicines or he would die. The group dispatched one of its most energetic members, a young Manila socialite named Ramona Snyder, with the supplies. She remained with Lapham for several weeks, nursing him back to health. After her return to Manila she stayed in contact with Lapham's headquarters, sending money and provisions and forwarding intelligence from the Manila cadres.

Mona Snyder, Bob Lapham assured me, was one of the most selfless and courageous people he had ever met. Diminutive, round-faced, with a frank, cheerful personality, she was absolutely fearless—indeed, she seemed to enjoy danger as something of a quaint diversion. An orphan from a Manila family, she had been adopted by a wealthy Spanish-Filipino couple, who provided her with an excellent education. She spoke Tagalog, Spanish, and English with equal fluency, and her potential seemed limitless.

Nonetheless, she became trapped in a bad marriage with a man who drank, squandered her money, and abused her. Though divorce was virtually impossible in the Philippines at that time, she persevered through all the archaic demands and rituals of Holy Mother Church and freed herself. For a few short months she remained at loose ends, and then the war came, and with it the death march. In the suffering of the prisoners she knew she had found her vocation, and from that point on she threw herself heart-first into the resistance.

Now in mid May 1943, it was Lapham's birthday, and he told me he had asked Mona Snyder to come up from Manila to help him celebrate. She would bring medicine and supplies for our camp and, Lapham confided to me, a birthday cake to rival the one I had had.

We spent the rest of that day preparing the camp for her arrival, and especially tidying up the big hut that served as our quarters. It was a lengthy single room of wood slats divided up by bamboo screens and crammed with clutter. Captured documents and copies of messages were strewn everywhere, along with castoff clothing, boots, weapons, and boxes of ammunition and supplies. But despite our fussing efforts, the place still looked and smelled like a makeshift warehouse on the morning Mona was to arrive.

Some of Lapham's men went into town to meet her. She had made the day-long trip from Manila jammed into an ancient bus with dozens of peasants and their animals and bulging bamboo bags. Nonetheless, when she came into camp with her entourage of heavily armed guerillas, she was fresh and fragrant.

She climbed the ladder into our hut bearing lovingly the box that held the cake for Lapham's party, and suddenly the gloomy depot was transformed. She shone. She wore a simple white linen dress that made deeper and more delicate the gentle brown of her skin. Her face was oval and open, and her brown eyes were filled with such frank cheer that I felt I had known her for a long time. She hugged Lapham and took my hand and sat us all down on the floor to tell us the latest news from Manila.

I scarcely listened. She was not beautiful in the conventional sense, but her charm was irresistible. I found myself observing her gestures and glances at Lapham in a jealous worry that took me by surprise. Had they become intimate during his convalescence? I wondered. She smiled at him frequently, but she also smiled at me. She touched his arm as she spoke, but she also turned several times and leaned toward me.

I could not take my eyes off her. How could such a small, delightful woman bear such burdens, take such risks? Like me she was a guerilla, exposed to every bit as much danger, and just as liable as myself to lose her head. Yet she laughed and chatted as amiably as if she were on a cruise. Indeed, the war for her seemed to be some hurried, complex journey on which she had embarked quite willingly, knowing that at any moment the fragile vessel on which we all depended might be destroyed.

I savored every moment of her company. By evening's end, after the dinner and the cake, I was in love with her. I was frantic, however, with wondering whether she felt anything for me. And if she were involved with Lapham, there could, of course, be no question of my approaching her.

We made up her bed at the far end of the room behind one of the screens, hung a mosquito net for her, and said goodnight. Lapham and I retired to the other end, each to a screened-in corner. There was no sleep at all for me. I lay all night thinking about her, worrying about Lapham and my vow of celibacy, wondering whether she felt for me anything of the attraction that now obsessed me.

It had been a year and a half since I had touched a woman. Now this brave, cheerful creature had appeared and upset all my resolve. I had made my promise to Joe Barker, and now Joe

Barker was worse than dead. But the point of the promise had been to smooth the growth of the organization, and now that organization had spread across Luzon.

No longer was I a rebel lieutenant hiding out in the hills, virtually alone. I was a major, the commanding officer of an army of twenty-five thousand that was growing stronger every day. My circumstances all had changed, but the desires in me had not. Would I risk everything to give into them now? Did I have the right to take that risk? And what about that other, more dreadful risk, that I would simply offend her, and be rejected? I struggled with myself until nearly dawn, when I fell asleep.

In the morning Mona was there making breakfast for us. I tried to avoid her eyes, but her manner was infectious. Soon she had us all in animated chatter about people and events in Manila. When we were done, she, Lapham, and I strolled outside, but in a moment one of Lapham's lieutenants approached and he was called away. I turned to Mona.

"I need to stretch my legs," I remarked to her. "Would you like to take a walk through the barrio with me?"

"Yes," she answered quickly, "I'd like to see what it's like."

We walked through the village to the river's edge, then turned and entered a grove of bamboo. It was shadowed and cool, and infused with the dry scent of the stalks. I paused, and she walked a few steps beyond me. When she turned I put out my arms to her. She was in them in an instant, kissing me.

"I wondered how long it was going to take you to do that," she said to me at last.

"I was worried about Bob," I answered. I was shaking. "About you and Bob."

"We're good friends," she smiled. "Nothing more."

We both laughed and hugged each other and kissed again. Then we walked on down the riverbank, our arms around each other. The awful tension I had felt was broken, and we now laughed at ourselves as we shared our feelings of the past two days. We had been drawn to each other with equal force, and we had been equally frightened by it.

"I was afraid you wouldn't make up your mind before I had to leave," she said. "I've been so lonesome I thought I would cry."

I told her how very badly I wanted her.

"Then why don't you come to me tonight," she answered simply.

I ached all the length of that day. Every time we came near to each other we managed a touch, furtive, hoping that no one would see. When night finally came we all withdrew to our beds. I lay for an hour until I heard Lapham's snoring. I could take the yearning and separation no longer. Silently I got up and crossed the room to where Mona lay. She drew back the mosquito netting and reached for me. We did not speak, nor did she release me until dawn.

We spent two more days together, and then Mona returned to Manila. As she was preparing to leave she told me that she moved in a prominent circle of the capital, including high officials of the puppet government created by the Japanese. Some of these were cooperating secretly with the Escoda Group, providing important information about the Japanese administration, and Mona offered to forward the intelligence to me. I accepted gratefully and made her promise to be careful. It was a dangerous game she was playing, and even the rumor of a connection with me would cost her dearly.

It was shortly after Mona left that I received word of the capture of Captain Ralph Praeger, commander of the mountain provinces of North Luzon. Praeger had been seen by one of our guerillas in Japanese custody at Cabanatuan, and there were reports that he was being tortured and put on display. This tactic was becoming more common: Guerilla leaders were being paraded before the public after having been tortured beyond endurance, and forced to make speeches denouncing the resistance and urging Filipinos to betray us. These piteous, ineffectual charades only served to deepen resentment against the Japanese.

Nonetheless, as I made the rounds of the cadres throughout the north that summer, I began to notice a waning in the popular will to resist. We had now been at war for nearly two years, and the occupation, though still hated, had begun to seem irrevocable. What was more, two years of oppression and resistance had played havoc with the nation's economy. Goods were in scarce supply, food was rationed, and the infrastructure of transport, commerce, agriculture, and trade was breaking down.

Present still was the conviction that MacArthur would return, but there was no sign of it, and the absence of that sign had begun to cause concern. It was not a movement toward the Japanese; rather, it was a subtle, slow withdrawal from struggle. People were becoming weary of the war and the price that it exacted physically and morally in their lives. It was a malaise insinuating itself not into the body of the resistance, which was still growing, but into its spirit.

Lapham saw it too, and he told me he thought it necessary to return to his headquarters. Our task now would be twofold, not only to continue expanding the resistance but also to sustain its morale. For this it seemed to me that a major revision was needed in both the structure and the philosophy of our guerilla operations. Our Maoist model of organization was proving inadequate. The Huks reinforced theirs with deceit, intimidation, and terror, thus keeping it vital through fear, but to us such tactics were alien and abhorrent.

A new approach was needed, one more suited to our goals, the nature of the struggle, and the character of the people. Unlike the Huks, we were not fighting for conquest but for liberation; ours was not a power struggle but one of freedom from oppression. Once the war was over and we had won, our organization would disappear. What replaced it must be capable of preserving the liberty we had fought for, or we who lived every day with the prospect of betrayal and death would have betrayed the whole nation and given it over to its death. That summer my thinking about the guerilla movement began to change, and I determined to take steps to implement that change.

Politics

F ollowing the invasion, in January 1942, the Japanese high command had created an executive commission of Filipino civilians to run the country's puppet government. Its chief aims were to execute the occupation policy and administer the day-to-day life of the nation. To give this commission credibility the Japanese induced some of the most prominent men in the country to participate. Some accepted as a matter of patriotic duty, hoping to blunt the excesses of the occupiers and retain some integrity for the government. Others simply refused. Among the latter was General Manuel Roxas, a leading prewar politician and a member of General MacArthur's staff.

Roxas, who had chosen to stay behind when MacArthur was ordered to Australia, was captured and sent to a prison camp. There he continued to refuse Japanese offers of freedom and a place on the governing commission, until his health had deteriorated to the point where he was near death. An old friend of his, Dr. Jose Laurel, who was cooperating with the commission, learned of Roxas's condition and pleaded with him to save his life by becoming an advisor. Reluctantly Roxas agreed, was released, and returned to Manila.

As soon as Roxas had recovered, he made contact with the resistance movement in the city and began providing our operatives with intelligence of great importance. In August 1943 he met Mona Snyder and asked her to act as intermediary between himself and me. In September Mona again traveled north to deliver Roxas's first communique to me, and to bring news that the commission intended soon to create a new Republic of the Philippines. The first act of its parliament would be to declare war on the United States.

Such disturbing and urgent information needed to be relayed at once to MacArthur's headquarters. I still had no radio contact with the outside world, so I sent two runners by different routes to our people in southern Luzon, with instructions to take the information immediately to both Colonel Macario Peralta on the island of Panay and Colonel Wendell Fertig on the island of Mindanao. Both of these guerrilla commanders, I knew, were in contact with MacArthur by radio and submarine.

Roxas also informed me that central Luzon was now the main reserve area for Japan's Southwest Pacific Army, and that there were no fewer than a hundred fifty thousand troops stationed there, with more to be sent. He warned me that I should thus expect my operations to become more difficult, and for pressure on our organization to intensify. My command, it was clear, was now at the very heart of the Imperial Army's Pacific theater.

Mona also brought word of the situation in the Manila underground. Ever since the capture of Barker and Santos, the Manila cadres had been reeling. Fausto Alberto had taken command, but he was so well known to the Japanese and under such scrutiny that he could not operate freely. As a result, the vacuum created by the January raids remained unfilled. Within it rivalries were developing among the clandestine groups, and their effectiveness suffered.

Something similar had been occurring throughout Luzon. Our movement had grown rapidly, now numbering over thirty thousand guerillas, and its structure was becoming unwieldy. Not only Manila but the entire East Central Luzon Guerilla Area force had to be reorganized.

Accordingly, in November 1943, I issued a series of general orders reconstituting my command. No longer would we follow

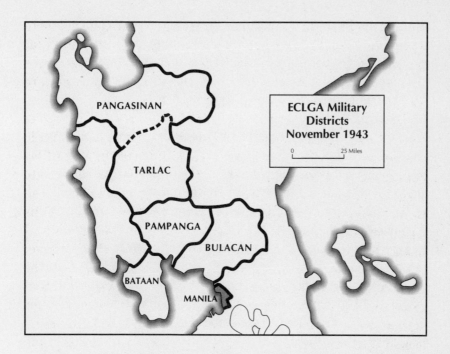

the Maoist model of cadres; instead, the resistance would be reorganized along military lines. I divided Luzon into military districts, redesignated our guerilla cadres as regiments, and assigned them numbers and names according to their districts.

There were five such districts: Manila, Bataan, Bulacan, Pampanga, and Pangasinan-Tarlac. Each had its own commander and its own regiments. These would report to my general headquarters, to which would be attached two special mobile combat regiments with responsibility for policing the districts. This structure did away with the inequities and vagaries of the cadre system, allowed for decentralized control, and made for a more efficient response to the increasingly grave military and counterintelligence situation we faced.

General Baba's efforts had severely damaged our leadership. Nearly all of the American officers had been captured, and their places had to be filled. I began issuing commissions and promotions to Filipino civilians and soldiers who had proved themselves in the resistance, and appointed them to command positions. Under the pressure of the kempei-tai manhunt for Americans, the command structure of the resistance was becoming more and more indigenous.

Another issue I had to address at this time was that of prisoners. Boone had raised the question with me on my visit to Bataan, but so far I had been reluctant to make a decision regarding it. The fact was, however, that the absence of a policy on prisoners was causing increasing concern as well as costing lives. Each unit was dealing with the issue on its own, which meant that some prisoners were being executed while others were being released. In the latter case the result was almost always raids, which meant the capture, torture, and killing of our own people.

The question of prisoners was the most difficult command decision I had had to deal with, and so I had tried to avoid it. Nonetheless, while I was in the north it was forced on me again, this time irresistibly.

I was spending the night in a barrio of Bayambong, where our men had captured a middle-aged married couple. The husband had collaborated with the Japanese and betrayed some of our men, leading to their arrest. He had confessed and been sentenced to die. The barrio lieutenant had carried out the execution, and then given the man's wife a stern warning against going to the Japanese after she was released. Instead of agreeing, she had become hysterical.

"You killed my husband!" she began shouting. "I will go to the Japanese! I will tell them where you are—I will lead them here myself!"

The lieutenant tried to reason with the woman, explaining to her that under such circumstances she could not be released.

"You have murdered my husband," she screeched in return. "I will go straight to the Japanese!"

The lieutenant ordered her held under guard, and all that day he pleaded repeatedly for her promise not to betray the guerillas, but each time she retorted with the same threats. She kept it up all night and into the morning. At last the lieutenant came to me for a decision. Camacho translated for me.

"Can't you make her understand that we can't let her go unless she swears not to betray us?"

The lieutenant shook his head. "She says we are murderers and we deserve to die," he answered. "She will swear nothing except that she will see us all dead."

"Doesn't she realize that she's making it impossible for us to release her?"

"She says that she will never promise to protect us; that we will have to kill her too."

In her desire for revenge the woman was threatening every-thing we had built in the north, everything our people there had sacrificed for and had yet to accomplish. If we were to let her go the woman would bring the Japanese to Bayambong. Even if we left, the Japanese would still sack the village and might arrest or even kill everyone there, including Camacho's family.

"What shall I tell him?" Camacho asked me quietly.

I could avoid a decision no longer. Indeed, it had been my failure to make it that had led to this.

"Tell the lieutenant that the woman's release would mean the death of our people," I answered. "Tell him . . . tell him that it is the policy of the guerilla forces to execute prisoners who threaten us. There is nothing else we can do."

Camacho translated this, and the lieutenant nodded and left. For a long moment I sat reflecting on the decision. I recalled Charles Putnam's remark that a guerilla commander was like a king, and that if I were to survive I must become one myself. There was truth in it: I did have the power of life and death in my hands. But it was a power that I had accepted, not sought, and my duty as a commander was to use it to protect the lives of my people. I had come to this decision reluctantly, but now there was no going back. I turned to Camacho.

"Draw up a dispatch about this new policy, to be sent to all units," I told him. "Bring it to me. I'll sign it myself. I don't want there to be any more doubt."

But I knew there was doubt, in my own mind, and though I understood the necessity of it, I could no more reason the point with myself than we had done with the woman prisoner.

One of the results of my revised organizational structure was that political and guerilla leaders from all over the country began contacting me, asking for liaisons, advice, and the sharing of intelligence and resources. I was now seeing my guerilla army taking on a larger, more political significance. What had begun as a provincial resistance was growing into a national movement. I communicated this fact to MacArthur's headquarters and urged him to send a general officer of established reputation to take overall command. To this request I received no reply, and upon reflection I was not surprised.

Despite the growth of our organization we were still war rebels, and my own position remained undefined. Sending a general officer to take charge of my command would have meant a formal recognition of it by the United States, and that, in turn, would have been tantamount to fomenting rebellion. Such a move would have destroyed any claim on our part, if we were captured, to be covered by the Geneva Convention, although I knew full well that such a claim would never be recognized by the Japanese in any case.

Thus, by November 1943, I was fighting on several fronts at once—reorganizing the army, resolving the conflicts in Manila, liaising with our political contacts, and improving our intelligence and counterintelligence operations.

One result of all this effort was that the stomach ulcers that I had been nursing for two years now erupted. They, together with the chronic dysentery and the malnutrition, represented yet another front to my war. But, enervating as it was, I came almost to be grateful for the illness, since it brought Mona more often to visit my camp with medicines from Manila.

I had come not only to desire her as a lover but to depend on her as a friend and confidante and esteem her as a courageous fighter. Though I knew she must be under great stress, her cheerfulness never failed her, and this served as an antidote to my own cares. She was as selfless in her solicitude for me as she was devoted to our cause, and I cherished every minute of the brief times we had together.

Each of her visits brought more news from General Roxas. He had now gained access to the Japanese authorities, including the kempei-tai commander, Colonel Nagahama. What was even more important, the chief of the Philippine constabulary, General Francisco, was now cooperating with the resistance, channeling intelligence from General Baba's office to Roxas. Roxas told Mona that Francisco had seen the composite drawing of me, which remained on Colonel Nagahama's desk, and that he had learned from General Baba himself that the reward for me had been increased to half a million pesos, or some $200,000.

It was through Roxas's communiques, carried by Mona, that I followed the dramatic struggle within the puppet government. Ever since I had established contact with Roxas, I had been urging him to encourage his friends to run for seats in the National Assembly. Far from denouncing the puppet government as the Huks were doing, we were determined to influence it as much as possible. Roxas had done so, and many loyal citizens had been elected.

Through the fall of 1943 our strategy was tested. A bill was introduced into the legislature to create a draft, a prelude to a declaration of war. The measure was debated hotly for weeks, the Japanese puppets arguing in favor of the draft, and our people fighting just as forcefully against it. I watched anxiously as reports of the debate flowed in from Mona. Then, in late fall, the draft question was put to a vote, and it was defeated. Our people had prevailed, and the news was celebrated across the country.

The more serious obstacle remained. The puppet president was pressured to appeal to the assembly for a formal declaration of war against the United States. Again there was furious debate when the Japanese attempted to force a vote.

We spent anxious days following the maneuvering in the assembly as the puppet legislators connived to impose a vote and our people struggled to block them. A declaration of war by the Philippines would be a severe blow, the precise consequences of which were impossible to predict. It might provoke a civil war in which, inevitably, we would have to take the leading role. In any case, it would mean even greater hardships for the Filipino people.

In late November a runner reached me in Bayambong with the news. The proposal to put the question to a vote had been defeated; the Philippines would not declare war. I announced this to my staff and called for an immediate celebration. The *tuba* and *bossy* were broken out, and everyone gathered in Camacho's house to toast the loyal legislators and the future of the resistance.

It was a tremendous victory, at once military and political. Two years of war, occupation, and oppression had not shaken the Filipino people's devotion to liberty and their loyalty to the United States. The Japanese would not have their puppet army; the resistance would continue.

As we drank, I wistfully recalled arguing with Joe Barker about Mao Tse-tung's concept of the guerilla struggle as essentially political, and how he had chided me on taking the "purely military viewpoint." Now our guerilla movement had won its most important victory so far, not in the jungles but in the chambers of the National Assembly.

I silently raised my glass to Barker, chained in the fortress at Manila. "Goddammit, Joe," I said to myself, "I've become a politician after all."

By the end of November 1943, my work in the north was finished. I had been away from my base in central Luzon for nine months, and I was anxious to get back and reestablish my headquarters. As I was preparing to leave Bayambong, however, I received a message from Manila that suddenly changed my plans. It was from Brigadier General Vicente Lim.

A graduate of West Point, General Lim was one of the most senior and respected officers of the Philippine Army. Like General Roxas, he had declined an American offer to escape, choosing to remain behind with his troops. He was captured on Bataan, interned, and later released. Since then he had been living in Manila under very close Japanese surveillance.

He wanted to meet with me in Manila to discuss the unification of all guerilla forces in Luzon. As he was being watched so closely, he explained, he could not travel to the provinces, so could I come to him? I jumped at the idea. General Lim was precisely the kind of officer about whom I had written to MacArthur. He had the reputation, prestige, and skill to coordinate the resistance and to put an end to dissention within the movement.

I had other reasons for going to Manila as well. My own network there was still in disarray, and I felt that only in person could I put it right. What was more, I had now spent two years in the jungles, mountains, rice paddies, and barrios, and I longed for a Christmas in the city. Finally, going to Manila would mean a chance to see Mona, and to spend a few precious days in her company. But it was a long trip, more than two hundred miles, and I was still suffering bouts of weakness and collapse. There was no question of my walking.

Over dinner one evening I casually mentioned my concerns to Claro Camacho. "I need a boxcar," I remarked half-jokingly.

Camacho thought a moment. "Sanchez," he said.

Jorge Sanchez, a Philippine Army major and my acting chief of staff in Manila, had contacts in the Manila Railroad Company. Camacho was right: It just might be possible for him to provide me with transport to Manila. I dictated a message for Camacho to send to him, and a few nights later Camacho announced that a boxcar would be waiting across the river.

"It'll be left on a siding in Bautista," he said. "Sanchez will be up tomorrow."

Camacho explained that the boxcar would carry a cargo of nipa palm leaves, but the inside core would be left vacant for myself and two bodyguards. It would be picked up in Bautista by a train bound for Manila.

"When do we leave?" I asked.

"Thursday, the 24th." He paused a moment, reflecting. "I think that's Thanksgiving," he said.

Cargo

The two men who were to ride with me in the boxcar, Sergeants Melicio Acosta and Candido Cornel, had been handpicked by Camacho for my headquarters guards and had been with us since Timbo. Camacho himself had made arrangements to ride in the locomotive, while Jorge Sanchez, who had sent the boxcar from Manila, would ride in the last car.

At midnight of November 23 we took a *banca* across the river and made our way up the far bank to the railroad siding. We brought with us food for two days, a pair of .30-caliber machine guns, and the Thompson submachine gun that I always carried. Camacho and Sanchez hid .45s of their own under their civilian clothes, as well as pocketfuls of Japanese war notes to use as bribes.

The boxcar sat hulking among the weeds, a dark, ancient affair made of weathered sheet metal stenciled with the name of the Manila Railroad Company. There was only one door, which slid on tracks and was closed with a padlock. Camacho crouched toward it to make sure that we would be undisturbed and then whistled for us to join him. We pulled back the door and were greeted with the wet vegetable odor of fresh palm leaves. A few dozen bales of the fan-shaped nipa shingles were stacked inside the door.

We hefted up the machine guns and their tripods, and then

Acosta, Cornel, and I climbed inside. With Camacho and Sanchez's help we piled the nipa bales chest-high against the door,
creating a barrier to discourage inspection from the outside.

"You okay, Major?" Camacho whispered.

"Yeah, close it up."

"Good luck, then."

Camacho slid the door shut, and we heard him pivot the
handle closed and padlock it. The interior of the car was plunged
into a dank, claustrophobic darkness.

We were now cargo, human contraband, and there was no
exit for us unless someone opened the door from the outside.
That someone could only be Camacho, who kept the key in his
pocket. If it were a railroad inspector or the Japanese at one of
the checkpoints on the Manila line, we would have to fight our
way out. We positioned the machine guns to face the door, and I
held a flashlight while Acosta and Cornel loaded them.

"If anybody forces the lock," I whispered to them, "open
fire. We kill whoever's near the door and make a break for it."

They nodded.

There was nothing more to do, and so we settled down among
the nipa shingles to wait for the train to arrive. The car was of
the narrow-gauge kind, and with the shingles and our equipment there was not much room. Acosta and Cornel lay curled
up by the machine guns, while I stretched out as best I could
next to the shingles by the door. Outside Camacho and Sanchez
moved off into the brush so as not to attract attention. Then
they too settled in for the night.

It was nearly 7:00 A.M. before we were awakened by the
noise of the engine approaching. There was little air inside the
car and even less light, and the heat and dampness of the leaves
were stifling. Through the gaps above and below the door we
watched the locomotive huffing toward us, then heard it stop,
give a grudging puff of black smoke, and back slowly onto the
siding. In a few minutes we felt the jar as it coupled on, and
then the to-and-fro tugging as the train started up again.

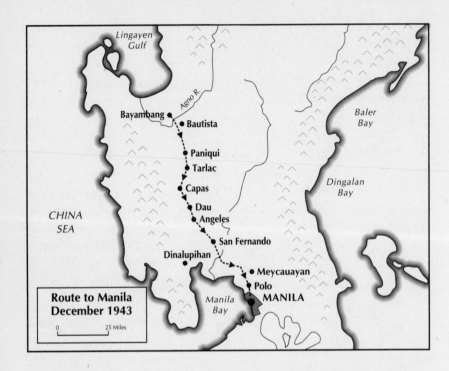

We gradually picked up speed and began the long, winding run into Tarlac City. From inside the car we could see almost nothing, just the strobing play of light shafts through the gaps and heaped shingles. After two hours we slowed into Tarlac, where the train was to pick up more cars.

While the engine chuffed back and forth collecting the cars, we waited on a siding. Every so often we could hear footsteps on the gravel, approaching, receding, occasionally pausing. The metal sheeting of the floor was loose and would buckle with the least movement, so the three of us were obliged to lie motionless.

An hour passed in the heat and suffocating humidity of the palm leaves, and then a group of men came crunching up to the car and stopped. We heard muted conversation from outside, and suddenly a hand was thrust in under the door. I glanced down quickly as fingers groped less than three feet from my legs. There was more talk outside, and the hand was withdrawn.

I carefully parted the shingles with my fingers and peered through the gap in the door. Outside, Camacho was arguing in undertones with an officer of the Philippine constabulary, who said he suspected the car of containing contraband. As I watched, Camacho slid a hand into his pocket and slipped the policeman a roll of bills. The conversation ended, and they moved off.

It was another two hours before the train began moving again. It was now near midday, and the heat inside the car was becoming unbearable. The metal floor braised our flesh through our clothing, making it impossible to sit still for more than a moment. As we bumped and jostled toward the next station, Acosta, Cornel, and I shared our rations, and we all gulped water from the canteens. In less than an hour, the train had stopped again.

This time it was at Capas, the site of a Japanese garrison and a notorious POW camp. We knew that the Japanese used Capas as a checkpoint for rail traffic moving north and south, and so it was this stop that we feared more than any other. Our people in the area had reported that the checks were random; some trains were allowed to simply pass through, while others were inspected closely. At first it seemed as if we were being ignored, and I began to hope that we might be passed through, but in a few minutes the whole train was surrounded by Japanese voices.

Acosta, Cornel, and I froze. There was pounding on the walls of the car, and then bayonet blades came jabbing in at the chinks. We would hear them ripping through the nipa shingles as the Japanese made their way along the side of the boxcar. Over and over the blades sliced in, twisting a moment, dripping mositure from the palms, and then slipping out again. I watched them approach, feeling like a magician's lackey locked in a box of swords, waiting to be impaled but unable to disappear.

Suddenly a blade thrust sliced in at the door, missing my leg by inches. There was a grunt from outside and another blade poked in, followed by another. When the blade points met no resistance, one of the Japanese soldiers gave a shout; there was a hurried conversation at the door, after which we could hear the men running for the head of the train. Acosta, Cornel, and I exchanged glances. We lifted ourselves to the machine guns, certain we would have to fight it out but knowing that since we were in the middle of a garrison there was little hope of escape.

At that moment, however, the train gave a lurch and began moving forward. We soon overtook the Japanese soldiers, who were still running and gesticulating toward our car. The train continued, picking up speed as it swayed through the switch onto the tracks for Angeles City, the halfway point to Manila.

For the next two hours we waited anxiously, sure that the Japanese at Capas had telephoned ahead to Angeles to have the car separated from the train. There was no sign from Camacho or Sanchez, so we sat helpless, the machine guns off safety, preparing ourselves for the moment when the door would be thrown back and the shooting would start.

As we slowed at Dau, the station on the edge of Angeles City, the three of us trained our guns on the door. The car grumbled to a stop, and for a moment there was silence. Then from outside we heard voices approaching. We strained to hear, but they passed by so quickly that we could catch only a word or two. It was Tagalog, not Japanese.

For five minutes more we waited, then ten. At any second we expected the padlock to be smashed and the door to be thrown back, and I whispered to Acosta and Cornel to get ready to open fire and make a run for it. We were soaked with perspiration, but we scarcely noticed; we were concentrating on the door.

There was more silence. Then the train gave a perfunctory shrug, the couplings clanked together, and we were moving again. There had been no search, only a routine check. Why the Japanese had not signaled ahead we could not guess; we could only be grateful.

Before we reached Polo on the outskirts of Manila, where we were to leave the train, there was another long delay. Instead of arriving at eight in the evening as scheduled, it was nearly ten before the engine slowed and stopped. The three of us waited anxiously for Camacho and Sanchez to open the door, but after a few minutes we started rolling again.

As we did, I could hear shouting from up ahead, and once more the train shuddered to a stop. There was a long, tense interval filled with muffled pleas and remonstrances, and then we were moving again, backward this time. In a few minutes the car had been shoved onto a siding and uncoupled.

After the engine noise had faded south toward Manila, whispers invaded the car. Then we heard the sound of the lock opening, and the door slid slowly back. Outside under the moonlight were Camacho, Sanchez, and a dozen armed men. They pulled aside the nipa shingles and signaled for us to get out. The three of us unbent our stiffened limbs and dropped to the ground.

Camacho introduced me to Colonel Benjamin Aquino, a regimental commander of the Manila military district, while his men removed our machine guns from the car. Together we set off across the rice paddies for Pugad Baboy, an isolated village where we were to remain until arrangements could be completed for my trip into Manila.

Over supper Camacho told us how close we had come to disaster. Because of the delay, the engineer had decided not to stop at Polo, but to continue on to Tutuban station in central Manila. That would have meant certain capture, for Tutuban was a major Japanese military installation.

Camacho had argued with the engineer and offered bribes, but he refused and began to pull out of the station. Camacho then produced his pistol, shoved it in the engineer's ear, and told him that unless he stopped and uncoupled the car as agreed he would be shot. It was sufficient prodding, and he shunted the car aside.

"You'll forget about this," Camacho said, putting back his pistol.

"Sure," the engineer replied. "How about the money?"

"What money?"

"The money you offered me before this didn't happen."

"I couldn't argue with that," Camacho told us, laughing, "so he got his bribe after all."

Manila

O ur immediate concern was my lack of papers. Although there was a large colony of Europeans in Manila, and the sight of a white man on the streets was not rare, Europeans were liable to be stopped and their papers checked. The problem had been confided to one of our key people in Manila, a Swiss national named Walter Roeder. Roeder was technical director of the Manila Gas Company and, though officially neutral, was actively involved in the resistance, offering his expertise to design sabotage devices for our guerillas.

Roeder was indispensable to our organization, and though I had never met him I had commissioned him a major of my staff and assigned him as our chief of chemical warfare. Roeder had artfully cultivated good relations with the Japanese authorities, who had allowed him to keep his post at the gasworks and his home inside its sprawling compound near the presidential palace. Nonetheless, because of its strategic importance, the Japanese had stationed a full company of troops inside the compound. Thus, at the same time that he was building our sabotage devices and sending us intelligence, Roeder was surrounded by hundreds of Japanese soldiers.

Using his knowledge of chemicals and dyes, Roeder had made over his Swiss passport with a false name and visas for me. This he sent to Colonel Aquino with equipment and instructions for making and affixing my photograph. Roeder had also sent a white tropical suit for me to wear.

(ABOVE) *Faced with growing resistance, the Japanese created a "wanted" list of American guerilla leaders. Here one of them, Colonel Hugh Straughn, is pictured upon his capture. Officially considered war rebels, the Americans' legal status remained vague. To the Japanese, they were bandits, and when captured were tortured mercilessly and beheaded.* (UPI/BETTMANN NEWSPHOTOS)

(LEFT) *Ramsey after the war with Fausto Alberto* (RIGHT) *and Alejandro Santos. In 1942, Ramsey sent Santos and Alberto into Manila to organize the guerilla resistance in the capital.*

Ramona Snyder, officer of the Manila resistance and one of Ramsey's most important intelligence assets. Her courage and love sustained him through some of the darkest months of the war.

Photo taken on the outskirts of Manila for Ramsey's Swiss passport. This picture could not be used because the kempei-tai (Japanese military police) had a composite drawing showing Ramsey with a mustache. Another was taken after he shaved.

(ABOVE) *Mount Balagbag, in the Sierra Madre Mountains, headquarters of the ECLGA. Its remoteness and dense jungle cover hid Ramsey's camp from detection by the Japanese.* (LEFT) *The entrance to Ramsey's camp was protected by this waterfall; atop it was a machine-gun nest.*

The "Balagbag Boys," Ramsey's personal bodyguards. Center, rear, is Processo Cadizon and front row left, kneeling, is Candido Cornel.

Jimmy Carrington (CENTER) with the headquarters security detachment.

My photograph was taken by Major Jorge Joseph, known as Jojo, one of our Manila officers, who owned a film studio as well as a nightclub. While he arranged the camera and lights, he told me that he was planning a party in my honor for New Year's Eve. Many Europeans would be there, he said, all of them connected with the resistance. The neighborhood around the club would be patrolled by guerillas, so there was no danger.

I was delighted and accepted with thanks. It was precisely the kind of thing I had hoped for in Manila; an antidote to my jungle existence. I was also looking forward to my reunion with Mona Snyder, who was making the arrangements in Manila for my visit.

Several photographs were taken of me in my stylish suit and tie, which were much too large for my emaciated frame. As we were finishing, Camacho reminded me that the picture that Colonel Nagahama kept on his desk showed me with a moustache. I had worn it since the war began and kept it proudly trim, but Camacho was right. I quickly shaved it off, and we retook the photos.

We spent two more weeks preparing for my entrance into Manila, choreographing my movements, finalizing the details of my transport and lodging. Much of the routine work was done by a young guerilla of Aquino's command, Pacifico Cabral. Just eighteen, Cabral was resourceful, energetic, and ferociously loyal.

He was especially anxious to please me and scarcely left my side, armed with an archaic bolt-action Springfield rifle that was nearly as tall as he. When it came time for me to go into Manila, I asked if he would like to come along. He beamed a smile from ear to ear and eagerly answered yes. I attached him to my bodyguard and put him in Camacho's charge.

On the evening of December 20, an old Chevrolet sedan pulled up in the road nearby the hut where I was staying. I climbed into the backseat between Sanchez and Cabral, while Colonel Aquino and his driver got in front. Each of us carried a concealed automatic pistol, and I wore a generous fedora pulled down over my face.

Our route into Manila had already been scouted for road-blocks, but in case we were challenged I had a cover story prepared. I was a Swiss businessman returning with my Filipino colleagues from the provinces, where I was considering buying mineral rights. If the Japanese soldiers did not believe this, we would open fire with our pistols as the driver sped away. As soon as we were out of sight, we would abandon the car and make our way across the swamps to one of our safe houses outside of the city.

We drove south along the main highway until it joined the Manila ring road. This we took east for a few miles, then turned south onto one of the major boulevards leading into central Manila.

All along our route we passed Japanese soldiers and constab-ulary officers on foot and in horse-drawn vehicles. Though they paid us little attention, I was extremely apprehensive each time we slowed or stopped next to one of their vehicles. If even one kempei-tai agent in Luzon had learned of my trip, we were all doomed.

The farther we drove into the city, however, the less para-noid I became. I was back in Manila, the city I had enjoyed so much as a young cavalry officer, and I found myself growing excited by its sights and sounds. It was nearly Christmas, and though there were shortages of everything, some of the shops were decorated for the holidays. There were lights on the boulevards, and people were out strolling and mingling. It was so far removed from the life I had become used to that I felt transported to a different world, at once fascinating and familiar.

The Chevrolet climbed the curving roads to the Santa Mesa Heights district and pulled up before the home of Narcisso Mabanta, an intelligence officer of the Manila network. Mabanta and his wife, Sofia, welcomed me with a warmth that over-whelmed me. Despite the shortages they had prepared an elaborate dinner, and afterward they served an excellent prewar rum that they had been saving for a special occasion.

We ate and drank until after midnight, when a hot bath was drawn for me. The sight of the steaming water and the soap in its delicate shell holder moved me deeply. I had not seen such luxury in two years. I removed my voluminous civilian clothes and eased myself into the tub, lay back, closed my eyes and relaxed. I was about to begin washing myself when I was stopped short by the sight of my naked arms and legs.

I had always been hefty—had even been chided for it by the cadets at OMA and my fellow cavalry officers. Now I wondered at the spare spectacle I had become. My flesh was dry and clung sepulchrally to my bones. My wrists, elbows, ankles, and knees bulged comically. All my ribs showed, and my groin was sunken between the gaunt ells of my hips. It was frightful, and I had to chuckle at myself in pity and dismay. The proud cavalry officer I had once been now resembled nothing so much as a broken-down nag.

For the next few days I conferred almost continuously with leaders of the Manila resistance, although the constant surveillance of General Lim prevented me from meeting him. I became concerned that the frequent visitors to the Mabantas' would attract attention, and so on Christmas Eve, Mona Snyder came to fetch me in a horse-drawn *carretela* to take me to the home of another of our officers.

She was the loveliest Christmas present I could have hoped for. We embraced for a very long time.

"You are well?" she asked me, her brown eyes smiling.

I held out my arms like a scarecrow. "As you see," I said.

"We will do something about that," she laughed. "We are invited to dinner at my relatives. They have prepared a Christmas feast in your honor."

We sat in the back of the little open carriage, I in my gangling white suit and she in a floral print dress, looking for all the world like lovers on an evening jaunt. I, however, carried my pistol in the band of my trousers, and the driver, one of our guerillas, had a submachine gun beneath the blanket at his feet. The boulevards bustled with horse-drawn carts and a few cars, and the sidewalks were busy with people. The Japanese had forbidden radios, and so every evening the streets filled up with people exchanging *balita*, something between gossip and news.

I was concerned about the number of Japanese soldiers patrolling the city center, each of whom, it seemed to me, scrutinized my white face. But Mona paid no attention, keeping up a cheery banter while the driver flicked the belly of the little horse with his whip and the shops slid by.

Her unconcern was contagious, and I found myself seduced by the joy of the evening. The night was pleasantly warm, and the air was perfumed with the scent of dama-de-noche and ilang-ilang. We passed down side streets deep in scent and tunneled by giant acacias. Behind their massive trunks ran the white-washed walls of the mansions of New Manila, and it was at one of these that we finally turned in. A servant waited at a huge mahogany door. Beyond, a handsome young couple held out their arms to Mona.

Tony and Mercy Gonzalez both greeted me with a hug before I was even introduced. There were no formalities, and I was made at once to feel at home. Dinner had been laid for us, and their little boy had been put to bed early to preclude his hearing our conversation or boasting of his parents' strange visitor. The meal was as exquisite as the company, and we ate and chatted and sipped wine until Mona motioned to me that it was time to go.

It was far too soon for me, but we could not risk being on the streets beyond curfew. I was a long time thanking the Gonzalezes, affected as much by their graciousness as by the wine. At last Mona bundled me into the carriage and again we set off across Manila, this time to the home of Narcisso Mabanta's brother, Pedro.

Christmas Day 1943 was devoted to celebration and meetings. Among my visitors was the former Czechoslovakian consul in Manila, a man named Schmelkis, who was serving in our propaganda section. Schmelkis bore a message from a Filipino he had recently met who claimed to have come to Manila by submarine from Australia. This man, who identified himself by the code name CIO-12, was able to supply Schmelkis with a number of accurate details concerning the submarine supply of our coastal networks.

"He is very anxious to meet you while he is in Manila," Schmelkis told me in his thick Slavic accent.

It struck me as a valuable contact, and I questioned Schmelkis closely about his conversation with the man. Schmelkis explained that they had been introduced by a woman who was known and trusted by the resistance, and whose son-in-law was a naval officer at MacArthur's headquarters. The man had produced papers to document his identity and had already met with several guerilla leaders in the southern islands.

I was routinely suspicious of unannounced contacts, but this one seemed genuine enough. Nonetheless, I asked Schmelkis to take me through the conversation once more.

"His bona fides seem to be in order," Schmelkis concluded. Then he paused reflectively a moment. "He did make one curious remark though . . ."

"What was that?" I asked.

"He said he understood from one of our intelligence people that you had come to Manila to arrange the killing of General Lim, to settle some dispute between you."

The suggestion immediately put me on my guard. Very few members of my organization knew my reasons for visiting Manila, and certainly nothing of that kind had ever been said. What was more, if anyone in my group even suspected that that was my motive, it would certainly not have been spoken of.

"I am to see him tomorrow, Major," Schmelkis continued. "What do you wish me to do?"

"I want you to take a message back to him," I answered. "Last night the Huks called a parley with some of our people in Malabon. It was a trap, and when our people showed up, the

Huks killed them all. Tell this man that I'm going up there for a few days, and that I'll contact him when I get back."

"Very well," Schmelkis said.

It was only half true. The Huks had massacred our people in Malabon, in the fish ponds north of Manila, and I knew that word of it would soon reach the kempei-tai, but I had no plans to leave Manila. I told Mona that I had planted this story with CIO-12, and asked her to alert her people to see if it surfaced inside the kempei-tai.

"If anything like it turns up," I told her, "then this CIO-12 is a spy."

Over the next few days I continued to try to meet with General Lim, but he warned me repeatedly that it was too dangerous. Meanwhile, I received word that Japanese agents had been patrolling the neighborhood of Narcisso Mabanta's house, where I had spent my first night in Manila. Then Mona arrived with even more unsettling news.

General Roxas had summoned her to tell her that General Baba not only knew I was in Manila but also roughly where I was staying. What was more, Roxas said, Baba had repeated to General Francisco, the constabulary chief, the story I had had Schmelkis relay to CIO-12, almost word for word. It was clear, then, that CIO-12 was a counterintelligence agent reporting directly to Baba. It was also clear that I would have to move at once.

Mona had brought a *carretela*, and we climbed quickly into the back. We drove at a trot toward central Manila, headed for the southern suburbs. As we reached the downtown district, traffic thickened. I was becoming more and more anxious, but soon we were caught in a crush of vehicles and we slowed almost to a stop. Then, in an instant, the *carretela* was surrounded by hundreds of Japanese soldiers carrying rifles.

I was stunned by their sudden appearance; they were everywhere, milling around and chattering at one another. It was a second before I could believe that none of them was taking any notice of us. I was also puzzled by the fact that their weapons were not at the ready, but were slung haphazardly across their backs or at their waists. Nonetheless, my body was taut with apprehension and I instinctively felt under my shirt for my pistol.

Mona regarded the soldiers casually a moment and then leaned over to me with a smile. "It seems we have joined a parade," she said.

It was true. We had driven into the middle of a military parade that was just breaking up. But instead of being relieved, I felt myself becoming angry. Mona was in as much danger as I, and yet she never lost her cheerful manner. She seemed to have no fear at all, and yet Ramsey, the professional soldier, was a mass of nerves.

"Isn't it wonderful?" she said suddenly.

"What?" I grumbled.

"Manila," she replied, slipping her arm through mine. The gesture calmed me. "And soon there will be a new year," she went on with a smile. "And you'll see, everything will be fine."

We spent that evening at the home of some friends of Mona's who lived near the waterfront. From there Mona telephoned Wally Roeder, told him that she had a Swiss friend staying with her, and asked him to come to fetch me. Wally understood and replied that he would be over at once.

Meanwhile, Mona's operatives at kempei-tai headquarters were reporting to her that General Baba had ordered a dragnet thrown over the city, and had set up roadblocks on all the routes leading out of it. Fleeing Manila would now be impossible, Mona said; all I could do was to bury myself deeper inside the city.

"You must go with Wally Roeder," she told me. "You can stay with him at the gas compound. It is the last place the Japanese will think to look for you."

"What will you do?" I asked her.

"I will go on as usual," she said. "Meanwhile, you must stay with Roeder until it is safe for you to leave Manila."

I told her that I did not think it would be safe for her in the city much longer.

She broke into a coquettish smile. "Nonsense," she said. "Who could ever suspect such a sweet girl as me?"

In a few hours Wally Roeder appeared at my hosts' door. He was a tall, thin-faced man with a shock of graying hair, a dry, formal manner, and clear blue, intelligent eyes. He had ridden his bicycle halfway across Manila from the gasworks, bringing a spare bike for me to use. His plan was characteristically audacious. I would stay as a guest in his home in the gasworks compound, literally under the eyes of hundreds of Japanese soldiers. Since Roeder was some twenty years older than me, and since our passports bore the same last name, I was to be his son, visiting from Zurich.

Mona left the house first, taking the little *carretela* back across the city to her home. Before she left I made her promise that if things became too difficult for her in Manila she would come and join me in the hills.

Roeder and I waited an interval before leaving the house. Before we did, he asked if I spoke any German. I told him I did not.

"Well," he said, "if you are to be my son, you must be able to converse with me. I will teach you a few words, yes?"

"Okay," I shrugged.

"Good. Now, please repeat after me," he said in a professorial tone. "*So . . .*"

"So," I said.

"No, not so, *tzo.*"

"Tzo," I mimicked.

Roeder cocked an eyebrow at me. "Yes, it will do," he muttered. "Now, *wie.*" I repeated it.

"Very good. Now say *Ja, so, wie so.*"

"*Ja,*" I said. "*So, wie so.*"

He made me repeat it several times until he was satisfied that my pronunciation could pass muster. "Now," he said, "I will carry the bulk of the conversation, yes? And you will contribute what you can."

"*Ja*," I agreed. "*So, wie so.*"

"Excellent," Roeder said. "We leave now, yes?"

It was a long ride to the gasworks on our bicycles, but the whole way Roeder chatted amiably with me in German, while I parroted "*Ja, ja, so, wie so*" over and over to everything he said. It was a mad charade, but I felt the very unlikeliness of it was a safeguard. As we pedaled the back streets of Manila, I began to make up German words of my own, causing Roeder to glance back at me over his shoulder. And each time he did, I responded with a solemn "*Ja, so wie so.*"

Despite my confidence in Roeder, I could not help but be dismayed when I saw the compound. It was a huge tract of machinery, storage tanks, and houses sprawling between two estuaries of the Pasig River in the heart of Manila. And crowded everywhere among the buildings were neat rows of Japanese infantry tents. The place was swarming with soldiers, and Roeder's own house was surrounded by them.

We pedaled on through the gates, where the sentries waved us past, I all the while nodding, "*Ja, ja, so,*" to Roeder's cheerful chatter. We maneuvered among the ranks of tents and pulled our bicycles up onto his porch.

"Congratulations, Major," he said to me when we were safely in his living room. I assumed he was referring to our successful trip across Manila, but he quickly corrected me. "No, no," he said. "You have made an even more impressive accomplishment: You have opened new frontiers of the German language."

For the next nine days the kempei-tai conducted a manhunt for me that virtually closed down Manila. All roads out of the city were blocked, and every vehicle was searched. Inside Manila there were continual patrols as well as random checks of pedestrians and vehicles from one end of town to the other. Our informants at kempei-tai headquarters, which was not more than a mile from Wally Roeder's house, told Roeder that Baba was determined that I should not escape, and that he was leading some of the patrols himself.

Meanwhile, I remained at the gas compound, keeping discreetly out of sight of the billeted soldiers. By the first week of January the pressure appeared to be easing off. Our informants reported that Baba had reluctantly decided I had slipped out of Manila, and he began reducing the patrols.

Throughout this time I had had no meetings, but word had reached me that some officers of the Manila resistance were in contact with an American from the Allied Intelligence Bureau who had arrived in Luzon via submarine. This man was waiting for me in a northeastern suburb of the city, I was told, with radio equipment and information from MacArthur's headquarters.

There was little more I could accomplish in Manila, and, given the surveillance, a meeting with General Lim was out of the question. On the other hand, the prospect of having my own radio was irresistible; a radio would be an invaluable asset to our intelligence operations. And so I decided to meet with the AIB man on my way back to my base in the mountains.

On the evening of January 7, Wally Roeder and I got out our bicycles and walked them across the compound, carrying on our one-sided conversation in German. At the gate the sentries passed us out, and we rode toward the bridge over the Pasig River. There were few lights, and by now it was quite dark. As I coasted down the far side of the bridge, I suddenly saw a group of Japanese soldiers coming toward me. I was almost on top of them before I realized who they were, and I swerved crazily to avoid knocking them over.

The soldiers threw insults after us as we turned onto the quai and began pedaling as fast as we could in the direction of the Malacanang Palace. The palace was ringed by sentries of the Philippine constabulary, but they took no notice of us as we rode by the arching, ornate gates.

We continued for over an hour, out into the rising ground of the San Juan del Monte district, pedaling as far as we could, then walking the bikes up the steep, brushy lanes. Several of Roeder's men were waiting at a house near the top of the district.

Among them was the chief of staff of the Manila military district, Colonel Patricio Gonzalez, known in the underground as Pat Gatson, one of our most daring operatives. I had known him only through communiques, but I had already promoted him twice for his fearlessness and efficiency. And now here he stood, a compact, handsome man of thirty with an ample moustache and black, searching eyes. He had recently made the long trek from southern Luzon, bringing with him the man I had come to meet, Sergeant Ben Harder of AIB.

Harder quickly told me that he had come to the Philippines with a senior officer, Major Lawrence Phillips, to establish a coast-watching station on the island of Mindoro. Since their arrival a month before, Phillips had been trying to contact me, and when he learned of my trip to Manila he sent Harder for a meeting. Shortly before Harder left, however, the station was raided, and he and Phillips had barely escaped. Phillips, he recounted, was now hiding out with guerillas on Mindoro.

"What about the radio?" I asked Harder.

"Major Phillips has it, sir," he said.

"Can he get it to me?"

"Not possible, sir. We've got our hands full just staying ahead of the Japs."

My heart sank. That radio would have meant not only direct contact with MacArthur's headquarters but also an end to the risks of my runners. I had never been to Mindoro and was not sure how I would get there. Nonetheless, I decided that I must go.

Pat Gatson agreed. "I'll take care of the arrangements," he volunteered.

So far as Harder knew, Major Phillips was on his way to a meeting with Ramon Ruffy, the guerilla commander of Mindoro. There was no guarantee that Phillips would be there when I arrived, but Harder assured me that Ruffy could provide me with guides to find him. It would be a long, difficult trip, first by boat across Manila Bay, then by land through southern Luzon, then by boat again across the island strait, and again overland to Ruffy's headquarters near Naujan on the eastern coast of Mindoro. I was not sure I was up to it physically, and I had been absent from central Luzon for nearly a year by now, but the chance of getting my own radio was simply too tempting to pass up.

I ordered Harder to return to Mindoro to locate Phillips and tell him I was coming, and I sent Gatson on ahead to prepare my trip. His job would be to scout the route I would take, contact the guerilla leaders along it, and arrange with them for my transport and security. I would be traveling through territory I had never seen, among guerillas I did not know, and my life would depend on the arrangements Gatson made.

Meanwhile, I began the long hike out of Manila to rejoin my headquarters guard. Wally Roeder accompanied me to the outskirts of the city.

"I must be getting back," he told me in his German accent.

"*Ja, ja,*" I replied. "*So, wie so.*"

We both laughed.

"You were a good pupil," he said.

"You were a good teacher." I shook his hand. "Maybe after the war I'll come back and teach you a few words."

"I hope for it, Major," he said. "Good luck." He swung his bike around, climbed upon it, and started pedaling back toward Manila. I watched him disappear into the darkness, and then began the trudge across the lowlands toward the watershed plateau of Novaliches, where my men were camped.

Camacho, Cadizon, and Cabral were waiting with the rest of my bodyguards. I had decided to take a security detachment with me, for the Japanese were still actively searching for me, and we had no idea how many Sakdalista spies might be in southern

Luzon. That night we all gathered at a hut in a barrio of Novaliches, where I briefed them on my plans.

"When do we leave?" Camacho asked.

"As soon as Gatson finishes the arrangements and we find a new base," I answered. "Maybe two weeks." I paused before going on. "But you're not coming, Claro," I added.

Camacho gave me a questioning squint.

"I want you to go back home," I told him, "and take charge of the regiment in Pangasinan. Putnam's too far north and Lapham's got his hands full in the mountains. When the invasion comes they're going to need a strong organization behind the Lingayen beaches. It's your province and your people. I want you to get them ready to meet MacArthur."

Camacho thought it over and nodded slowly. "Okay, Major," he said. Then he gave a glance around at Cadizon, Cabral, and the others. "But do you think I can trust these guys to look after you?" They all laughed quietly together.

"You just look after MacArthur," Cadizon answered him.

"It's true," I said. "If they do come through Lingayen, you'll be behind the Japs on the beaches. How many of our people get ashore, or even *if* they get ashore, may depend on you."

"I understand," Camacho said. "I'll get started in the morning."

While we were speaking a face suddenly appeared at the top of the ladder leading into the hut. Our conversation stopped immediately, and with some puzzlement we regarded the intruder, who seemed as surprised as we.

In a moment he had composed himself and climbed up into the room. He was, he declared, a member of the Makapili, and he had come with a Japanese patrol to arrest me. He advised me not to try to resist, as the kempei-tai had the place surrounded.

I was standing by the back wall, taking in this speech with some amazement. My .45 was hanging in its holster nearby, and the spy made a move toward it. At that instant Cadizon drew a bolo knife from his scabbard and struck the man full in the forehead. The blow split his skull from the bridge of his nose to the crown. He dropped to his knees, his head fell forward, the matter oozing from it, and he pitched onto his face at my feet.

Stunned by the sight, I watched in horror as he writhed violently on the bamboo slats, a sticky purple puddle edging toward me. In a voice trembling with anxiety, disgust, and anger, I ordered my men to get rid of him. They grabbed him by the arms and legs, which still twitched with an electric rhythm, and dragged him down the ladder. There were a few urgent whispers in the dark and then a moist thud as they finished him with an axe. The body was buried in the brush behind the hut.

There was no Japanese patrol. The spy had run into my sentries by accident and had begun asking about me. When my men were sure he was alone, they led him to the hut for my bodyguards to dispose of. Though there had really been no danger, I was shaken by the spy's sudden appearance, and his even more sudden death. The walls of the hut were splashed with his blood and brain matter, as were my own clothes.

I ordered the men to wash the place, and we moved farther back into the hills for the remainder of the night. The first thing I did when we camped was to scrub my clothing, over and over again. And though after an hour of effort I managed to remove most of the stains, I did not sleep that night, nor many others to follow.

FILIPINO
PATRIOT

1944 (January–May)

MEDAL ON PRECEDING PAGE:
Silver Star with Cluster (AMERICAN)

Water

E ver since the loss of Timbo, the East Central Luzon Guerilla Area force had been without a general headquarters. While I waited for Gatson to return with the details of my transport to Mindoro, I began to scout for a new site. With both the Japanese and the Huks in force in the Fort Stotsenberg area, I ruled out the central plain.

My trip to Manila had impressed me with the strategic importance of our network there: The intelligence on Japanese intentions that flowed from the city was essential to the plans and security of our operations. I was now known there and had been accepted as the military commander both in Manila and throughout central Luzon. Promixity to the capital was an asset at once of geography and morale. One of the principles of guerilla warfare was that the guerilla leadership should assert itself as the only legitimate authority; if we could not be in the capital, we should be as near to it as possible.

North and west of Manila were the plains and fish ponds of south central Luzon—flat, difficult, exposed ground. To the northeast, however, rose the rolling rain forest of the Sierra Madre Mountains. Its ridges were steep, its giant canopy of trees and jungle was impenetrable, and even the peaks overlooking Manila were remote and inaccessible. It was forbidding territory, inhabited only by Negritos, but somehow, I felt, I must make a home within it for the guerillas.

The desolate, sprawling foothills were a patchwork of huge haciendas where wild cattle foraged among the scrub and jungle fringes. The largest of these ranches belonged to the com-

mander of our Mountain Corps Regiment, Colonel Eduardo
Manahan. A small, spare Filipino of fifty, Manahan had dark,
wrinkled skin and the sinewy forearms of a farmer. His head
was shaved, and he bore upon it the deep, puckered scar of a
Japanese sword slash, a remembrance of the death march of
Bataan when his head had been laid open and he had been left
for dead. His hatred of the Japanese was profound, and he
welcomed my proposal to establish our headquarters in his hills,
as well as the job of protecting it with his guerillas.

Manahan led us north from the Novaliches watershed plateau and then east in among the foothills. The ground rose
sharply, and with just a little elevation it became tangled in
scrub. Above us towered the giant acacias and lauans of the
upper slopes, some spreading straight up for hundreds of feet
in dense umbrellas of branches. In an hour we were deep into
the wilderness. The air was thick and blue with moisture,
everything hung heavy with vines, and though it was midday,
we found ourselves in the cool dark of a cathedral.

We struggled up a rise to a small clearing and surveyed the
scene. Below us lay Manila across the foothills and plain, its
barrios crowding in a crescent around the business district to
the bay. Behind us bulked a mountain of jungle as remote as
any in the range. Down its precipitous slopes thick with trees,
a waterfall rushed within a gash of white rock. Near the top of
the falls was a shelf of slabs that gave onto a broad shoulder,
and above it a forested valley sloping toward the mountain's
summit.

"What moutain is that?" I asked Manahan.

"That?" he said. "Balagbag."

It was, I recognized, the perfect place for my headquarters.
The rocky shelf was an ideal defense position, the valley beyond
it would be the site of the camp, and the rise beyond that would
be our observation post for Manila. All we had to do was find a
way to it.

"Balagbag," I repeated. "Well, now it's home."

We spent the rest of the day exploring the base of the

mountain, hacking through the jungle with bolos, following the streambed in search of a trail to the waterfall. At last, up a steep slope, we found it. We cut our way across to the falls and began climbing them. The rock was slick with moss and in places nearly vertical, so that we had to pull ourselves up by vines. After hours of labor we reached the rocky ledge and turned right onto the shoulder.

"This is it," I said to Manahan. "We'll set up the machine guns on the shelf and begin building here. When I get back with the radio we'll put our signal station up on the hill."

It was settled, and for the next few days we planned the camp. My chief of staff, Colonel Amado Bautista, had been an officer of the Philippine Army Corps of Engineers, and I assigned him to oversee the work in my absence. Building and defending the camp would be the duty of Manahan's Mountain Corps Regiment. Supplies would have to be carried up from the plain: food, medicine, equipment, and weapons. There were to be no trail markers, and the men were to leave the vegetation undisturbed as far as possible. Only our headquarters troops were to know the path up the falls to the camp, for Balagbag's very isolation was to be our principal line of defense.

It was an unlikely place with an unlovely name—Balagbag— but our army would have a base again, and I left for Mindoro with the reassurance that I would have a home to come back to.

I returned to Polo outside Manila on January 15, 1944. Pat Gatson was waiting with news that my route to Mindoro had been prepared. He had arranged for guides and lookouts as far as the coast and a boat to take me across Manila Bay. Most important, he had contacted the guerillas in Cavite province, where I would land.

I knew that the guerilla factions in southern Luzon were in disarray, and that fighting sometimes broke out among them. I had no intention of becoming caught among the rivals, and so Gatson's assurance that he had smoothed my way was calming. He had spoken personally to the leader of the Cavite guerillas, a notorious bandit who called himself General Ernie. Tishio Ernie had been a renegade for years, and neither the prewar government nor the Japanese had been able to suppress him. A colorful, half-wild character about whom legends were told and songs sung, he was also an effective resistance fighter, for he hated the Japanese as much as he loved thievery.

Ernie's men were at war with the other guerilla bands in the area, but Gatson had arranged a truce during the time I was to be guided from one to the other. I would have safe conduct to the southern coast, where an interisland cargo sloop would meet me and take me to Mindoro.

That night my bodyguards, Gatson, and I set out across the fish ponds to Manila Bay. It was intricate, slow going. The moon was big and brilliant, and we could not take the trails, so instead we had to balance our way along the dike tops in a hasty single file, threading a half circle around one and then the next in the opposite direction. The ponds were a giant flooded labyrinth that stretched for miles in every direction, the moon glinting off the salt cisterns and the big bangus fish slapping impatiently against the water. It took us most of the night to make the few miles to the coast, and when we reached it we were exhausted.

Nonetheless, it felt good to face the sea again. The air was clean and the moon busked brightly upon the water. A *banca* was waiting, bobbing in the mist a few yards offshore. It was a shallow fishing boat some thirty feet long and four wide, with a pair of spindly bamboo outriggers. There was a single bamboo mast with a square sail much weathered and patched, and a tarpaulin stretched across the beam to protect the catch. Under this I, Gaston, and my four bodyguards—Cadizon, Cabral, Acosta, and Cornel—would be concealed.

The captain and his two mates poled away from shore and rowed out into the bay, where they raised the threadbare sail. The farther we went the thicker became the mist, until we could see nothing beyond the gunwales of the boat. It was an eerie sensation, for the moonlight infused the mist, shrouding it around us with an opal glow that lent the aspect of a dream.

Silence reigned, save for the rustling of the sail and the echoing horns that warned shipping away from the points at the entrance to the bay. I sent the two mates forward as lookouts, while the rest of us huddled under the tarp—Cadizon and Cabral on either side of me; Gatson, Acosta, and Cornel opposite. We stretched out as best we could, our legs overlapping, and went to sleep.

It was daylight when Gatson gently shook me. "Major, look . . ." he whispered.

I lifted the canvas and peered out, squinting against the glint. There, not fifty yards from me, was the massive gray hull of a Japanese destroyer, its guns bristling against the light. Beyond it lay another, riding implacably at anchor, and then a cruiser and a freighter. In the darkness and the mist we had drifted in among a convoy of enemy ships, and now we were virtually walled in by steel.

All six of us crouched beneath the tarp, clutching our weapons while the captain and his men steered toward the open water beyond. There was nothing we could do. At any moment a cutter from one of the ships might hail us to inspect. If that happened, we were dead. If we fought, we would be blown out of the water in an instant, and if we surrendered . . .

We maintained our deliberate pace, passing one by one the sheer armored cliffs of the destroyers, keeping the curving headland of Cavite on our left. We were to land not far beyond, but I told the captain to sail on until we were well beyond the sight of the Japanese ships. Only when I was sure it was safe did I have him turn in toward the beach.

No one was there to meet us. We disembarked and headed inland toward the first barrio. I wanted to be through it before its people had awakened, so we moved quickly in among the huts. As we were emerging on the far side, two horse-drawn *carretelas* come trotting toward us, each bearing a pair of heavily armed guerillas. Gatson recognized them as General Ernie's men. We continued our route, riding with them as far as the main road. Then we climbed down and hiked a jungle trail to an isolated village from which the general himself came out to meet us.

"Major Ramsey!" he beamed at me. "Welcome to my headquarters!"

He was a small, wiry man in his fifties, austerely dressed, his thick black hair slicked back, his moustache trim. His skin was dark and deeply weathered, and his eyes had a dull, dirty look.

I saluted him, which evidently pleased him, and shook his hand.

"You will do me the honor to inspect my troops," he said. He gave a shout, and thirty or forty men formed up in line before us. A lieutenant snapped them to attention, and then General Ernie motioned me toward them. Together we walked the length of the line while I studied each man cursorily. They were a ragged, predatory group, bandits like their leader. None had any semblance of a uniform. What they wore had been stolen on raids and represented every sort of clothing, from bits of evening dress to dancing shoes to football shirts with numerals. But every one was armed to the teeth with a wicked collection of weapons old and new.

I completed the inspection and declared myself impressed with the platoon. Ernie smiled and nodded to the lieutenant, who dismissed the men. We walked across the village, which was inhabited by the soldiers and their families, to Ernie's house. He said he had prepared a breakfast for us of fish, eggs, fruit, and rice, and he invited us to spend the night with him.

The general's house was suitably large and distinctive in that it was constructed of milled lumber rather than bamboo. It was exceptional for another reason as well: Before it stood three wooden posts driven into the ground, some six feet high and a foot in diameter. To these were tied a woman and two men, each gagged and blindfolded. They were badly dehydrated; their heads lolled, and their blue tongues swelled grotesquely from their mouths. They had evidently been tied up and tortured for several days. Their bodies, half naked, were covered with welts and bruises, and they moaned continually as they slumped against the ropes.

"Japanese spies," Ernie remarked. "We have been interrogating them, but without much success."

As I watched, one of Ernie's soldiers moved among them with an axe handle. He stopped before the woman, shoved his face close to hers, and barked a question at her. She groaned in reply, a deep, pitiable pleading for water. The soldier straightened, swung the axe handle, and struck her across the stomach. The breath coughed out of her in a long, dry gasp, and she began to sob, though no tears came.

"They think they can infiltrate *me*," Ernie said contemptuously as he led us up the ladder to his house, "but here in Cavite we know how to deal with them."

The *sala* was large and airy and filled with an extraordinary assortment of furniture culled from raids. As in some bizarre showroom, the collection of sofas and chairs, tables and armoires were crowded and grouped together. Along one wall ran a closet with slatted folding doors. These Ernie threw open with a flourish. "My wardrobe!" he declared. The closet was lined with men's and women's clothing of every style. Bolts of cloth were also heaped up, and among them I could see silks and brocades that must have been worth a small fortune.

Ernie sat me down and handed me a tumbler of rum. "Now, Major Ramsey, tell me about your forces in Luzon," he urged. "We have heard much about you."

I briefed him on the situation and the status of the ECLGA. He listened carefully, his dirty eyes, the whites yellowed almost to the brown of the pupils, registering a dull approval.

"Impressive, most impressive," he nodded. "I am very glad that you are here, Major. We will talk, officer to officer."

He was certainly not my idea of an officer, but I forbore telling him so and asked instead about guides.

"Of course, of course!" he exclaimed with a wave of his hand, "but there is no hurry. You will be my guest."

It was not an idea I relished, but I had no choice. That night my men slept in a hut adjacent, while beds were made for Gatson and me in the general's house. I could not sleep, however, for the unbroken moans and pleading for water of the three captives who were still being beaten outside. It kept up hour after hour far into the night, while I wrapped my shirt around my ears and struggled to ignore it.

At last I got up and went in search of Ernie, whom I found drinking with some of his officers in the *sala*.

"Could you please put a stop to that noise so that I can get some sleep?" I asked.

"Of course," he smiled, and he called an order in his dialect to a guard outside. Within minutes there was silence. I returned to bed grateful for the quiet, contenting myself with the thought that I had spared the prisoners at least a few hours of torture.

In the morning I went outside to confer with Cadizon and the others. As I passed the prisoners I saw that their faces were covered with flies and their chests were soaked with blood. Ernie had not ordered the beatings to cease; he had ordered the prisoners' throats cut.

I was horrified. Far from sparing them torture, my request had caused the prisoners' deaths. I told Cadizon that we were getting out that morning and to prepare the men. This trip to Mindoro was becoming a grotesque nightmare, one with its own fatal logic. A word, even a casual gesture, could be enough to prompt murder, and I was anxious to be finished with it. When Ernie appeared, I explained that while I valued his hospitality, I was obligated, if I were to have any chance of finding the AIB man at Major Ruffy's headquarters, to move quickly.

Ernie answered that he would provide the guides, but first he had a request. "I would consider it an honor," he said, pulling himself up to his inconsiderable height, "if you would accept the services of me and my troops under your command."

I had had no intention of doing anything of the kind, and I certainly did not want to be responsible for the general's behavior, but at the same time I felt that it would be indiscreet—not to mention imprudent—to refuse. A bandit who would slit the throats of three prisoners to enable a guest to sleep was capable of anything. And so I accepted his offer with as much semblance of gratitude as I could manage.

Again General Ernie assembled his troops, and I swore them in as guerillas of the East Central Luzon force. When it was done the general, striding back and forth in front of the buzzing corpses, gave a speech about the virtues of patriotism, loyalty, and freedom. He grabbed my hand and hoisted it up over his head while the men gave three cheers. Then he assigned a lieutenant and a squad to guide us, and we marched out of camp.

I was anxious to be on my way. We had a long hike ahead of us, and after my experience with General Ernie I no longer had any idea what to expect. Our maps had shown our route across Cavite province to be easy, the ground rising slightly to the vast, flooded caldera of Lake Taal. Instead, beyond Ernie's camp we encountered thick jungle and broken ground that heaved and twisted in a series of ridges and ravines.

For the next three days we fought our way through, hacking trails with bolo knives. We dared not attempt the terrain at night, and so we sweated and suffocated under the daytime heat and dampness. Our clothing was continually soaked through to the skin, we could never see more than a few feet in front of us, and the whole jungle was alive with snakes, monkeys, and vermin of every description.

When at last we emerged from the jungle onto the slopes above Lake Taal we were exhausted, and desperate for water. While we rested, Ernie's guides went ahead to locate the local guerilla chief, who returned with them and led us to his village. He was a squat, elderly Filipino who had lost an eye in his bandit days, and his troops, like Ernie's, were comprised of a vile assortment of thieves.

A meal had been laid for us and for Ernie's men, who ate quickly, wished us well, and set off back to Ernie's camp. They had not been gone for twenty minutes when we heard gunfire

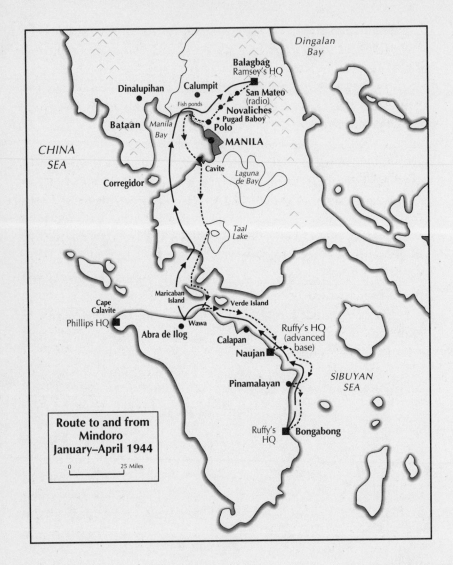

**Route to and from
Mindoro
January–April 1944**

0   25 Miles

from down the trail. We grabbed for our weapons, but our hosts seemed unconcerned.

"Not to worry," the guerilla chief grinned at me. "It is nothing. Some of our people have ambushed Ernie's men."

I sent Cadizon back down the trail to check.

"It's true, Major," he reported on his return. "They're all dead, shot in the back and their throats cut."

"I told you," the guerilla chief nodded at me, his empty eye squinting mischievously. "Cavite is not like Manila. Down here we have our own ways."

In the morning we were guided south from the lake toward the coast, where we would hire a *batil*, an inter-island cargo schooner, to take us to Mindoro. The going was easier as we followed ridges that sloped gently toward Balayan Bay, but once we reached the lowlands our guides stopped short. They would go no farther, they declared, since the guerillas in that area were at war with them, and they had no intention of becoming victims as Ernie's men had done.

We thus had to make our way among the patchwork of partisan groups along the southern Luzon coast, and though the guerilla leaders were kind to us they were deeply suspicious of one another. None would cross into the other's territory, and so we had to find our own way through the no-man's-lands between them. The result was that a trip that should have taken two days at most consumed a full week, leaving us frustrated and weary.

When at last we arrived at the coast I sent Gatson to find a *batil* while the rest of us waited in a barrio near the beach. Worn out from the days of trekking, we took the opportunity to rest, swim, and sunbathe. It was good to see the men enjoy themselves for a change, and to enjoy the hospitality of the villagers who shared with us their fruit and sweet coconut-milk beverages.

Gatson returned next day with news that a *batil* would pick us up after dark. The island passage was heavily patrolled by the Japanese, he said, and so we must make the crossing at night. The captain had told him that it would take two days at most to reach Ruffy's headquarters at Naujan. It was welcome news. In a few days I would have my radio and be done with his hellish trip.

That evening Gatson and I strolled along the beach, discussing the future of the Manila district and our plans for MacArthur's return. Though we had no idea when it would come, we spoke of it with urgency. Our regiments must be ready throughout Luzon to aid the invasion, we agreed, for every bit of intelligence or logistical support we could offer would mean time and lives saved.

We talked quietly and earnestly as the day faded into the sea and the lights of the Japanese ships on the horizon became visible. Gatson had an instinctive grasp of the importance of our organization both for the occupation and beyond. The present was a crisis that called for immediate action, but the future too would be perilous. Fighting for freedom and winning it were difficult enough; sustaining it would be far more complex.

I was moved and impressed by Gatson. He was an excellent officer—intelligent, dedicated, and courageous—and though he was a patriot devoted to the ideals for which we were fighting, he spoke always in the most pragmatic terms. In that I felt a kinship with him; he seemed to be waging the same struggle I faced of balancing the poetic with the practical. He understood that liberty was above all hard work that had to be attended to in its details. And though he kept the ideals always in view, the test of a patriot was to translate them into a program of action. At this Pat Gatson was brilliant and tireless.

As we walked back up the beach to the barrio where my men were standing guard, I realized the talk had affected me in a way I had not expected. Gatson was a patriot fighting for the freedom of his native land, the Philippines. But what was I? I was an officer of the United States Army; but had I not become a Filipino patriot as well?

Through the darkest days, through the sickness and the isolation and the years of organizing, the sustaining note of my consciousness had been that I was a soldier doing my duty. Whenever I would find myself outcast in some barrio, or buried deep in the jungle, I would answer the inevitable question of what I was doing here, how I had gotten here, with the simple,

sobering assurance that it was my job. But the guerilla movement had grown far beyond a job, and its goals and ideals had
surpassed duty's ability to explain them.

I was no longer merely *with* the Filipino people; I was *of*
them. I was not simply organizing among them; I had grown
organically to be a part of them. Their struggle had become my
struggle, and their liberation, inevitably, would be mine as well.
It was a vague reality and a foreign one, but somehow, through
two years of shared suffering and danger, the professional and
private faces of my war had become superimposed.

In the faces of people such as Mona Snyder, Claro Camacho,
and Pat Gatson, whose love of liberty and devotion to duty
mirrored my own, I saw myself reflected. And though their
faces were brown and their accents were foreign, their struggle
was identical to mine. We were one people fighting for a single
ideal within the quotidian labyrinth of guerilla organization.

Guerilla struggle, I began to realize, had altered not only
my understanding of tactics but also my whole concept of the
nature of war, from that of a conflict fought by rules with
conventional weapons to one fought by instinct, with faith and
devotion above all. And, inescapably, it was altering my understanding of myself, not only as a soldier but also as a man.

The *batil* curved in toward the beach, its big sail bobbling like a
hand before our faces in the dark. We gathered up our weapons
and waded out to it, handed them up to the ragged crewmen,
and said a hasty good-bye to Gatson. I promised to contact him
as soon as I got back, and to bring him out to the new headquarters for our first radio transmission. For a moment as we shook
hands I considered taking him with us, but he was far too
important in Manila to be absent for long. He stood for a few
minutes by the water's edge until he saw us out of sight and
then started back on the long trek to Manila.

None of us would ever see him again.

Teeth

D ark fists of cloud had been gathering all day, and as we set
sail the wind picked up. It was not the typhoon season, so
we welcomed the rain as a blind to protect us from the Japanese.
We sailed south, making good time before the rising wind, and
turned east among the dozens of islands that dotted the strait.
The captain was anxious to be free of them, for they harbored
Japanese patrol boats, but the wind was beginning to blow a
gale and the sea was lurching furiously. By the time we cleared
the islands and turned out into the broad passage toward Mindoro, we were full in the teeth of an extremely early and violent
typhoon.

The wind roared around us and the rain swept down in thick
curtains. Huge walls of waves heaved up, threatening to roll us
over, until we tumbled down their backsides into the black
troughs. My men and I, below in the crowded cabin, struggled
to hold down our equipment as we were tossed wildly from side
to side, together with the crew's belongings and the galley pots
and pans. All of us were sick, clutching at ourselves and vomit-
ing. At last I could stand the confining chaos no longer and I
groped my way up on deck.

The whole world was black and bellowing. Thick clouds
cascaded over one another, spewing rain in deep-chested gusts.
The captain was lashed to the wheel, which strained against his
arms, and the crew were tied down to the rails. I grabbed at the
ladder and held on.

The ship shot straight up into the air, its bow parting the
rain for an instant, and then swooped down again. We were all
pitched backward, then onto our faces, and then backward once

more as the waves thundered over us. I was both terrified and fascinated; I had never seen nature so angry, all its force and fury seemingly concentrated in this gale. I could not imagine that the ship would not be torn to pieces.

We rode the storm all night, beating back and forth across the passage, until just before dawn we reached the islands off the coast of Mindoro. We sheltered among them, dropping anchor in a cove, while the storm raged on around us. By nightfall the wind had relented a little, and we crept from our covert back out into the passage. No sooner were we at sea, however, than the full force of the typhoon returned and we were again fighting for our lives.

We could not regain the shelter of the islands, and so the captain steered toward the point at Calapan, the site of a Japanese naval base. I hollered to him that we must pass the point by daybreak, but he only waved helplessly back. All night we fronted the typhoon, swinging in great arcs between the coastline and the open sea. When light came we were still at it, and I searched the landward side anxiously for the cranes and masts of the Japanese base. There were none.

"Are we past?" I called to the captain.

He scanned the coast through his bleary eyes.

"See there?" he yelled back, pointing toward a clutch of islands. "We are back where we began!"

It was true. Ten hours of fighting the storm had gained us not a yard of progress. We turned again toward shore and spent the day recovering at anchor. The night came on calmer, and we set out again. The seas were high but the wind had slackened, and we ran furtively along the coast toward Calapan. We spied the naval base as the sun rose, and were about to head in to shore when the wind suddenly died, becalming us in the bay opposite the Japanese.

I cursed in frustration and ordered everyone below. Again we crossed into the cabin while the ship lolled pointlessly and the channel came to life with motors. A Japanese patrol boat buzzed by, and then another, their wakes rolling beneath our hull. The air inside the little cabin was stifling and I seethed and sweltered. Once again I was helpless, just as I had been in the Manila boxcar, only worse. If any of the patrol boats swung by to inspect us, there would be no chance of escape. I hated the inertia of it; it was the opposite of cavalry—no mobility, no shock, no surprise. We were marooned amid the enemy, hidden by a few planks of wood, wholly at the mercy of their curiosity.

"What the hell is that?" I said aloud in spite of myself.

From on deck came a whistle—low, insistent, and hissing. It was joined by another and then a third, and in a moment the breathy whistling was everywhere around us.

"The sailors," Cadizon whispered. "It is an old superstition. They are whistling up the wind."

It was an eerie ululation, half aspiration, half mournful song, and it was sustained, to my amazement, for hours. The effect of it all was hypnotic. There was the heat, the close confinement, the suffocating sea air, and the whistle. Together they produced a strange, disembodying sensation, and my mind began to wander across the events of the past two years and the trip that I was now embarked upon.

Where was I going? a voice within me asked. To Mindoro, I answered. Why? To meet an officer who had brought a radio for me by submarine. But was that really the answer? How had I come to be here, in this place, among these people, becalmed within a sea of enemies, whistling for wind?

It was not healthy to brood upon such questions, I knew, but at some point it was necessary. What was I now: an officer or a rebel? And who was I now: that Ramsey boy from Wichita, the cavalryman, or a Philippine guerilla? I was all of these things, and, in a sense, I was none of them, for at any moment, just on a whim, I—all of us—could be annihilated.

I fought to keep my mind in focus as the whistling cloyed around it. I must find Phillips, get the radio, and return. To where? Balagbag. For what? To keep the movement going. But why? Because MacArthur was returning. That much we all knew and all believed. MacArthur was reality, the long, unfail-

ing cable that bound us to the outside world. He had promised
to return and he would return, and when he did he would need
our help.

The idea of MacArthur consoled me, and I began to enjoy
the feeling of being adrift in my own thoughts. Though I had
often been lonely in the past two years, I had not been alone
within myself for a long time, and as I lay in the bottom of the
boat, soaked with sweat and panting under the suffocating air,
I allowed my mind to float free.

For a few moments it seemed to rise above my body and
look down at it, kindly, indulgently, and with a pity for the poor
thing it had become. It was a tingling, titillating sensation, more
pleasant than strange, and I wondered if this was what death
was like. Perhaps this was what Hardwick had known, perhaps
it was what I would know if the Japanese discovered us. And
perhaps it was not so terrible, to float like this, fascinated at the
furious past, enthralled by the formless future. Perhaps in my
boyhood my thinking had not gone far enough. Brooding was
death, I had decided, but was not death also release?

The boat began to stir, its ropes and cleats creaking against
the ponderous calm. We were moving, and the air inside the
cabin freshened faintly. The whistling stopped; there was a
breeze. I lifted myself onto an elbow, my sweat-soaked khakis
clinging to my skin, and squinted out the porthole. Calapan was
sliding past, slowly at first and then more quickly, until I saw it
disappear behind the point.

For the moment the danger was over; we would be in Naujan
by dark. I shook myself to be rid of the trance into which I had
fallen. That, too, was danger. Death was not release, I told
myself, it was the enemy, just as surely as the Japanese were
the enemy. And just as the Japanese had their propaganda
about prosperity, death had its own propaganda of release. By
neither must we content ourselves to be lulled; against one as
against the other we had a duty of resistance.

The *batil* slid southward along the coast, the palms nodding
before the warm wind. The end of this dreadful trip was in

sight. Soon I would be back in Luzon at my own headquarters. And what was more, I would have a radio—contact with the world, and a chance to rejoin the wider war.

Major Ruffy's men met us on the beach. We stayed the night in their barrio, and next morning we were escorted to one of Ruffy's command posts in the jungle. There we were told that neither Ruffy nor Major Phillips was in the area. Ruffy was a hundred miles down the coast at his southern headquarters, and Phillips had left a month before to return to his observation post at Calavite on the western side of Mindoro.

I was furious with frustration. I now must either return to Luzon, having wasted a month's time and without a radio, or else push on farther from my base in search of Ruffy and Phillips. Grumbling and cursing, I called my men together and marched them back to the beach where the *batil* was waiting.

"South," I snarled at the captain. He looked incredulous. "Yes, dammit, south!" I said. He shrugged and we set sail.

For the rest of the day we tacked back and forth, running before a capricious wind. As darkness fell I told the captain to put in to land, for I had no intention of spending another night on board. There was a little cove at the village of Pinamalayan, and we eased into it. While I waited on the beach my men went inland to scout a handful of shacks among the coconut palms.

In half an hour they emerged from the jungle some fifty yards farther up the beach. With them was a tall, skinny black man dressed in native clothing, well into his sixties, his skin deeply wrinkled and his hair ashen white. When he saw me his face burst into a smile of anticipation and disbelief. He hurried to me, leaving my bodyguards behind, and threw his arms out to greet me.

He was a startling apparition, another bizarre encounter on this endless trip, and I stood stunned a long minute in his embrace before I managed to free myself.

"Sir," the old black man panted out before I could speak, "if I didn't know you was an officer, I'd kiss you."

His name was White, he told me, Sergeant White, from New Orleans. He drew himself up and saluted.

"Tenth U.S. Horse Cavalry," he announced. "Buffalo Soldiers."

He explained that he had arrived in the Philippines in 1907 with an expedition sent to put down the Moro insurrection. "I served under Arthur MacArthur," White declared proudly, "General Douglas MacArthur's father." After his term was up, White had chosen to remain behind on Mindoro. For over thirty years he had lived in a remote village in the jungle, where he had married several Filipino women and sired dozens of children.

"You're the first American I've seen in all this time," he told me. "I can't hardly believe it. What branch you from, sir?"

I told him that I, too, was cavalry.

He paused a long moment, his yellowing eyes clouding. "Well, now, I'll just be damned," he said at last, and the tears brimmed over.

White took us to his village, which indeed was populated by his sprawling family. There were children everywhere whose bright faces reflected that of the old trooper. Three or four of his wives made a feast for us, and for the rest of the evening we sat swapping stories of the cavalry, the guerillas, and our shared loneliness for fellow Americans.

White knew little about the war. He lived in almost total isolation among his family and had not been bothered by the Japanese. His clan was completely self-sufficient, with ample rice, chickens, pigs, and fruit. Since nearly everyone in the vicinity was related to him, he had no worry over spies who might denounce him or bandits who would steal his produce.

He was eager for details of the Twenty-sixth Cavalry and its role in the fighting. As I told him about the battles in Luzon and on Bataan, he wagged his head in sympathy.

"What become of your horses?" he asked me.

"When the food ran out they were butchered."

He nodded and lowered his head. "My, my," he sighed. "Now that is a terrible thing. Surely terrible. I do feel most keenly for you, sir. I mean, a cavalryman without his horse, now, what is he? Just another footslog, sir, ain't that so?"

"No, White, I don't think that's true," I said. "I think the cavalry can survive the loss of its mounts. I think it has to. Because one way or another they're going to take away the horses—that's inevitable."

White nodded ruefully, and then his face brightened. "But they can't take away the spirit, can they, sir?"

"No," I answered. "Old troopers like us are proof of that."

I spent the night at White's village, and when it came time for me to go in the morning he was again in tears, and it was a long while before he would leave off hugging me and shaking my hand. He pressed food and herbal remedies on us, and he and a dozen of his children accompanied us to the beach.

"God bless y'all," he cried as we climbed again onto the *batil*. "I'd volunteer to join you, but I fear that I'm too old to fight. But I'm at peace, Major; I have my home here, and I'll die among my family." He looked at me a long moment in thought. "That's what we all fight for, ain't it, Major—to live in peace in our home, among our own people. I pray that God may bring you safely to it, sir."

I thanked him, wished him well, and said good-bye.

All that morning we made our to-and-fro tacking way along the coast. I was sick of this meandering before the wind that was taking me farther and farther from my base. There was no guarantee that Ruffy would be at his camp, nor even that the camp still existed. I made up my mind that at the next disappointment I would give it up and return to Luzon.

At a cove below a coastal town we climbed over the side and waded ashore. While Cadizon, Cabral, and I waited on the beach, the others went inland to scout. In a short while they were back with some of Ruffy's men, who told us that indeed their chief was at his advance base, a few hours' hike into the jungle.

I was impressed with Ruffy's camp. It was large and well organized, with a kind of permanence I did not associate with guerilla forces. Rows of well-built thatch-and-nipa barracks stood on streets that had been edged in stone, and there was even a parade ground. Major Ruffy emerged from his house to greet me, a dark-skinned man in his forties, of medium height. He had been a constabulary officer before the war and bore himself with an easy habit of command. Open and gregarious, he was popular among his troops.

Ruffy had evidently been in the middle of a meeting, for in his house were three other officers, and as soon as I entered I sensed an atmosphere of tension. The officers were introduced to me as Major Jurado, aide to Colonel Peralta, the overall commander of the southern islands resistance, and Captain Galang and Lieutenant Songco of Major Phillips's detachment. Phillips had left Galang and Songco behind to coordinate with Ruffy. Jurado had come on quite a different mission, and it was not long before the source of the tension became apparent.

Colonel Peralta had appointed Ruffy to command Mindoro under Peralta's authority. When Phillips arrived from Australia, however, he had urged Ruffy to establish an independent command under the authority of the Allied Intelligence Bureau. When Peralta learned of this he dispatched Jurado to bring Ruffy back into line. Now Jurado and Galang were disputing each other's authority, and Ruffy was caught in the middle.

It had nothing to do with me, and so I kept carefully out of it. Instead I asked about Phillips; how might I meet him and get the radio he had brought for me?

Major Ruffy sighed. "We have heard rumors that Phillips's camp was raided," he said, "and since then I have had no radio contact with him. No one knows if he escaped or is even still alive. I am waiting for my people in Calavite to report."

Again there was nothing I could do but wait. If Phillips were alive and in hiding he must be found so that the radio could be transferred to me. If not, and the radio was still available somewhere, I would have to find it myself.

For the next week my bodyguards and I remained at Ruffy's camp, marking time and trying to avoid the daily round of arguments among Ruffy, Jurado, and Galang. Occasionally I was asked to mediate, but I declined, merely counseling calm. No purpose would be served by discord, I told them; perhaps after I had had a chance to confer with Phillips a solution might be reached.

We were having lunch in Ruffy's house on the tenth day of my stay when a commotion arose outside. From the window we could see a man dragging himself across the parade ground, half-naked and nearly prostrate with exhaustion and malnutrition. Two of Ruffy's men grabbed him, questioned him quickly, and then helped him over to the house.

"My God; that can't be Wise," Ruffy gasped, and he hurried outside to meet him.

Warrant Officer David Wise had been a member of Major Phillips's staff. He had been with Phillips at Ruffy's headquarters at Naujan two months before, and now Ruffy scarcely recognized him. His hair was matted and filthy, and his sun-baked skin was caked with dirt and dried blood. The clothes he wore were rags, so badly shredded that they hardly covered his battered body.

Ruffy ordered Wise brought into the house and lain upon one of the beds. He was given water and a little food, and while a doctor attended to him he explained what had happened.

Phillips's camp had indeed been raided. Scarcely had they returned, Wise rasped out, than the Japanese had surrounded the place and opened fire. Phillips and Wise were operating the radio and were caught completely by surprise. After a furious gun battle in which most of their men were killed, the two of them escaped into the jungle, leaving the radio and all their supplies behind.

For a week Phillips and Wise clawed their way through the jungle trying to make it back to Ruffy's headquarters at Naujan.

With no rations and no compass to guide them, they were becoming hopelessly lost. One steaming noon they stopped to bathe in a river near the village of Abra de Ilog, a little less than halfway to Naujan. A Japanese patrol stumbled across them.

The two Americans were helpless as the Japanese opened fire. Wise managed to scramble to the bank and disappear into the jungle, but not before he saw Phillips hit by several bullets. Wise was now alone, naked, wandering desperately through the jungle pursued by the Japanese. After two days he found a Filipino farmer who fed and clothed him, and he again set out for Ruffy's camp.

For the past month he had walked all the way across Mindoro, dodging Japanese patrols, crossing the mountains and lowland swamps, sometimes guided by local guerillas, sometimes alone. That he had even attempted it had been heroic; that he had survived was a miracle.

I asked him if Phillips was dead.

"I don't know, Major," he answered. "The last time I saw him was in the stream. He was hit, but I don't know if he was killed."

"What about the radio?"

"We lost it in the raid, sir. I'm sure the Japs got it."

So that was that. The whole awful trip had been for nothing. I had come over three hundred miles to meet a man who had been dead before I started out, and to get a radio that had been lost even before he had died. I walked out of the house with Ruffy and crossed the parade ground.

"You'll be going back to Luzon?" he asked.

I told him I would, but first I would make a detour through Abra de Ilog.

"What for?"

"I came all this way to meet Phillips. I can't go back without confirming whether or not he's dead. Australia will need to know, and besides, I suppose he's got family."

The next morning, as we were preparing to leave, Ruffy

received a radio signal from Colonel Peralta on Panay that a submarine would arrive in two weeks at the southern tip of Mindoro bringing money and equipment for the guerillas. And there was a message for me.

"Peralta says that the sub can take you out," Ruffy told me. "But you'll have to leave at once if you want to get down there in time. Jurado is going; he'll take you."

It was an idea that had never occurred to me, and for a moment I was speechless. In two weeks I could be on a submarine bound for Australia. I would be an American officer again, safe behind my own lines; my war in the Philippines would be over.

It was tempting. It was tantalizing. But I knew I could not leave. I had too much invested in Luzon to walk away—everything I had, everything the Filipino people had. For better or worse, I was the leader, and I had no idea whether there was anyone to replace me. I had been out of touch with Lapham and Putnam for months and did not even know whether they were still alive. And if nothing else, I had learned from this trip how important an acknowledged leader is to a guerilla movement, and how dangerous and undermining rivalry and dissention can be.

Besides, my people trusted me and counted on me. It was my war as well as theirs. How could I explain it to them if I left now? How could I explain it to myself? No, I would have to stay and see it through to the end. I had volunteered for this job; I would not give it up now.

"Tell them no, thanks," I replied.

Ruffy smiled and nodded. "I should not give you this," he said, handing me a folded piece of paper. "My instructions were to show it to you only if you decided to leave."

I opened the paper and read it. It was a radio signal from Australia addressed to me. *MacArthur to Ramsey*, it began, *Request that you return to Luzon and command of your resistance forces*. It was signed by General MacArthur himself.

My first real contact with the outside world had come from

MacArthur personally. I was deeply moved. He knew of my work, and evidently he valued it. In all those months of messages and those scores of couriers, something had gotten through. I had been right to go on and not give up. It all had meant something, MacArthur was affirming. And it must continue.

I thanked Ruffy, folded the paper, and put it in my pocket. Outside, Cadizon, Cabral, Acosta, and Cornel were waiting for me. They had followed me across Luzon and Mindoro, they had protected me, borne everything with me; at times they had kept me alive. They had killed for me, and I knew they would die for me. There was no question of my leaving. We were not just officer and men; we were compatriots.

I told them that Major Phillips was probably dead but that we were going to look for him anyway. There would be no radio, and all we were likely to find would be a corpse.

"When do we start?" Cadizon asked.

"Right away."

"Let's go," he told the others, and they went to collect their gear.

Jurado and I left at the same time, he to the south and I to the north. I had given him a packet of intelligence documents and maps for delivery to MacArthur, together with a note requesting a radio, arms, medical supplies, and money for my organization. We retraced our route in the *batil* around the Mindoro coast, but instead of crossing the passage to Luzon we pushed on to the northern coastal town of Wawa. There we disembarked and hiked inland to Abra de Ilog, a village in the lowland swamps between two ranges of hills.

While Cadizon, Cabral, and I waited in the jungle, Acosta and Cornel went into the village for information about Phillips.

"The people say that an American was killed nearby," Acosta reported. "They buried his body in the village cemetery, but none of them knows who he was."

"Alright," I said. "We'll wait until dark, and then we'll go in."

That night we made our way into Abra de Ilog. On the far side of the huts was a little fenced-in cemetery dotted with wooden crosses, some hung with wreaths of flowers. We pulled aside the gate and searched under the moonlight.

From some of the graves carved saints stared back at us, their wooden faces warped and swollen with the humidity. One or two crosses bore the picture of the deceased—cracked, faded portraits in porcelain. Near the fence on one side was an unmarked grave, the moist earth still heaped. While Acosta and Cornel kept watch, Cabral and Cadizon began digging.

It was mournful work. The grave was shallow, hastily dug. A few feet down they struck the body and carefully scooped out the dirt from around it. Our flashlights showed the effects of the heat and the dampness of the jungle earth. The corpse was naked, the face unrecognizable, and there were no dog tags.

Having come this far to confirm Phillips's death, I felt there was no choice. I told the men to use their knives and to extract the teeth. They bent over while I held the light and worked meticulously, tapping with the handles and prying. When they were done I put the teeth into a little box and slipped it in my pocket.

Back on the coast I turned the box over to the local guerillas with instructions that it be taken to Ruffy's headquarters and delivered to Warrant Officer Wise, who, I knew, was to be taken to Australia by submarine as soon as he recovered. We, meanwhile, started back for Luzon.

I learned later that Wise did receive the box and took it to Australia. By that time, however, MacArthur's headquarters had been removed to New Guinea, and so Wise continued on to deliver it. His task completed, he requested permission to return to Mindoro to reestablish Phillips's coast-watching station, and he took the next submarine out.

Somewhere between Panay and Mindoro the submarine was

attacked by Japanese destroyers and sunk. Everyone was lost. As for Phillips, I never learned the results of the examination of the teeth, nor, so far as I knew, was the body in the little graveyard at Abra de Ilog ever retrieved.

Rain

I faced the long trek back across southern Luzon with dread. It was April and the rainy season had begun, so we would have to slog and sail through the thickness of it. It rained steadily the whole way across the passage to Luzon, and we waded ashore, soaked and miserable. I was looking forward to a rest at the little coastal village where we had sunbathed a month before, but when we reached it I was shocked.

Some of the huts had been burned down, and the rest were in shambles. Walls had been kicked out and furniture and clothing lay sodden under the rain. Only a handful of villagers remained. They told us that a few days after our departure for Mindoro the Japanese had raided the place, ransacked the village, and then bullied and tortured the people for information about me. What was more, the raid had been led personally by General Baba.

As we pushed inland we found that Baba had traced our route, and every village through which we had passed had been raided. His kempei-tai had been ruthless in their search for information about me; crops had been destroyed, food stores and supplies had been confiscated, and entire villages were burned to the ground. Hundreds of people had been threatened and intimidated and dozens arrested.

Our whole route to Manila Bay had been devastated, and the people were now too frightened to help us. The Japanese had been everywhere; they had come without warning and departed just as suddenly, and everyone was terrified that they would return. We moved as quickly as we could, for we had few supplies with us and we had no idea where Baba might be. Word reached us that he had followed me to Mindoro and had raided all along the coast. Without knowing it, we had been only a week, or even just a few days, ahead of him.

By the time we reached Manila Bay in early May we were half starved and exhausted. I had sent word ahead to Pat Gatson in Manila, but there was no boat waiting. It was not like Gatson, and this worried me. I dispatched Cornel to Manila to make the arrangements, and the rest of us withdrew into the jungle. By now we had no food left, and even the local guerillas were reluctant to help us. In our brief contacts with them they reported Japanese patrols throughout the area, and we saw one ourselves as we sought a refuge inland.

For three days we waited for Cornel to return, constantly on the alert and weakened by hunger. When at last he arrived, he brought with him a boat and bad news. Shortly after his return to Manila from southern Luzon, Pat Gatson had been captured. The Japanese had known exactly where to find him, and the raids had not been limited to his headquarters. Dozens of our people in Manila had been arrested, including some of our highest-ranking officers. For the second time, our Manila network had been stripped.

It left us in a bad position. We now had to make the risky trip across Manila Bay and then the long trek north of the city to my headquarters on Balagbag, all without support. The worst of it was that we could not count on Manila for intelligence about the Japanese patrols. It began to look as if the nightmare trip to Mindoro would be my last.

We climbed aboard the fishing boat and set off into the night. A steady rain was falling and the wind was against us. It took us all night to cross the bay, and when we landed next morning we had no choice but to hide out until dark among the fish ponds. There was nothing nearby but a derelict shack, and in this we spent the next twelve hours, soaking under the downpour and with nothing to eat. All the next night we slogged our way through the rain, wading across the marshes and hacking the dripping jungle to my advance command post at Polo, north of Manila.

Here, six months before, I had left the boxcar and had had my photo taken en route to Manila. My Christmas there with Mona Snyder had been a happy one. Now so much had changed. My command had suffered badly in my absence, and I had no idea what I would find on my return to Balagbag. More than ever, I cursed the trip to Mindoro. It had all been for a radio, but I had managed to survive for over two years without one. I had taken a chance, and I had lost; but what I had lost was incalculable—not time only, but people.

I was disgusted and depressed. I lay in the hut at Polo remonstrating with myself and sorting out in my mind what I must do. First it was necessary to determine the extent of the damage to the Manila organization, and so I sent Cabral to Jorge Sanchez there, asking that he come to me immediately. Manila would have to be reorganized, and I would have to get back in touch with all the other districts as well.

I tried to sleep but I could not. The rain poured down, rustling the nipa shingles and splashing in through the chinks in the walls. I began to feel feverish, and all my joints ached. I cursed myself and I cursed the rain, the radio, and the war. When would it end? I had forgotten what a normal life was like, and peace was an abstraction that no longer had any real meaning for me.

The fever grew worse as the rain washed down in waves. It was like being back on the *batil* in the storm. I could have gotten out by submarine, I told myself. I could have reported to Mac-Arthur and then come back, fortified by a few weeks of rest and proper medical attention. I thought of the old cavalryman, Sergeant White, and could not help but laugh at how much like him I was: isolated, out of touch, surrounded by my huge adopted family, but still longing for home. We were just a pair of cavalrymen stripped of our mounts and yearning for the old days, which both of us were helpless to retrieve.

Colonel Sanchez came out next day and was as reassuring as possible. He had already appointed a replacement for Pat Gatson and had begun the reorganization of Manila.

"What do you hear about Gatson?" I asked.

Sanchez smiled faintly. "Our people at Fort Santiago say he has given up nothing, and so far we have not lost one person. When they ask him about you, he says that you took a submarine from Mindoro to Australia."

Sanchez added that Gatson was not the only one telling this to Baba. Evidently the same story had reached him from Mindoro and he had believed it, for he had halted the patrols that had been hunting me for two months.

There was bad news as well. Colonels Noble and Moses had both been captured in the northern mountain provinces. They had been tortured and put on display just as Ralph Praeger had been. Despite the abuse, none had given up information damaging to the organization, but their loss was a severe blow.

"They have been replaced," Sanchez added, "and most of the damage has been repaired." His tone, however, had lost its reassurance. "There is other news," he went on more quietly. "Our operatives in Fort Santiago reported that Colonel Thorpe, Colonel Moses, Colonel Noble, Captain Praeger, and Captain Barker have been executed."

He fell silent, staring at his folded hands.

"Is it certain?" I asked. Sanchez nodded.

He told me that in December 1943 they had been taken together from the cells of Fort Santiago to the old Chinese cemetery in Manila. There they had been made to dig graves for themselves under the pouring rain, and then forced to kneel over the graves. One by one, they were beheaded.

It put an end to a year of cruel suffering they had all endured in silence. None of them had betrayed the organization, which had lost not a single man or woman as a result of their captures. I was living proof of their fortitude, for any one of them might have given information and names sufficient to lead to my death. They had behaved like soldiers, and they had died like martyrs.

Though I had known Joe Barker was a dead man the moment news of his capture reached me a year before, the fact of his death still stung me. I missed him and I felt his loss keenly, but I could not mourn for him—I dared not. He was only one of over twenty-five hundred guerilla fighters who had so far lost their lives, and though he was closer to me than the others, and his face was clearer in my mind, I allowed him to take his place among them in my memory.

Joe was gone, I would never see him again; but the movement we had built together was still alive. I packed my gear to move on. I now had more than thirty-eight thousand men and women under my command, and I had been absent a long while. It was time for me to get back into the fight.

I walked out of the hut under the steady rain and turned my face up to it. It was cool and it eased my fever. "Good-bye, Joe," I said aloud while the rain poured down. "I'll see you on Fiddler's Green."

If General Baba truly believed that I had left the Philippines, then I would have to move quickly to make the most of this advantage. My first job was to finish organizing the headquarters on Mount Balagbag, and to establish a ring of advance posts in the lowlands to protect it. I sent Cadizon on to Balagbag to oversee the work there and let them know that I was coming. Meanwhile, I instructed the lowland guerilla units to set up a series of outposts between Manila and the foothills to monitor Japanese patrols and alert the headquarters to impending raids.

I established one of these posts myself at Novaliches in the watershed area north of Manila. This was a rugged plateau, thick with cogon grass and dotted with the lakes and reservoirs from which the city drew its water. It was too close to Manila for a headquarters but was an excellent spot for observation.

Another post was set up inside the leper colony of Tala to the north of Novaliches. It was a lonely, outcast little place that neither I nor the Japanese had ever visited.

I spent the next few weeks supervising the creation of the other outposts until I was satisfied that we had an effective screen against surprise attacks, reaching right up into the foothills of Balagbag. It was absolutely essential work, but also trying and tedious under the rainy-season downpour, and it sapped the little strength I had left after the Mindoro trip. The fever and aches I had felt at Polo had increased, and once again I had to be dragged from post to post on a carabao sled. Outside the village of San Mateo, midway between Manila and Balagbag, I collapsed.

I was taken to the home of the local Catholic priest, where I spent the next ten days alternating between delirium and raucous games of poker with the priest. Sometimes the two became blurred, and I found myself demanding a dozen cards or a hundred, and then flinging them around the room while my head caught on fire and my whole body throbbed.

It was somewhere within that aching, fitful time that Captain Casey arrived. His real name was Modesto Castaneda, and he had come from the far southern island of Negros, across Panay and Mindoro, to find me. The trip of nearly a thousand miles had taken him four months. He had crossed some of the roughest country in the islands, endured monsoon rains and typhoons, and dodged dozens of Japanese patrols, all to bring me a gift: an Allied Intelligence Bureau radio.

The radio had arrived in Negros by submarine while I was still in the north organizing, and Casey had been on his way to me at the very time I was making the trip to Mindoro to meet Phillips. Casey had taken a boat to Mindoro, and had I stayed there longer I might have met him. He then made his way to southern Luzon, where he commandeered a truck, filled it with crates of vegetables, and hid the radio beneath them. He then drove the truck into Manila, where he contacted Mona Snyder.

I had kept her up to date on my movements, and she told Casey where he might find me.

With the priest's help I hobbled outside to where the truck was parked under the rain. Both the old, prewar pickup and its cargo were much the worse for their trek across Luzon. Casey and my bodyguards began hefting dripping crates of vegetables from the back, and there, embedded among them, was the radio.

Cabral lifted it down reverently and carried it inside. It was an unimposing device to have caused such anticipation and sacrifice, an olive-drab metal box some two feet long, six inches high, and eight inches wide. I carefully opened the lid. Inside were a transmitter, a receiver, a coil of antenna wire, a little speaker, and a telegraph key. With these we could signal to Colonel Peralta on Panay, who would relay our messages to MacArthur's headquarters.

For us it was the beginning of a new phase of the war. There would be no more runners risking their lives on the long journey to Panay, no more endless delays to receive replies, no more isolation. We were back in the wider war, in touch with the world. I told Cabral to pack up the radio: We were going to Balagbag. Though I was still sick, I was anxious to get started.

I shook Captain Casey's hand and thanked him. I knew what he had gone through to reach me.

"It's okay, Major," he said. Then he smiled mischievously. "You can thank Mao Tse-tung."

I was taken aback. "What do you mean by that?" I wanted to know.

"Didn't you read his book?" he answered, and then intoned: " 'Communication is the lifeblood of guerilla warfare. Every guerilla unit must have radio equipment.' "

"You're an admirer of Mao?" I asked.

Casey frowned theatrically. "Hell, no, I hate the commie bugger. But you can't argue with the logic."

THE
"OLD MAN"

1944 (June–October)

MEDAL ON PRECEDING PAGE:
Distinguished Conduct Star (PHILIPPINE)

Signals

The camp at Balagbag was almost ready when I arrived in early June 1944. Half a dozen nipa huts had been erected for barracks, and there was a large, airy mess hall and a hospital. My own quarters were set apart, a small bamboo hut on a slope above the camp. Everything was overarched by towering lauan and narra trees, making the buildings invisible from the air. We were high enough that the humidity was not oppressive, and a stream bubbled through the camp, freshening the air.

The approaches, however, were daunting: thick jungle slopes, vertical ravines, and a dizzying, spray-slick climb up the waterfall. At the top we had posted two .50-caliber machine guns salvaged from a downed American fighter plane, as well as a detachment of my headquarters security troop under Lieutenant James Carrington.

A young Marine corporal, Jimmy Carrington had escaped from a POW camp and been rescued by our guerillas. He was an able, amiable soldier who adapted easily to guerilla tactics, and I commissioned him as lieutenant in charge of headquarters security. With his big, boyish grin and Marine esprit he was instantly popular with the security troops, some of the best-trained and toughest of my combat veterans.

I gave orders for a communications hut to be built high on the hill behind the camp to house the radio and its operators. Then on June 27 we carried the precious thing up to its throne on the summit, which we christened Signal Hill. While some of the men strung the antenna wire among the trees, my signal officer, Lieutenant Colonel Leopoldo Guillermo, set up the radio on its little bamboo table.

"Ready, Major?" Colonel Guillermo asked me.

"Sure. What do we do?"

"Start cranking."

Cabral and Cadizon stepped to the generator. In a moment it was whirring, and Guillermo switched the set on. He gave me a thumbs-up sign, and I returned it. Then Guillermo began tapping at the telegraph key: *NAL this is LRT . . . over. NAL this is LRT . . . come in, please. . . .*

There was a static silence through the speaker while Guillermo eased the knobs left and right, and then he began tapping again. *NAL this is LRT . . . come in, please. . . .*

He switched the receiver on again, and we strained to hear a signal through the static. Suddenly, a high-pitched whistle broke into a series of rapid dots and dashes.

Guillermo listened and then turned to me with a grin. "It's Colonel Andrews, Major. He says congratulations, we're in business."

Edwin Andrews, a Philippine Air Force officer, headed the Allied Intelligence Bureau network on the southern island of Negros, and was one of our conduits to MacArthur's headquarters. A cheer went up from the men, and I patted Guillermo on the back. We were connected, we had arrived; the Luzon Guerilla Force had joined the war.

From that evening we began broadcasting regular intelligence reports, which were relayed by Andrews's station in Negros to MacArthur's headquarters. But we were not only sending now, we were receiving as well, and I was as hungry for news of the progress of the war as MacArthur was for our intelligence. During those first few heady weeks after our radio post went on the air, I pieced together a brief history of the previous two years of the war, and I was both shocked and encouraged by what I learned.

In the months after the fall of Bataan, while we had been organizing in the isolation of Luzon, we had come frighteningly close to disaster. The Japanese had moved both northeast and southeast from their new base in the Philippines across the vast crescent of islands stretching from the Arctic to Australia. I was stunned at the scope of their conquest. Two of the Alaskan islands had been seized; Formosa, Malaya, Singapore, the Dutch East Indies, and Hong Kong had fallen in quick order. The Japanese had then pushed on across the atolls spanning Australia. Borneo, the Celebes, New Guinea, the Bismark Archipelago, and the Solomons all had been attacked. Australia had been cut off, and we in the Philippines were surrounded. I could only be grateful that I had not known.

After his departure from Corregidor, MacArthur had arrived in Australia expecting to mount an immediate offensive to recapture the Philippines. Instead, he found fewer troops in Australia than he had left behind on Bataan. They were largely untrained, ill-equipped, and without naval and air support. The Australian military had favored a withdrawal into the southeastern corner of the continent in the face of the Japanese onslaught that seemed inevitable. MacArthur refused, insisting instead on taking the offensive.

His first target was New Guinea, which the Japanese had planned to fortify as a base from which to invade Australia. Far from ceding it to them, MacArthur determined to make a fight for it. Weeks of bloody war in the thickest jungles of the Pacific followed, but the Japanese were driven out. Now MacArthur planned to use New Guinea as a base to reverse the Japanese tide of conquest, hopping from one island to the next toward his ultimate and unalterable goal, his return to Luzon.

The navy, however, had other ideas. Admiral Chester Nimitz, commander of the Pacific fleet, urged Roosevelt to allow him to bypass the Philippines and strike for Formosa as a prelude to an invasion of Japan. MacArthur argued hotly that the Philippines could not be abandoned. If Formosa were taken first, they would represent a massive enemy garrison in the American rear. The Philippines, he insisted, were the key to success in the southwest Pacific, just as the Japanese had understood in

1941. To take and hold the southwest Pacific, an area larger than the United States itself, it was necessary to possess Luzon.

What was more important in his thinking, however, was the fact that he had given his solemn pledge to the Filipino people that he would return, and Roosevelt had backed this pledge. MacArthur would not abandon the Philippines; it was his home, the home of his friends, and the prison for his boys from Bataan.

I could only guess at the details of the strategic debate in which the future of the Pacific war, and of the Philippines, was being decided. What was clear, however, was that as the argument heated, we were being asked for more detailed information on the strength of our guerilla forces and their readiness to support an invasion. These requests, to my surprise, were being made by MacArthur himself, in a series of urgent messages addressed to me.

MacArthur to Ramsey, the signals would begin, and he would ask for details on the number, dispersement, armament, and training of our regiments. I responded instantly and in kind, addressing my replies *Ramsey to MacArthur*. This concentrated, abstract relationship continued for weeks, composed of figures and place-names and framed by the dot-dash-dot of our signals. But it was no less exciting for that. MacArthur was coming closer—liberation was coming closer—and I labored to keep the line between us vibrant and alive with as much information as the commanding general could possibly require.

What I did not know was that MacArthur was preparing for an offensive not only against the Japanese but against the American Navy as well, and for it to succeed he needed all the information possible about the situation inside Luzon. In July 1944, he flew to Hawaii for a summit conference with Roosevelt and Nimitz. In fact, however, it more resembled a gladiator contest, in which the general and the admiral took turns before a huge map of the Pacific, bashing at each other for the approval of the president.

Nimitz argued for his Formosa plan, while MacArthur insisted on the Philippines. Roosevelt, a partisan of the navy, was inclined to support the admiral. He wanted to recapture Manila Bay, he admitted, but he asked MacArthur if it were not true that an invasion of Luzon would cost too many lives. MacArthur replied with the guerillas.

There were, he said, tens of thousands of partisans prepared in Luzon at that moment to support the invasion. The Japanese would be caught between the Americans to their front and the guerillas to their rear. They could not resist; they would be forced to capitulate or cede the island to the Americans. The guerillas of Luzon were a secret weapon ready to explode in the Japanese' faces, and they would save thousands of American lives.

Roosevelt was swayed. MacArthur's arguments, along with his pointed suggestion that abandoning the Philippines a second time might cost Roosevelt votes at the coming election, turned the tide. Army Chief of Staff General George C. Marshall agreed to MacArthur's plan; the first landing was scheduled for October 1944. The Philippines would be retaken.

Sound Effects

We knew none of this as we frantically sent out the signals, with Guillermo and his chief operator, Captain Marcus Contreras, taking the transmissions in turns. I often spent the night shift with them while they rapped out the endless ribbon of intelligence that flowed from our forces across Luzon, and then jotted down the rapid-fire responses. The signals sped back to us on the night sky with a high-pitched pulsing that before many seconds managed to arouse the cicadas and frogs.

There were millions of them in the Balagbag jungle, and

they rose up in a powerful hidden chorus that quickly drowned the signal. Their gutteral chirruping, as dense as it was strident, made it difficult to hear the incoming signals or concentrate on the outgoing ones.

It became a contest: our data on infantry concentrations and depot locations versus their clamoring protest. They invariably won, and I grew to hate them for it. Then, gradually, my attitude changed, and at times when the radio was silent I would lie on the ground and listen to them with a grudging pleasure.

I was the intruder, I reflected; I was the one disturbing the night peace of which they were a part, with my strange staccato piping. Before long I learned to adjust to the sound, and even to welcome it. In the end, I took no notice of it all, except when it stopped.

I knew that the sudden silence meant Japanese foot patrols. Our continual transmissions had drawn the attention of the Japanese, who had begun triangulating our signal and sending spotter aircraft low over the jungle in attempts to locate our base camp. But when these efforts failed, General Baba began scouring the area with foot patrols.

We could see them from our observation post, groping their way through the foothills. It was a job they must have hated, for the Balagbag jungles were alive with snakes and leeches, and the rains had swollen the streams to torrents. Had they found us they would surely have been furious and hacked off all our heads, but they never came near to us in our waterfall sanctuary.

In Manila, on the other hand, the pressure was mounting. Mona Snyder was by now indispensable to our intelligence operations, with contacts that reached into the highest levels of the puppet government and the Japanese high command. From her came some of our most vital intelligence, which we now relayed directly to MacArthur's headquarters. But inevitably the kempei-tai became suspicious of her, and in June she sent a message to me requesting permission to leave Manila and join me in the hills. I agreed at once, for I knew it might only be a matter of days until she was arrested.

Mona joined us on Balagbag, moving into the nurses' and visitors' quarters. She continued her intelligence activities, maintaining her contacts through a small army of couriers moving between Balagbag and Manila. She also took charge of organizing the camp and sustaining its morale. I was delighted to have her with me; she was as lovely and as vibrant as ever. But the circumstances would not permit us to resume our intimacy. I was now the commander of an army of over forty thousand troops, with a busy headquarters camp and a large staff. More than ever I had to set an example, and my liaison with Mona might have provoked resentment and undermined my authority.*

Though Balagbag became our base, Manila remained our nerve center, and my intelligence chief there, Lieutenant Colonel Liberato Bonoan, kept us supplied with a constant flow of information. Known in the underground as Colonel Obie, Bonoan was a boyish-looking twenty-nine-year-old, small and slight in stature but brilliantly energetic and efficient as a secret agent.

He was wanted in Manila under five different aliases, but the kempei-tai never suspected that any of them was Obie. Twice they had arrested and interrogated him, and both times he had been released because of his innocent teenagé appearance. Obie would then return to his network of agents and continue feeding us some of the most damaging intelligence we received about the Japanese.

---

*It was at this time that I appointed as my chief of staff Colonel Amado Bautista. Known in the resistance as Colonel Abe, Bautista had been a career officer in the Philippine Army corps of engineers. After the fall of Bataan he was interned in a POW camp, but was released at the request of the puppet government that appointed him district manager for Luzon of the National Rice and Corn Administration. Bautista used his position to supply our guerillas with food, as well as intelligence gathered on his travels about Luzon. By early 1944, however, the Japanese had become suspicious of him, and I ordered him to join me on Balagbag where he reorganized my headquarters staff with his customary energy and efficiency.

As the occupation wore on and the quality of life in Luzon declined to desperation, the Japanese responded with a strident campaign of racist sloganeering. The Americans were white devils and tyrants, they declared, and we in the resistance were bandits leading a small gang of "misguided elements."

In response we were publishing a regular newsletter, *The Voice of the Misguided Elements*, which contained excerpts from British and American news reports, as well as speeches by Presidents Roosevelt and Quezon and General MacArthur, with messages from them to the Filipino people. Distributed by couriers to the villages and towns, they were then handed around discreetly among the populace. They were in great demand as the only available source of outside information, and people read and reproduced them at the risk of their lives.

Mona reinforced our counterpropaganda efforts with a steady stream of morale-boosting bulletins, slogans, and keepsakes. Among the last were matchbooks, candy bars, pencils, and sewing kits bearing the motto I Shall Return. Tens of thousands of these were smuggled in by submarine, and they became the magic charm of the resistance.

It all infuriated the Japanese, who could do nothing to stop it. Despite the radio triangulations and the patrols, Balagbag remained untouched, the busy switchboard of the resistance. Couriers made daily trips up to the mountain and back into Manila and the provinces. Intelligence poured in, was organized and analyzed, and then was channeled out again to Australia. Meanwhile, our permanent staff grew to fifty, and then to a hundred officers and men, engaged in every aspect of intelligence, training, planning, and operations. Our organizing and intelligence work was going well, but by the end of June I had decided that more direct action was necessary.

To this point in the war our guerilla forces had engaged in sabotage only occasionally and with great care. Joe Barker and I had adopted it as a principle of our organization that sabotage was to be conducted only when it posed no risk to the civilian population, and MacArthur had seconded this in his dispatches to us. The reason for this policy was twofold: First, we could not risk alienating the population directly through wanton acts of violence, and second, we were determined to avoid any action that might provoke Japanese reprisals. Instead, individual units were instructed to engage in sabotage only when clear, low-risk enemy targets presented themselves.

The result was a random pattern of low-key acts directed mostly at Japanese military installations. Operatives would pour pure cane sugar into the gas tanks of planes and vehicles, set fire to depots, or attack military convoys in the countryside. Sabotage served a valuable morale-boosting purpose, but it had always remained subordinate to our main goals of organizing and intelligence gathering.

By midsummer 1944, however, our organization was stronger and more secure than it had ever been, and I felt the time had come for a visible display of our presence. The Filipino people needed a sign—something to sustain them through this third year of occupation. What was more, it was only a question of time before General Baba realized that I was still in Luzon and the mobility I had enjoyed would end. If we were to strike, it should be now.

I therefore sent a series of sealed, secret orders to my commanders in Manila to prepare for a sabotage offensive in mid July. Among them was a message to Wally Roeder assigning him technical supervision of the operation. In the past we had received sabotage devices by submarine from Australia, but our experiments with these had been disappointing. The arming mechanisms were too complicated, the fuses too unreliable. Operatives had risked and lost their lives placing these devices, only to have them fail. I was determined that this would not happen again.

I asked Roeder to devise an explosive that would be effective and foolproof. It was short notice with scant resources, but he responded with characteristic cleverness, and in late June he came out to Balagbag to demonstrate his device.

From a Manila toy manufacturer Roeder had obtained a mold for forming lead cylinders. These cylinders were four to six inches long and open at both ends. His sabotage device consisted of two of the cylinders soldered together with a thin copper plate between, forming a pair of hollow chambers separated by a layer of copper.

Roeder laced on his spectacles and held the device in his fist as he explained.

"Into one end we put a dozen match heads so that they rest against the copper plate, yes? This is the primer. We then fill the tube with black powder. The end of the tube is sealed with wax if it is to be an incendiary device, or with lead if it is to be an explosive."

I asked where the powder would come from.

"I have all the chemicals necessary at the gasworks," he answered.

"You're going to make it yourself?" I said.

Roeder glanced at me over the top of his glasses like a schoolmaster.

"Black powder is a very simple substance to produce," he said, as if it were something every child should know. "And besides," he added with a dry smile, "if I run short, I can always 'borrow' some from my guests."

"What about the trigger?" I asked.

He turned the device around. "That is what the second tube is for. This end is left empty until just before the weapon is put in place. Now this is the tricky part, because at that point it must be filled with sulfuric acid and sealed. This means that the saboteur must carry a vial of acid with him in addition to the device, and that he or she must have sufficient time to fill the tube at the site where it is to be placed. It will involve preparation, and some danger."

I nodded. "How exactly does the thing work?" I asked.

Roeder gave a dismissive shrug. "Oh, the theory is really quite simple—childish, in fact. The sulfuric acid eats through the copper plate until it reaches the matches. It ignites them, and they in turn explode the powder."

"How much of a bang will we get?"

"If it is placed in an oil drum or near flammables, one device should be sufficient to start a chain reaction. But proper placement is crucial. Our people must be carefully trained, and the targets must be selected with a view to maximum effect."

I was satisfied. "You've done a great job," I said.

Roeder resisted the flattery and raised a warning finger. "There is one problem, however," he said. "Timing. How long it takes the acid to burn through depends upon the thickness of the copper plate. I have experimented a good deal with this, but I am afraid that I cannot gauge the timing to within less than two hours. Perhaps if I had more time . . ."

I told him there was no more time to spare; the operation must go forward as soon as possible.

"As long as you're sure these things will work," I told him, "I want you to start producing them and training the teams. Make as many as you think can safely be distributed in one day."

"How much time do I have?"

"Ten days."

Roeder slipped the device into his pocket. "Very well," he said. "I will ride back to Manila at once."

"Ride?" I repeated, incredulous. "You rode your bicycle out here?"

Roeder fitted his spectacles meticulously into their case. "Of course," he replied. "You did not expect me to walk."

Through the following week, Roeder supervised the construction of the devices and the training of the sabotage teams. The saboteurs were drawn from among our operatives who worked in strategic areas in and around Manila. The selection of them and of their targets was carried out under strict security, and their training in the use of the explosives was conducted by Roeder and his most trusted deputies. It was a tense and dangerous time. If any of our saboteurs were caught and the details of the plan exposed, General Baba would close down Manila with raids to prevent the operation.

By the second week of July everything appeared to be ready. The teams were trained and equipped and anxious to go into action. Meanwhile, our counterintelligence in Manila had found no sign that the Japanese suspected what we were doing. I therefore gave the order for the devices to be placed during the morning and afternoon of July 15, with the fuses set to go off at midnight.

That day, as they went about their business in Manila, our operatives carried the lead tubes with them, arming and placing them at installations throughout the city. Meanwhile, at our camp on Mount Balagbag, we received brief coded reports on their progress. At around nine o'clock that night, Wally Roeder came out to the camp to report that all the devices were in place. His long face was drawn, and there was an anxiety in his voice that I had not heard before.

"I used several different thicknesses of copper," he said, "and dispersed them according to the time of day they were to be placed. But this is not a Swiss clockwork device, Major, and I offer no guarantees of accuracy. I hope you understand."

I patted his arm reassuringly. "*Ja, ja,*" I said. "*So, wie so.*"

Near midnight my staff, Roeder, and I gathered up a telescope and a few bottles of rum and made the long, steep climb up to Signal Hill. There was no moon, and we sat in total darkness, quietly sipping the rum and gazing out over the lights of Manila, reflected ghostlike in the bay. We talked quietly, but we were worried and apprehensive.

When midnight came we all looked expectantly toward the city, but there was no disturbance. Then twelve-thirty passed, and then one o'clock, but far from erupting, Manila was sinking deeper into the warm stillness of the night. We had been drinking steadily to ease the anxiety, but after an hour more I felt depression and anger stealing through me. I turned to Wally

Roeder to ask him if it was possible that none of the devices had worked, when suddenly a column of flame shot into the sky.

There was a mushroom of silent smoke, and then the sound of the blast reached us. More explosions followed, spraying fire and flares across the startled city, and the boom, rumble, boom echoed off Balagbag and back over the bay.

Roeder snatched up the telescope and trained it on the flames. "Tanque," he said, and then he turned to me and grinned.

Tanque was the main Japanese fuel oil depot, and now it was exploding in a broadening fan of fireworks. Then from the far edge of the city rose a fence of flame. One orange picket after another spiked up, merging finally into long rows of fire. These were the tanker cars in the Manila railroad yards going off one by one, with precise, punctual explosions.

Behind me, Wally Roeder burst into a raucous German folk song, and in a moment he had jumped to his feet and started dancing. Cabral and Cadizon joined in with him, linking arms and kicking at the dirt, and soon my whole staff was dancing and singing while the glow from Manila flickered over their faces.

I was sitting on the ground in a stupor of rum and excitement, my legs thrust out before me, leaning back on my hands and trying to decide whether to laugh or cry. With each new concussion Roeder whooped again, and soon I too was shouting and laughing and pointing at the marvelous show unfolding below us.

All through the night the explosions followed one another. Just before dawn, the oil lubricant tanks at the Philippine Manufacturing Company went up with a tremendous roar, lighting the whole length of the Pasig River and raining burning debris onto its sluggish back. Then, as the first light came, there was a blinding explosion in the bay.

For a moment the docks were thrown into amber relief as flames shot hundreds of feet into the morning sky. A device dropped into a fifty-gallon oil drum had been loaded onto a

Japanese tanker, and now the whole 10,000-ton ship heaved up at once.

When the sound reached us it was thunderous, a huge ball of blast sparkling with smaller individual explosions. Berthed next to the ship as it sank was another tanker that quickly caught fire and began rumbling. Then a third ship, a cruiser, ignited with the debris, and it too roared and rustled with flame.

We remained atop Balagbag celebrating the spectacle until 8:00 A.M., and then started down to the camp. Beneath us, as I encoded a message to MacArthur, fires burned all over Manila, and sirens rattled from the suburbs to the bay. The effort had been a success more flagrant and more blazing than any of us had expected.

Ramsey to MacArthur, Captain Contreras tapped out as the horizon thickened with oil smoke and the flares flashed within it. *Sabotage successful stop Jap installations in Manila up in smoke.*

All that day reports poured in about the effects of the sabotage. The Japanese, taken completely by surprise, had dashed about the city trying to determine what had happened. Roeder's unpredictable fuses had been an inadvertent asset, imposing a randomness on the explosions that made it impossible for the Japanese to coordinate a response. Meanwhile, our operatives informed us, the Huks were clamoring to take credit for the coup.

Altogether we had destroyed hundreds of thousands of gallons of fuel and lubricant oil that the Japanese would be hard-pressed to replace. We had sunk two ships and crippled another, and had disrupted both shipping and rail traffic across Manila. But most of all we had damaged the Japanese' pride and presented to the nation a vivid reminder that the spirit of resistance was alive and active.

There had been losses too. At least half a dozen of our operatives had been captured while placing the explosives and in the wave of arrests that followed. These brave people were tortured mercilessly, and from them General Baba learned that

I had never left the Philippines, and that it was I who had ordered the sabotage.

He responded with a fury fired by hubris, ordering Manila closed down with roadblocks, the patrols doubled, and a broad-range confiscation of food supplies as a punishment for the people of the city, many of whom were already starving. Despite this, no one betrayed us, and we remained untouched on Mount Balagbag, watching the storm of fire and smoke slowly dissipate above Manila.

That night I made my way up to Signal Hill with a follow-up report to MacArthur. In it I summarized the extent of the damage and reported the names of those who had been captured. I recommended each of them for medals, but though I said nothing about it in the tap-pause-tap of the transmission, I knew that the medals, if they were to be granted, would all be posthumous.

The Executioner

I n the wake of the sabotage, the pressure to find me intensified. Reports came from all over the Manila area of raids, arrests, and interrogations. Many of our people were swept up and sent to Fort Santiago, where they joined the hundreds of other torture victims, but as fast as the Japanese captured them they were replaced. After the fireworks of July 15 the whole spirit of resistance was lifted, and minds were set more than ever on victory.

It was a spirit seconded by our radio communications. More and more frequently we received signals that indicated that an invasion was coming, and that we should be ready on a moment's notice. MacArthur had conquered the bulk of New Guinea, and in August 1944 had established his headquarters there. With every passing week the battlefront moved closer to the Philippines.

In June 1944, in a furious two-day battle in the Philippine Sea, the Fifth Fleet had virtually destroyed the Japanese naval air force. At the eastern edge of the sea, American troops invaded the Mariana Islands and battled the Japanese garrisons in desperate hand-to-hand fighting. On the northernmost island of Saipan, three thousand Japanese made a suicide charge in which nearly all were killed, while civilians behind their lines leapt over cliffs to their deaths, many with their children in their arms. The bloody tide in the Pacific had turned in our favor, and it was sweeping inexorably toward Luzon.

In the face of this, General Baba's efforts against us stepped up even more. In September I received word that Charles Putnam, commander of the northern provinces, had been captured and executed. It was Putnam who had likened the guerilla leader to a king, and now he had met a king's death: beheading. Then from Manila came a tale of tragic heroism.

For seven months Colonel Pat Gatson had suffered all the torments of Fort Santiago. The highest-ranking resistance officer in custody, he had been the object of special cruelty—fire, water, electricity—but none of it had broken him. After the sabotage campaign in July his torment redoubled, and he was tortured almost to death. It was only a matter of time before he made the trip to the old Chinese cemetery.

One of our men had been made a trusty in the cellblock where Pat was held, and this man conspired with Pat's cellmate to kill the night guard and steal his keys. The trusty smuggled an iron bar into the cellblock, and when the guard reached Pat's cell on the evening meal round, the trusty struck him over the head and killed him. He seized the keys and unlocked the door.

The trusty then began hurriedly opening the other doors, but despite warnings to be silent the freed men panicked. A platoon of Japanese soldiers was billeted in the courtyard above, and the prisoners rushed madly for escape. The trusty grabbed Pat's arm and told him they must get out at once. Pat shook himself free and demanded the keys; he was not leaving before the other cells had been opened.

The trusty handed them over and joined the fleeing men. Pat went down the cellblock unlocking the doors, but by this time the riot of escaping prisoners had raised the alarm. Shots exploded in the prison yard above, and the cellblock erupted in chaos. Men began tearing at one another to get to the stairs, only to be thrust back with bullets and bayonets. Some got to the yard and escaped; others were shot down as they clawed their way up the stone walls.

Pat was seized with the keys in his hand, having opened all of the doors. After a perfunctory hearing before the prison commandant, he was taken into the yard and shot as an example. His body was left for several days, tied to the execution post in the courtyard. Then it was cut down and thrown into a grave somewhere beneath the prison. The grave was left unmarked.

I was stunned when I heard the news, as deeply moved as I had been by Barker's death. I had known Gatson as a courageous man, but he had given his life with a selflessness that I had thought was confined to legend. I did all that a commander could do under such circumstances. I sent a message addressed *Ramsey to MacArthur*, describing Pat's heroism and recommending him for a Distinguished Service Cross—next to the Congressional Medal of Honor, America's highest military decoration. It was little more than a gesture, I understood; a formality fraught with awe, a final salute to a man who had laid down his life for his friends.

Through the eventful summer of 1944, Balagbag remained inviolate in its misty isolation. Our life there had become familiar and fixed. While the Japanese patrolled busily below, we went on with our training, organizing, and intelligence work. I enjoyed the respite and the continuous activity of an administrative headquarters camp. Though only twenty-seven, I had by now become the "Old Man," the senior officer in charge. It was a strange condition. I was still a major, yet I regularly commissioned lieutenant colonels and colonels, all of whom reported to me.

One of them was Colonel Manahan, the commander of the Mountain Corps Regiment. When I had established the radio station on Signal Hill, I had asked Manahan to detail a guard to protect it. Among the men he sent was a short, stocky fifteen-year-old boy who had served as executioner for the Mountain Corps.

Ever since the incident with the woman prisoner in the north, it had been the policy of our organization not to keep prisoners. Consequently, whenever one of our units captured a Japanese or a Filipino collaborator or spy, he was interrogated briefly and then killed. It was a policy I had adopted reluctantly, as a measure to save the lives of our own people, but enforcing it continued to be a heavy burden for me.

The boy was a simple, taciturn peasant who had wandered into Manahan's camp and volunteered. He had neither education nor skills and was put to menial jobs. But then, when a prisoner was taken and sentenced to die, only the boy was willing to perform the execution. Handed a rifle, he declined it and asked instead for a bayonet. The boy walked around behind the prisoner and made him kneel. He then jabbed the point of the bayonet in behind the prisoner's left collarbone and thrust it straight down into his heart. The man died almost instantly. The boy pulled out the bayonet, wiped it on a palm leaf, and handed it back. Then, without a word, he returned to his chores.

After that, he carried out all the executions for the regiment. In between these assignments he kept to himself and concentrated on his routine of washing and cleaning for the men. Far from being accepted by them, however, he became even more ostracized. Rumors began to spread abut him that he was a demon and that he had unnatural powers, and the men became uneasy about his presence in the camp. When I asked Manahan for guards for the radio, therefore, he was grateful for the opportunity to transfer the boy out.

I knew none of all this until one night when Cadizon went up to Signal Hill to check the radio post. He returned to report to me with a worried look.

"What's the matter?" I asked

"That boy . . ." he began.

"What about him?"

"The other men will not sleep in the hut with him."

I asked why not and Cadizon told me about the boy's job as executioner. It reminded me of my own struggle with the whole question of prisoners, and I felt myself become suddenly angry.

"We all have to deal with things we don't like," I growled. "It's not the boy's fault. What's their problem?"

Cadizon shuffled his feet uneasily. "They say that when he sleeps his eyes are open," he replied, "and in the dark, they say his eyes glow red like coals."

I was struck by the remark. If it had been anything less, anything more rational or arguable, I would have angrily dismissed the incident. As it was, the dark fear it implied somehow made sense to me.

"Very well," I said to Cadizon. "Send the boy back to Colonel Manahan in the morning."

I could not sleep that night. Like the man on Signal Hill, I realized, I too was haunted by the boy. But in my case there was more to it. He was the executioner, but it was I who had created the policy. He was merely the instrument of my own decision, one that involved a violence more intimate and personal than anything else I had experienced in the course of the war.

I did not know what effect such a choice would have on my life, but instinct told me that it would remain in my system like the other infections, though more subtle and less subject to cure. For the time being, however, every time I closed my eyes I saw the two red dots, and I forced myself to stay awake. And as I lay there alone, I wondered whether Charles Putnam had seen them too among his Igorots and Ilongots, and whether they had haunted his king's conscience until his death, as I supposed they would do with me.

Stitches

Through the summer and fall of 1944 I made regular trips to my advance posts in the lowlands around Manila. Such trips were necessary for planning and coordination, but I found that I craved them for another reason. In the weeks of routine activity at Balagbag I had become restless and my health had declined. I could not account for this until I made my first trip into the lowlands, where the Japanese were swarming and meetings were held in huts by candlelight. I realized then that I needed danger as a stimulant to my system, and from that time on I made the routine rounds of the posts myself.

It was a strange self-realization. My old love of risk had not disappeared; indeed, it had become essential to my well-being. I could not command without risk; I could not function normally without it. I had lived in such danger for so long that danger itself had become indispensable to me. I craved it like a drug and savored it like a sexual adventure. Once down among the Japanese patrols, my health picked up and my spirits sharpened. Danger was a cathartic, a cleansing of my system, the key to my enjoyment of command.

Each of the advance posts was different, with its own character and its own mix of personalities. One of my favorites was at Bagbag, a barrio on the outskirts of Manila. Bagbag was the personal haunt of Major Jorge Joseph, known as Jojo, who owned the nightclub in Manila where I was supposed to have celebrated

New Year's of 1944. Jojo had heard years of stand-up comedy, and in the evenings at camp he kept us all in stitches. He would mime and mug the comics, some of whom must have been terrible, as he went through his repertoire of raunchy jokes.

It was on a visit in September, while he was unleashing some particularly scatological one-liners, that I first felt the pains. They were piercing and deep in the pit of my stomach. My temperature shot up, and in a minute I was doubled over. This was not malaria or dysentery, I knew; this was different. It was a stab, a spike, a hot shard shredding my intestines. I had no idea what it was, but I was grateful when it finally eased off. Jojo insisted on going into Manila to fetch a doctor, and I was scared enough to agree.

Next morning he was back, accompanied by a huge, muscular man who looked more like a wrestler than a physician. Teng Campa, the son of immigrant Basque parents from the Pyrenees, had a massive chest and a bull head, and was one of the most formidable creatures I had met in three years of war. As he bent his bulk over me, Cadizon and Cabral eyed him with dark suspicion.

Dr. Campa questioned me closely for a few minutes, then began poking at my midsection. It felt as if he were touching an electric switch inside me, and with every jolt I howled.

The doctor grunted and poked some more. "Acute appendicitis," he declared, tugging down my shirt. "You must be operated on immediately."

"Operation?" Cadizon shook his head. "Impossible."

"Alright," Dr. Campa shrugged. "He dies."

Cadizon reached for his pistol. "Hold on," I groaned, "I think he's right. But we can't do it here . . . too close to Manila."

Cabral interposed himself between the doctor and me.

"What do we know about this guy?" he whispered. "Let's get somebody we trust."

"Jojo says he's alright," I answered, "and besides, I don't feel like waiting. The damn thing's gonna burst."

"Well, at least let's go back to headquarters," Cabral said. "Can you make it?"

"I think so."

I told Dr. Campa that I would travel back to Balagbag with my men while he and Jojo returned to Manila, collected the necessary supplies, and came up to perform the operation at our hospital.

"It'll take a day or two," Dr. Campa said. "You're not strong enough for chloroform, so I'll have to get a spinal anesthetic on the black market."

"Well, get it as quick as you can," I said. "We'll be waiting."

Cadizon borrowed a little Filipino pony, and on this I set off through the dense, head-high grass above the watershed of Novaliches. The pain, however, compelled me to stop every few minutes, and it was nightfall before we reached the base of Balagbag. I knew I could go no farther that day, and so we spent the night in a cowherd's lean-to in the foothills.

It was a rude and lonely place, huddled under a hillside overgrown with cogon grass and jungle, and I passed as miserable a night as I had had during the war. The pain was intense, riding surges of nightmare every time I fell asleep. I enjoyed risk, I had come to crave danger, but this anatomic betrayal infuriated me. For three years I had dragged and coaxed my body through the war, and now it was turning on me again. I spent the night clenching my teeth and cursing and waiting for the dawn.

When it finally came, I grumbled at my bodyguards to get going, and they helped me back onto the pony. I rode as far as the steepening trail allowed, then got down and began the hike-climb-crawl up the streambed to the camp. Over the months it had become familiar, even welcome, but now I hated every slimy, slipping inch of it. By the time we arrived at the machine-gun post atop the falls, I was delirious with pain and fever.

Jojo and Dr. Campa came up early the next morning with the supplies for the operation. Campa quickly took charge, ordering a squad of men to disinfect the hospital shack and barking out instructions to our medical staff, which consisted of a dentist, a chaplain, two nurses, and Mona Snyder. I was in too much pain to object to the usurpation, but my guards were clearly resentful of Campa's manner, not to mention mistrustful of his intentions.

By eight o'clock he was ready. Cadizon and Cabral carried me to the table and stood by while the nurses shaved my groin and scrubbed me with alcohol. When they had finished, Campa moved toward me, a syringe poised in his gloved hand. As he did, Cadizon and Cabral stepped between him and me.

Cadizon slipped his .45 from its holster and held it discreetly down his side. He fixed the doctor's eyes above the surgical mask. "If he dies," he said in an undertone, "so do you."

Campa regarded him for a moment, then grunted and elbowed past him to the table.

The nurses rolled me onto my side, Campa stooped, and he jabbed the needle into my back. I could feel the pressure of the fluid as it was forced in. In a few minutes, he began pinching me to test the effect. There was none. For half an hour he pinched and poked, but I could feel every bit of the pain. At last, he grumbled under his breath that the black marketeer had cheated him. The vial had been filled with water.

Cadizon jerked out his .45 again.

"That's it," he growled. "You're through."

I grabbed at his arm. "It's too late to argue now," I said, "the damn thing's got to come out, anesthetic or no."

Cadizon glanced from the doctor back to me again and slowly put the pistol back. I told him to go to my quarters and get a bottle of old Tanduay rum, which I was keeping in my locker for the celebration of MacArthur's return. He threw a dark scowl at Campa and hurried out of the hut.

In a moment he was back with the rum. He popped the cork, poured a deep mugful, and held my head up while I drained it. I handed the mug back to Cadizon and grumbled at the doctor: "Now get that sonofabitch out of me."

While the nurses held me down, Campa leaned over me with

a scalpel. He sliced open the flesh above my groin, and I winced and tightened with the sudden slick pain. Then, as Mona cradled my head and talked quietly to me, Campa began cutting through the muscles of my abdomen. I screamed and groaned and bit at Mona's arms.

Campa reached in with a gloved hand, and I could feel the fingers pushing aside my organs, probing for the swollen appendix. It was a horrid intimacy, a searching shoving among my viscera, an obscene invasion of myself. I swore as loudly as the pain would allow, in protest and indignation, and in a moment I was joined by Campa's own Spanish swearing.

He could not find the appendix among the bloodied giblets of my insides. As he searched, the Spanish curses degenerated to Basque, a string of mutterings muted by his mask, buzzing with guttural Xs and Zs. He probed and cursed and I cursed and snarled back, but by now I was slipping beyond protest, stupefied with the fever, pain, and rum and sliding hypnotically into a slough of shock.

At last, with a grunt of satisfaction, Campa located the appendix, leaned his big bulk over, and snipped it clear. He was lifting it out upon his fingers with a gesture approaching triumph when the thing bloated suddenly and burst over his gloves. Campa gave another grunt and handed the vacant flesh sheath to a nurse.

Then there was the stitching of the intestine, which went on for nearly an hour. While Campa jabbed and slipped the blood-soaked thread, the nurses powdered the sutures with sulfanilamide. Then when he was done, for good measure, Campa dusted my insides again with sulfa, pinched the flesh together, and sewed it shut.

After an hour and three-quarters he straightened, swabbed his brow with a meaty forearm, and announced that it was done. Then he threw a glance at Cadizon, turned his back on him, and walked out.

I was now in total shock; I felt nothing as my bodyguards lifted me and carried me to my hut. For the next five days, while

I passed from coma to a delirium fueled by fever, I was cared for continuously by Mona and Dr. Campa. They fed me broth and soft rice and cleaned and comforted me. Campa proved to be kindly, solicitous, and extremely competent, though he clung assiduously to his gruff demeanor.

"Your hospital is a joke," he grumbled to me one day when my head was clear. "You need a surgeon."

"Are you volunteering?" I asked.

"Naturally," he said.

"Alright, I'm commissioning you major and assigning you as chief of our medical corps. Pending approval from MacArthur, of course."

Campa grunted disdainfully. "I am not a military man," he said.

"You are now," I told him.

For another week I lay on the cot in my hut, regaining strength. So far we had been spared the Japanese patrols, but word of the operation had reached Manila, and General Baba ordered an all-out effort to find me before I could be moved. The radio triangulations were stepped up, and every so often I could hear the burr of spotter planes above the trees, but there were no alarms from our waterfall outpost and I spent the long hours dozing and daydreaming.

One morning I was awakened by a rustling in the brush behind my hut. I pulled myself up onto an elbow and reached beneath my pillow for my pistol. The side panels had been pulled up to admit the faint morning breeze, and I peered into the jungle that tangled up the slope toward the summit of Balagbag.

We were sure the Japanese could not approach us from that direction; the slopes were nearly vertical and impassibly over-grown. Yet if they had somehow come over the summit of Balagbag, they might even now be preparing to attack us from both sides.

While I watched, the brush shifted, swayed, and then parted. Not a dozen yards from where I lay appeared the

massive head of a wild boar. His black shoulders bulked as he
shuffled toward me, and the ragged mane between them
twitched with flies. A pair of yellow tusks tined up about his
snout, which shoved and grunted against the ground as he
rooted for food, oblivious of me.

I raised the .45 and leveled it with the dirty, downcast eyes.
Meat was rare in our camp, and here were hundreds of pounds
of it. My eyes would not focus, however, and I could feel the
pistol twisting in my hand. The boar moved closer, still snuffling
the ground, until it was no more than ten feet from me. I could
not possibly miss. I made an effort to steady myself and then
squeezed the trigger.

The shot exploded in my ears, and the recoil shoved me
onto my back. The tops of the trees lifted all around as big
fistfuls of birds startled up. I scrambled to my side again in time
to see the boar crash away unscathed into the jungle.

In a moment Mona, Cadizon, Cabral, and the headquarters
guard were all piling into my hut, bristling with rifles and
machine guns.

When I waved them off, Cabral regarded me with relief.
"You are alive, Major Ramsey?" he said.

"Of course I'm alive. What did you think?"

He looked shamefaced a moment. Mona, carrying a big
Garand rifle, stepped to me. "We know the Japanese could not
come from this side," she said. "We thought you had blown your
brains out."

Then, for the first time since Jojo had entertained us at the
advance post, I laughed. "Not possible," I told her. "The way
I'm shooting these days, I would have missed."

October 20, 1944: Americans invade the Philippines. This photo was taken minutes after the first American troops stormed ashore at Leyte. The landings here were a prelude to the invasion of Luzon. (UPI/BETTMANN NEWSPHOTOS)

January 9, 1945: MacArthur wades ashore at Lingayen Gulf, making good his promise to return to the Philippines. He was met on the beach by Ramsey's guerillas. The intelligence they had supplied and their presence behind Japanese lines helped MacArthur persuade Roosevelt to invade, rather than bypass, the Philippines. (UPI/BETTMANN NEWSPHOTOS)

As the Americans pushed toward Manila, guerilla units guided them and participated in the fighting. (UPI/BETTMANN NEWSPHOTOS)

Resistance to the drive south was sporadic. Around Fort Stotsenberg, the Japanese had to be blasted out of fortified caves and tunnels. (UPI/BETTMANN NEWSPHOTOS)

January 31, 1945: Ramsey (CENTER) the guerilla commander, rejoins the U.S. Army. Standing beside him is Claro Camacho; behind, the jeep that Camacho captured from the Japanese.

Major Ed Ramsey on the outskirts of Manila during the liberation. Claro Camacho is at the extreme right. After three years of guerilla warfare, Ramsey weighed less than a hundred pounds. Unable to support the weight of a pistol around his waist, he carried a snub-nosed .38 across his shoulder.

(LEFT) *The guerillas join the American army* (UPI/BETTMANN NEWSPHOTOS). (ABOVE) *With Colonel Luis Villarael, his Chief of Operations, Ramsey oversaw the incorporation of his forty thousand-member force into MacArthur's Sixth Army.*

(OPPOSITE, TOP) *May 9, 1945: Ramsey celebrates his twenty-eighth birthday with his headquarters staff at Mecauayan on the outskirts of Manila. Mona Snyder* (CENTER) *wears her captain's uniform.* (ABOVE) *Among the presents, an inscribed portrait of General MacArthur.* (OPPOSITE, BOTTOM) *The party continued far into the night, attended by Filipino and American dignitaries. The following morning, Ramsey suffered his first breakdown.*

June 13, 1945: Ramsey and John Boone after receiving their Distinguished Service Crosses from General MacArthur at the Manila City Hall. MacArthur ordered Ramsey to remain in Manila to rest and recover. Three days later, after a second breakdown, MacArthur ordered him home.

Lieutenant Colonel Ramsey in Manila with his General Staff and district commanders of the ECLGA.

The hero returns home. Flown from San Francisco by Nadine, Ramsey is met in Wichita by his mother (RIGHT) and family friend Walter Beech, owner of Beechcraft Corporation.

From cadet to commander, Ramsey's journey to manhood was marked outwardly by medals and inwardly by the scars of more than one war.

TRIUMPH

1944–1945

MEDAL ON PRECEDING PAGE:
Distinguished Service Cross (AMERICAN)

Leyte

Radio traffic had been growing hectic through the fall of 1944. After recapturing the Marianas, MacArthur's forces had pushed westward through the Caroline Islands to Palau, just five hundred miles from the coast of Mindanao. From Palau, American navy planes launched a series of raids on the southern and central Philippines to test the strength of the Japanese defenses there. Admiral William Halsey, commander of MacArthur's Fast Carrier Force, was surprised by the feeble resistance to these raids, and he recommended that the planned invasion of Leyte, some hundred miles to the south, be moved up. MacArthur was only too happy to agree.

As a result, his demands on us for intelligence became even more insistent and pointed. Were the Japanese stripping Luzon to defend Leyte? Were their ships moving south? How many planes were serviceable in Luzon? Were munitions being stockpiled or shipped?

We began working overtime, channeling information in from Manila and the provinces, evaluating it, analyzing it, and sending it on in unbroken shifts of transmission. Though we had learned that the new Japanese commander in the Philippines, General Yamashita, had been ordered to mount his main defense in Leyte, our agents reported that he appeared reluctant to carry out the order. All of our intelligence indicated that Yamashita wanted to fight in Luzon, not Leyte, and that he was resisting the pressure to shift his forces southward. We relayed this information to MacArthur: Luzon, and not Leyte, remained the main enemy stronghold.

☆ ☆ ☆

As the American forces approached, Japanese activity aimed at thwarting us increased. Raids in Manila became almost a daily occurrence, and we noted much more patrolling in the watershed area of the foothills below Balagbag. Though they still had not located us, our fear was that our lines of communication would be cut by the growing numbers of troops. Couriers to and from my headquarters now ran greater risks—risks compounded by the fact that MacArthur was demanding more and better intelligence every day.

I could no longer afford a convalescence. On the eighth day after the operation I had Cabral whittle me a cane, and I began exercising on the trail outside my hut. I had lost a lot of blood and I was chronically weak from malnutrition and dysentery, but if an invasion was coming I was going to have to be ready for it.

By the middle of October 1944, we were flooded with demands for information about Japanese troop strengths and intentions in Luzon and instructed to prepare to render all assistance possible to Allied forces. It was clear from the urgency and specificity of the messages that the invasion was coming, and coming soon. I dispatched secret communiques to all my unit commanders to be on alert and to stand by for emergency orders.

Then, on October 20, MacArthur's forces invaded Leyte. It was the beginning; American troops were now in the Philippines and fighting desperately for a foothold. The Japanese responded by massing the bulk of their fleet around Leyte, and General Yamashita, faced with a large-scale invasion and the wrath of his high command, finally began shifting troops south. The whole war in the southwest Pacific was now focused on the Philippines.

While MacArthur's troops poured ashore, the Japanese and American navies locked in a series of battles around Leyte Gulf. Hundreds of carriers, battleships, cruisers, destroyers, submarines, and patrol boats dodged, feinted, and blasted at one another, as the Japanese staged a last-ditch effort to destroy the assault force, cripple the American fleet, and save the islands.

Three Japanese task forces attacked from the south and west, while a third, as decoy, attempted to lure the main American battle group away to the north. For a time the ruse worked, and the American flank was exposed, opening the way for the Japanese to destroy the landing force. But the remaining American ships, though outnumbered and outgunned, drove off the Japanese and saved the landings. By the time the sea battles were ended, the Imperial Japanese Navy was dismembered and had virtually ceased to exist.

For us these battles were the signal to frantic work. Leyte was an important island to the south, but we knew that the landings there were merely a prelude to the invasion of Luzon. The moment that we had organized and planned and struggled and sacrificed for over the past three years was now nearly upon us.

The Japanese realized it too, and before long our area was overrun by them. At first we assumed the activity was part of a massive effort to find us, but it soon became clear that they were busy at some other operation. Heavily armed parties of troops began stringing miles of telephone wires through the Sierra Madre Mountains toward the north, the main lines of which ran behind Mount Balagbag. It was puzzling and disquieting; any of these parties were liable to stumble accidently on our camp, or to intercept our couriers streaming back and forth. We therefore increased security and put our outposts on high alert, but we could not afford to decrease activity.

In the meantime I sent orders to Obie Bonoan in Manila to find out what the Japanese were planning. The answer came when some of his men ambushed a Japanese staff car on its way out of the city. From the body of a young officer they recovered a packet of top-secret documents, which were brought to me on Balagbag. I recognized their importance at once.

The papers made it clear that the Japanese had been com-

pelled to revise their plan for the defense of Luzon. Their
original intention had been to fight a major battle for Luzon on
the central plain north of Manila, but the presence of our
guerilla army made this impossible.

In 1942 MacArthur, facing a similar invasion, had been able
to establish five successive defensive lines across Luzon. Now,
three years later, no matter what defensive position the Japanese assumed on the plain, there would be thousands of guerillas
at their rear, cutting their lines of communications and supplies,
sabotaging their equipment, and sniping at them unseen. They
had failed for years to destroy us, and now, at this most critical
time, they would pay a high price for their failure.

Our sources told us that Yamashita had decided to abandon
Manila and the entire central plain and establish his defenses on
a long line stretching through the eastern and northern mountains. To be called the Shimbu Line, it would protect their rear
from guerilla attacks and force the fight against the American
troops to assume a definitive front.

This information was at once vital and threatening. If the
Japanese were establishing a line in the mountains, Balagbag
would be in the middle of it. I therefore gave orders to my staff
to prepare plans for an emergency evacuation of our headquarters to the lowlands when the Japanese shift began. I also
collected every peso of currency we possessed and instructed
our communications people to contact the loyal Negrito tribes in
the Sierras and pay them to cut the Japanese telephone wires
on my signal.

Everything was now happening very fast. Our regiments all
over Luzon began reporting major movements of Japanese supplies and troop concentrations, and in light of the captured
documents the pattern was clear. The Japanese were preparing
to pull back into the mountains in a gigantic crescent from
Manila to Lingayen Gulf. This, too, could only mean that an
invasion was imminent.

I sent orders to all of my commanders to step up both their
sabotage efforts and intelligence operations. While the Japanese

were on the move they would be vulnerable as never before, and we must not miss the chance to inflict all the damage we could. In the process, a premium was to be placed on captured officers and documents, and every scrap of information about enemy intentions was to be sent at once to my headquarters.

By November Bonoan's spies in Manila began to pick up signs of dissention within the Japanese hierarchy. While General Yamashita had determined to abandon Manila and fight in the hills, some of his subordinates violently disagreed with his strategy. They felt that the defense of Manila was a matter of honor, and that the city should not be surrendered without a battle. This information, too, I forwarded to MacArthur, for it might mean that there would yet be organized resistance in Manila. Our equation in the guerillas had always been that intelligence equaled lives saved. Soon that equation would be put to the test.

In the midst of all this, the kempei-tai launched its most vicious effort to date to break our organization. Our agents in their hands were tortured savagely, and whether they relented or not they were executed. Meanwhile, anyone even suspected of ties to the resistance was arrested in massive sweeps through Manila.

One European woman associated with our movement broke under the brutality and identified a key female operative. That woman in turn was tortured mercilessly until she revealed the names of dozens of our agents. Both women were then beheaded, and the kempei-tai snatched up over fifty of our people.

Under this pressure, Obie Bonoan labored mightily to keep the Manila organization going. It was our critical time—intelligence had never been more important, and no break in the flow could be allowed. Every operative who was taken was immediately replaced, and when the replacement was captured, he or she, too, was replaced. People were coming forward all over Manila to volunteer, sometimes making their way through the kempei-tai patrols to meet Bonoan's agents. They knew that the danger was more acute than ever, but they also understood that the life of their nation was at stake.

I followed Bonoan's efforts day by day, and then, as the arrests mounted, hour by hour. He was one of my most valuable officers, and the risks he had run already were legendary. When it was clear to me that the danger for him was simply too great, I sent word for him to leave Manila and join me on Balagbag. I was careful to leave him no choice; it was a direct order. After the liberation, the nation would need men like Obie Bonoan, and I was not going to see him lost so near to it.

We were now in a desperate fight against time. General Baba was sparing nothing and no one in this last drive to destroy us, and with each operative who collapsed under the pressure, more of our organization was exposed, bringing him closer to locating us.

There were other enemies as well. In their preparations to defend Luzon, the Japanese were stockpiling supplies and confiscating the scant foodstuffs that were left. Rice and vegetables disappeared, and meat became impossible to find. The situation in Manila grew critical; in the midst of these shortages, people began dying of starvation.

Our condition in the hills was not much better. We were forced to forage for anything we could find. Through October and November we began eating monkey, birds, and the indigenous *kamoting kahoy*, a pasty wild tuber. We were all losing weight, and by mid November I was dangerously thin and debilitated. I was down to less than a hundred pounds, and so weak that I could no longer support the weight of my .45 around my waist. Instead I began to carry a little snub-nosed .38 in a belt slung over my shoulder, and even that became a burden.

At about this time American planes from Leyte began bombing and strafing Luzon. To us they were a miraculous sight, and we waved and hallooed to them as they passed overhead, cheering every concussion of the bombs. They hit the airfields around Manila, the docks and storage depots, and the Japanese top-secret underground fuel bunkers, using the intel-

ligence we had been sending for months. Because of the preci-
sion of the raids, there were few civilian casualties, and only a
handful of American planes were lost, our people rescuing most
of the downed airmen.

The Japanese, who had lorded it over us for so long, were
now being paid back, and we were anxious to add our part. Our
people slipped into the airfields and blew up planes; they cut
railroad tracks and ambushed patrols; they attacked truck convoys and mined the roads that the Japanese were using to fortify
the Shimbu Line. After three years of occupation, the Filipino
people were on the offensive.

The Attack

They found us finally on January 2, 1945. Between the radio
triangulations and the clues tortured from the agents he
had captured, General Baba pieced together our location on
Balagbag. Patrols were sent scouring the foothills, and for a few
days we watched them hacking blindly through the jungle. Then,
without orders, the Negritos cut the Japanese phone wires
behind our camp, and the patrols began converging on us. When
one got as far as the waterfall, Jimmy Carrington opened fire
with the machine guns.

The Japanese fell back, leaving several bodies behind, and
we waited, keeping up our transmissions but ready to move. On
the 4th they returned, not just a patrol this time but an entire
battalion backed up with mortars.

The soldiers clawed their way up the streambed to the base
of the falls and then started climbing. Again Carrington opened
with the .50 calibers, spraying the lower basin of the falls, which
soon was stained with blood. The Japanese withdrew, and then

came the chug-chug of the mortars. The shells squealed up, arching against the falls, blasting into them, and sending rock and water spuming.

All that day and the next the Japanese kept up their attack, gaining a foothold on the rocks. A mortar round landed on the edge of the camp and then another on the cliff above. They were probing for our range, and their infantrymen were already firing up the slope toward us. I posted the security detachment along the perimeter to return the fire, and soon we were enveloped in a racketing battle.

Meanwhile, we were evacuating the sick and wounded from the hospital and carting our supplies and papers out through the jungle behind the camp. Our men followed the meandering Negrito trails across the ridges and then down toward the shelter of the cogon grass plateau above Novaliches.

Our next priority was to evacuate the radio. I was still a semi-invalid and so, on the night of January 5, I sent Cabral up to Signal Hill with a message to Colonel Guillermo.

"Signal MacArthur that we may be closing shop," I wrote him. "Say that we'll resume transmissions as soon as we relocate."

Alarms were kept up all through the night as the Japanese crept closer, were fired on by our men, and slipped back into the jungle. Around midnight Obie Bonoan came to see me.

"They've cut our communications lines into Manila," he said. "Somebody has got to go down and tell our people not to send any more couriers."

"Who'd you have in mind?" I asked, knowing full well what his answer would be.

"I'm the only one who knows where everybody is," he grinned, his face more boyish than ever. "I guess it's me."

It was a dangerous mission, but absolutely necessary: Any couriers sent now from Manila would run straight into the Japanese battalion that was besieging us. They would be captured or killed, a thought that Bonoan, in his keen solicitude for his men, could not abide.

"Alright," I said, "but be careful, and get out as soon as you can. You'd better take Teddy Fernando with you—he knows the hills."

"Okay," he said. "I'll see you downstairs."

"Obie," I told him, "good luck."

He saluted, gave me a charming, childlike wink, and left.

Bonoan gathered up a few supplies and set off into the night with my aide-de-camp, Captain Fernando. They would follow the Negrito trails to the cogon grass, cut their way through, and cross the Novaliches watershed at night into Manila. So far our men going down to the plateau had managed to avoid the Japanese. I prayed that Obie would too.

At dawn next morning the Japanese resumed their attack. This time they opened with the mortars while the infantry inched forward. I knew that Carrington was running low on ammunition, and so, with Cadizon's help, I hurried to the falls for a situation report.

"This is it," Carrington hollered over the rattle of the guns.

"How long can you hold out?"

"How long do you need?"

"Till 0:400 tomorrow. Can you do it?"

"Sure . . ." he drawled as a shell decapitated the palm trees over us, "no sweat. . . ."

As I made my way back to the camp, leaning on Cadizon's shoulder, I reflected that if Carrington held out that long it would be a minor miracle. I gathered up my staff and gave the order to evacuate.

"Where to?" Mona Snyder asked.

Of the several contingency plans we had, I was now forced to choose one. We would have to move to the lowlands but stay close to Manila. That meant that no matter where we went, we would be in the line of the Japanese movement to the mountains. I ran through the advance bases in my mind. There was only one place where we were liable to be safe, undisturbed by either the Japanese Army or the kempei-tai.

"Tala," I said.

Mona nodded. "How long do we have?"

"Till 0:400, if Carrington can hold."

"Okay, we'll get the wounded out."

We still had a dozen sick and wounded men in the hospital and only a few hours to get them to safety. Some of them could walk with help, but others were too badly hurt to move. Mona, Dr. Campa, and a squad of men began carrying them on stretchers into the jungle behind the camp. From there the headquarters troops took them down the circuitous route to the shelter of the cogon grass below the foothills.

The Japanese, meanwhile, were working their way up the slopes toward the camp. Shells burst in the trees overhead and bullets ricocheted noisily through the huts, thumping into the wattle walls. Japanese reinforcements had arrived, and now they were fanning out across the slopes below the camp, threatening to surround us.

I yelled to Dr. Campa to get the last of the wounded out, and he threw me a furious glance as if to say *I know*. Mortar shells were dropping straight into the camp, bursting among the huts and hospital. There were only a few wounded men left, but they were unable to walk. I watched Campa heft one of them onto his back and run with him crouching toward the jungle. A mortar round pounded into the earth nearby, and he dropped to his knees. He knelt there stunned for a moment, then got to his feet again and continued running. A minute later he was back, dodging the bullets and shells to get another man, and then a third and a fourth until the hospital was cleared. Then he began ferrying them on his back down the slopes to safety.

Everything was out now but the combat troops and the radio station. I left a skirmish line along the edge of the camp and told the other men to start down. Then I sent Colonel Bautista up to Guillermo with instructions to signal MacArthur that there would be no more transmissions for a few days, and to pack up the radio and get out.

Guillermo rapidly tapped out the signal. While he closed up the radio, Contreras unstrung the wire, and together they carried it back down the slope. By now the Japanese were pouring fire into the camp from three sides, and the whole place was heaving and shuddering with explosions. Again with Cadizon's help I made my way back to Carrington at the falls, and shouted to him over the racket to hold on as long as he could and then pull back through the camp.

"You asked for 0:400, Major," he yelled back, "and that's what you'll get."

"Burn everything as you go through," I said.

Two or three mortar rounds went off at once, and Carrington fired a long burst down the falls. Then he gave me a thumbs-up signal and resumed firing.

I made one more quick check of the camp to be sure that everyone was out, and then told Cadizon to pull the skirmishers back with Carrington. I was clutching at my stomach now, barely able to breathe for the pain and dizziness. I hobbled across the camp among the bursting shells, fighting to stay on my feet. I made it into the jungle and then groped my way along the path to where my staff was waiting for me. We started the long trek down the slopes, but soon I had to be carried between Acosta and Cabral. After a few miles I could go no farther.

"Go on into Tala and set up the headquarters," I told them. "I'll come down with Carrington."

They argued with me, but I knew their having to carry me would slow them dangerously. Carrington and the others would not be along for a few hours, and I hoped by then to have rested enough to continue. I insisted, and they left me in the jungle by the trail while they went on.

I lay under the jungle cover until nightfall, listening to the distant thud and crackling of the battle at the camp. I had not eaten for two days and was by now so weak, my senses so dulled by the pain in my groin, that I could not summon the strength to sit up. It began to occur to me that perhaps I had reached the end. Once Carrington and the others were out, all my people would be safe; they could reestablish headquarters in the lowlands and carry on until the invasion.

I took stock of myself as I lay there. I was emaciated, scarcely more than a skeleton, and too worn out to move. I had driven and tormented my body through three years of war, I had seen the organization to the brink of the invasion; perhaps I had earned the right to let go, to lie down and rest. My work was done, I told myself as I drifted into sleep; I simply could not go any farther. If I were captured, there would not be much left of me for the Japanese to find.

I was awakened by boot steps on the trail. The firing had stopped, replaced by the heavy lifting silence of predawn. I drew out my pistol and listened for the voices.

It was Carrington's men, and I called to them. Cadizon's was the first face I saw.

"Are you hit, Major?" he asked, kneeling beside me.

"No, just bushed," I said. "Is everybody out?"

Carrington came over to us. "Didn't lose a soul," he said. "C'mon, let's get you down. Can you walk?"

I told him I could not and that I would need more rest before I could go on. His men had stripped the huts before burning them, loading themselves with supplies, and so I instructed him to go on to Tala and come back for me after dark.

"I'll stay," Cadizon said.

I was too fatigued to argue, and so as Carrington and his detachment continued on, Cadizon remained behind with me. During the long daylight hours he cooked a few handfuls of rice and held my head as he fed them to me. I dozed fitfully for a few hours, then woke with a start. For one terrifying moment I had no idea where I was. Cadizon put his hand on my shoulder and then began talking quietly.

"It will not be much longer," he said calmly. "The Americans will be here and then everything will be over. That will be strange. I cannot remember what peace is like, or a normal life without hiding and fighting."

His tone had a soothing effect, and I relaxed. As the

daylight faded and the air grew chill, we talked about the people who had become close to us in the resistance—Mona, Camacho, little Pasing Cabral, and the others. We remembered the friends we had lost: Joe Barker, Pat Gatson, and a dozen more. He asked about my mother and sister.

I thought of them aloud, how they had survived their own struggles, Mother fighting for years to sustain her family and Nadine battling back from the crash.

"You are all fighters," Cadizon said. "And your father? He too must have been a fighter."

I had never spoken of him, and indeed, except as a warning to myself had scarcely thought about him the whole length of the war. Yet I realized now that Cadizon was right: He had been a fighter, in a long and lonely war of his own. The battlefield had been his spirit, and the stakes had been his sanity. It must have been every bit as terrible as my war, for its isolation and its unequal odds. But in the end he had lost, succumbed to desperation, chosen death.

I asked Cadizon to give me a lift up, and I got to my feet. The night was coming on, deepened by the shadows of the huge trees. I took a few steps, nearly fainted, grasped his shoulder, and walked on. Carrington's men would be coming up soon, and I wanted to meet them on the trail. I leaned on Cadizon as we made our way into the dense sea of cogon grass. I was not finished yet, I reflected, but neither was I alone.

Tala

I had never visited Tala, the leper colony that was to be our
new base. I was anxious for the chance to rest and to begin
our work again, but still I was extremely uneasy as we made
our way down from the watershed plateau toward the village. I
had never encountered leprosy before and knew of it only as a
disease mentioned in the Scriptures and the lives of the medieval
saints. I had images of horribly disfigured creatures haunting
shadows out of the sight of men. The many ills to which I had
succumbed and the evils I had witnessed in three years of war
had inspired in me anger, depression, and disgust, but leprosy
caused an instinctive dread.

Our men were camped in the rice paddies beyond the
village, but that night I was to have dinner with the director of
the leprosarium. Tala itself was a collection of ramshackle dwell-
ings ranged around his large wooden house. Its layout was less
orderly than most Filipino villages and the trails leading in were
deeply rutted. It struck me as a ragged place, grown up out of
necessity rather than choice.

Most of the residents were asleep in their huts as I led my
headquarters guard down the dusty main street. From under
some of the huts, however, I caught eyes peering at us as we
passed, but I was careful to take no notice. I knew nothing
about the disease, and the ignorance made me all the more
fearful.

I mounted the porch of the director's house and knocked on
the door frame. I was greeted by a quiet, rather solemn Filipino
of about fifty in shirtsleeves and broadfall linen trousers. He
wore sandals and spectacles and introduced himself as Dr.
Amador.

"I am very honored to welcome you to Tala, Major Ramsey," he said, putting out his hand.

As I raised my own to shake his I hesitated momentarily, chastised myself inwardly, and took his hand. A nurse was laying the table for dinner, and the doctor warmly invited me to stay. I asked if my staff could join us, and he agreed at once, adding that he had arranged for the other men to be fed at their bivouac.

Over dinner he told us about Tala. It was a government project established before the war and largely neglected since. Under the occupation it had become even more isolated; now there was little medicine for the patients and few staff to care for them.

I asked if they had been bothered by the Japanese.

"Never," the doctor replied. "The Japanese are terrified of leprosy, as are most people. We have been fortunate in that regard, at least."

He told us that many of the lepers had fled but that about forty were left, together with their families. It was rare that a leper arrived at Tala alone. Often when a villager showed signs of the disease, he or she was exiled together with the entire family. Thus, he explained, all sorts of people lived at Tala, including children. Most were not lepers, though many would eventually contract the disease.

"Leprosy is actually not very contagious," he continued. "It is the disfigurement that makes it so frightening. But it is only a disease and not, as some people think, a punishment from God. It is the ignorant who make outcasts of lepers, but lepers are just sick people—people like you and me."

Carrington asked if there was a cure.

"No," the doctor replied, "though we can slow its progress and, to a certain extent, limit the disfigurement. The best we can do, especially under the circumstances now, is to keep the patients clean and try to prevent the spread of the disease."

I told the doctor that we would probably remain in the area for a few days while we reestablished communications with our people and with MacArthur's headquarters, and I asked if there was anything we could do.

"On the contrary," he said, "please let us know if there is anything we can do for you. These poor people are no less patriotic than others."

At the doctor's urging I spent that night in his house, and in the morning we made our way through the village to our new base camp. Most of the people were out working in the little communal vegetable garden or gathering wood and water.

In some the disfigurement was plain and pathetic. One woman whom we passed had no nose, merely a stub of decaying bone; another, an old man, sat mute with the stump of an arm upon his lap, the crusted flesh a powdery whitish pink. In others it was more subtle, hands twisted into talons wrapped in ragged bandages, or legs drawn up into knobbly bows. Some seemed ashamed and sought to hide themselves from us, but others went about their business in a sullen silence.

In contrast, little children ran and played among the huts, chasing one another or darting around makeshift toys. They seemed healthy though undernourished, but a few already showed the first signs of the disease, a scaly, ashen graying of the skin. One, a boy of six or seven, sat watching us from the fringes of the garden, his bony arms bowed inward, his hands curled into claws, and his eyes brown and vacant like an old man's.

Even he was an exile, I reflected, an outcast on that sad, silent island of sickness, decay, and death. He had been doomed by forces within and beyond himself to suffer and, probably, to die. And I thought as we turned our backs on Tala that the doctor was right, and that the boy was no different than me.

I too had been exiled, I too had felt outcast among sickness, decay, and death. And while he bore the marks of his disease upon his body, I almost certainly would bear them on my soul.

Invasion

B y early January 1945, MacArthur felt secure enough in his bases on Leyte and Mindoro to launch the final phase of his Philippine campaign, the invasion of Luzon. To that end he assembled a flotilla of 164 ships accompanied by 3,000 landing craft and including 280,000 troops. Confronting these were General Yamashita's force of 275,000 men, who had had three and a half years to prepare. Behind them, however, were our guerillas, over 40,000 of them, armed with every kind of weapon from machine guns to swords, and all eager to join the fight. The battle for Luzon was now to become the climactic struggle of the war in the southwest Pacific.

On January 8 we were installed in our temporary head-quarters near Tala, and our radio was back in operation. That afternoon I received an urgent message from MacArthur. *Mac-Arthur to Ramsey*, it began. *Starting immediately, destroy enemy wire communications, railroad tracks, rolling stock and trucks, planes concealed in dispersal areas, ammunition, oil and supply dumps. . . . Unleash maximum possible violence against the enemy.*

It meant invasion, the moment we all had been working and waiting for. I called my staff together and gave them the news. The anxiety that had been building for weeks now became translated into concentrated action. Couriers were sent to every part of Luzon to tell our commanders that the moment had come for all-out sabotage against the Japanese. No effort was to be spared; the time to avoid risk was over—the Americans were coming.

Simultaneously in every province the guerillas rose up,

cutting enemy communications, attacking convoys and troop concentrations, destroying supplies and equipment in the depots. Because of the massive shifts in Japanese forces to the Shimbu Line the campaign was difficult to coordinate, but it did not matter. The guerillas were now doing what they had trained for these long years: attacking the enemy at every opportunity; disrupting their preparations to meet the invasion; harassing, crippling, and killing them all over Luzon. The body of the guerilla resistance that for more than three years had lain quietly, sending intelligence through its vast nerve system and occasionally flicking a finger at the Japanese, was now on its feet and fighting.

Our makeshift base near Tala was the center of furious activity. Messages streamed in from MacArthur, demanding updates on our activities and yet more intelligence on the Japanese. Couriers rushed into camp by the dozen every hour to report on the damage inflicted and to get the latest news of the invasion.

Almost lost among them was a lone figure who stumbled from the cogon grass fringe into the camp, bent nearly double. I caught him out of the corner of my eye and watched him come toward us, his clothing caked with dried blood, clutching at his chest.

It was my aide, Captain Teddy Fernando, whom I had sent into Manila with Obie Bonoan. Cabral and Cadizon ran to help him, and I was at his side in the next instant.

"Major Ramsey," Fernando gasped, "Colonel Bonoan is dead."

They had gotten as far as the cogon grass on the plateau below Balagbag, where dozens of our men had already passed in safety. The luck had run out, however. In the suffocating thicket they walked straight into a Japanese patrol, which opened fire. Bonoan was shot repeatedly point blank and killed outright. Fernando was also hit several times, but managed to lose himself in the grass. For the next few days he crawled and dragged himself down off the plateau, across the watershed hills, and over the lowlands to our camp.

It was a particularly bitter blow in the shadow of the invasion. In a few weeks, or perhaps days, we all might be safe behind our own lines, but it was characteristic of Obie Bonoan to have volunteered for so dangerous a mission at so critical a time. His first thought had been for the safety of his people in Manila, and no doubt it was his last.

Cabral, Cadizon, and Dr. Campa carried Fernando to the field hospital while I walked over to where Contreras was transmitting intelligence to MacArthur. I took a small sheet of paper from my pocket, smoothed it on my knee, and wrote out a message.

"Send this as soon as you're through," I told Contreras, as I handed him the slip. He glanced at it quickly, nodded, and began tapping it out.

Ramsey to MacArthur, it began. *Request posthumous Distinguished Service Cross for Liberato Bonoan, colonel guerilla forces, for volunteering to cross Japanese lines to reestablish communications. Killed by enemy action.*

Once again it was all that I as commander could do. Another medal for another dead friend.

On the morning of January 9, 1945, MacArthur's forces arrived at Lingayen Gulf, where the Japanese had landed four years before. All that day his battleships and planes pounded the shoreline, and early on the morning of the next day the troops of General Walter Krueger's Sixth Army clambered over the ships' railings and down the mesh ladders to the landing craft. At 9:50 they hit the beaches.

The Japanese had withdrawn into the mountains, and Krueger's troops poured ashore, meeting little resistance. In five hours the landing was secured, and Krueger ordered the advance toward Manila. Meanwhile in the gulf, the kamikazes had appeared, and as the infantry pushed south the ships fought desperately for their lives. Loaded with explosives and fuel, the suicide planes dived straight into the guns of the battleships, destroyers, and carriers. None was sunk, though scores of kamikazes hurtled crazily into their iron bulks and spewed blasts over the water.

In the meanwhile, after the first wave of landing craft had buzzed in toward the beach, General MacArthur boarded a Higgins boat and headed toward shore. The boat had too much draft to reach the sand, but the general impatiently waved off a suggestion that they land at a pier that the Seabees were hastily building. Instead, he ordered the coxswain to make straight for the beach, and when the landing craft bumped against the bottom, the ramp was dropped and he stepped out into the water. A few guerillas were waiting on shore, and they watched MacArthur wade toward them. They sent up a cheer and rushed to meet him, and in a minute more the word was racing inland and across Luzon that MacArthur had fulfilled his promise to the Filipino people: He had, indeed, returned.

As Krueger's Sixth Army rolled south in two long arms, the troops were welcomed with wild celebrations by our guerillas. In every village the American officers were greeted by organized, armed regiments that formally attached themselves to the Sixth Army. For many of our people it was the first time they had been regular troops, and they eagerly volunteered to take the van of the advance. The Americans were astonished by their number and discipline, and grateful for the information that they provided.

Pockets of Japanese were pinpointed and wiped out with their help, guides shortened their route by miles, and valuable time was saved as the guerillas fanned out before the army, alerting the villages and scouting the terrain. But most important of all was the absence of Japanese before them. As the Americans pushed forward, there was little organized resistance. MacArthur had been right: The Japanese had not attempted to fight the Americans in front and the guerillas in the

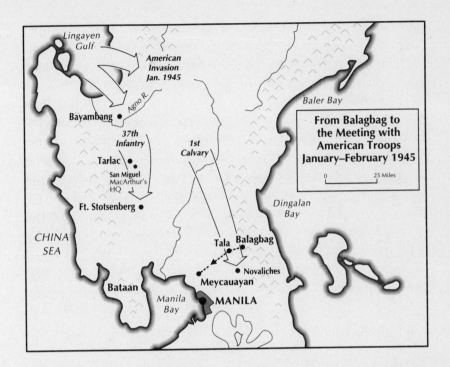

Lingayen
Gulf

American
Invasion
Jan. 1945

Agno R.

Baler Bay

**From Balagbag to
the Meeting with
American Troops
January–February 1945**

0   25 Miles

Bayambang ●

37th
Infantry

1st
Calvary

Tarlac ●
San Miguel
MacArthur's
HQ

Ft. Stotsenberg ●

Dingalan
Bay

CHINA
SEA

Tala Balagbag

● Novaliches

Meycauayan

Bataan

Manila
Bay

MANILA

rear. The way to Manila had been thrown open, and the roads were lined with friends.

Still, General Krueger moved with deliberate speed. Though there were few Japanese ahead of him, there were tens of thousands in the mountains on his flank. Thus while he pushed south, he was careful to fortify his left against the Shimbu Line in the Sierras. In this regard our job was to keep him apprised of Japanese strengths, concentrations, and defenses, which threatened at any moment to split his lengthening line of communications and supply to the fleet in Lingayen. Now, suddenly, our whole world was reversed, and it was we who began patrolling the foothills and probing the jungle slopes in search of the hidden Japanese.

Ironically, however, the dangers to our people had never been more acute. The Japanese were still shifting their forces to the north and east, and any movement by civilians was considered to be suspicious. Couriers and intelligence patrols were in

constant danger of encountering enemy troops as they forced
their way across the central plain to the mountains.

The situation in Manila was particularly acute. General
Yamashita had declared it an open city, evacuated the government to the northern mountains, and left only a small garrison
behind. Manila was not to be defended, he ordered; it had no
strategic importance, and he would not be responsible for its
destruction. Admiral Sanji Iwabachi, commander of the Manila
defenses, disobeyed the order and occupied Manila with seventeen thousand marines and sailors who were sworn to defend
the city to the last man. Manila, which had suffered under the
years of occupation, was now being savaged under the frantic
preparations for siege.

Civilians became prisoners in the city, and anyone suspected of disloyalty was arrested and summarily shot. People
were being rounded up by the hundreds, and then by the
thousands. A massacre was in motion, propelled in its brutal
logic by the certainty of the doom for which the Japanese were
preparing. They had volunteered to die, and Manila, they decided, would die with them.

Meanwhile, the Sixth Army pressed on, encountering resistance
mostly from Japanese who had failed to reach the Shimbu Line.
These barricaded themselves in barrios and at river crossings,
or attacked the columns from ambush. But everywhere they had
to contend not only with the driving columns of American tanks
and infantry but with the guerilla fighters behind them as well,
and they were systematically swept away.

The stiffest resistance was at Fort Stotsenberg and Clark
Field, the chief targets of Krueger's advance through the central plain. There the Japanese had embedded themselves in a
network of fortified caves and tunnels in the Zambales foothills,
and it was weeks before they could be rooted out.

MacArthur, traveling with the vanguard and sometimes in
front of it, was chafing to get into Manila. We received reports
from John Boone in Bataan that American forces had landed in

Zambales on the 29th, quickly secured Subic Bay, and begun a rapid drive north. The north central plain and Bataan were now safe, and our guerillas in those areas had already been attached to the U.S. forces. Only we in the plain north of Manila remained on our own, waiting to be swept up in the advance.

Then, on January 31, I received a message from MacArthur at our camp near Tala. *To Ramsey: All Luzon guerilla forces will now pass under the control of Sixth Army commanded by Lieutenant General Walter Krueger*. The message included Krueger's call sign and directed me to report to him by radio. I did so at once.

Ramsey to Krueger, I signaled. *I am reporting for duty as per orders of the commanding general received this date.*

After nearly three years as a guerilla behind Japanese lines I was formally back in the war, and once again an officer of the United States Army.

Confrontations

My people were not yet safe, however. Tala was nearer to the Shimbu Line than to Krueger's advance, and so I decided to relocate my headquarters closer to Manila. Advance units of General Robert Beightler's Thirty-seventh Infantry had already crossed the Pampanga River and were headed toward the town of Meycauayan just north of Manila. Our guerillas there had driven the Japanese out and had saved the railroad bridge, which was the main approach to the town. It would not be much longer until they reached it. I therefore signaled General Krueger that I was moving my headquarters to Meycauayan so that we could welcome Beightler when he arrived.

I set off west across the dried-up rice paddies of the lowlands toward the main road into Manila. I was still weak from the operation and my usual ailments, but I could make the trek in easy stages. With me was my headquarters staff and Carrington's security detachment, some fifty men in all. It was a march of only about fifteen kilometers to Meycauayan, but we were extremely wary. I had not crossed this ground with so large a group in many months, and with the dramatic changes of the past weeks, I had no idea what to expect.

Most of the barrios through which we passed were deserted. The Japanese had devastated the area on their way to the mountains, and now there was little left. They had not done all the damage themselves, however. In their wake the Huks were moving in, expropriating the land and demanding that the villagers join their movement. Those who refused were driven out and their property confiscated; others, who had supported us, were killed. Now the whole area was like a ghost town, haunted by the emptiness of villages terrorized, of rice paddies abandoned, of vegetable gardens stripped and trampled underfoot.

We were about halfway to Meycauayan when we came across a sprawling, deserted barrio. I led my men down the narrow dirt trail that crossed the village into its heart. The little nipa palm shacks were derelict, and there was not a living thing in sight. We were about to pass through on the far side when from our right a column of Huks suddenly appeared.

Their lieutenant seemed just as startled to see me as I was to see him, and for an instant we stared at each other. Then the Huks threw themselves into a ragged line along the trail and trained their weapons on us. My men deployed just as quickly, and we confronted them across the dirt track with dozens of rifles and machine guns.

There were about fifty of them to Carrington's twenty fighters, and we eyed one another for a long moment in silence. Had anyone pulled a trigger there would have been a massacre that few of us could have survived. I put my hands out in front of me as a signal that I did not intend to shoot, and then stepped forward onto the trail to confront the lieutenant. He was a small, wiry Filipino in his twenties, barefoot and dressed in the same ragged clothing as his men.

I asked if he spoke English. He nodded.

"Do you know who I am?" I said.

"Ramsey," he replied.

"Tell your men to put up their weapons."

He glared at me a moment and shook his head. "Put up yours," he demanded in a voice tight with anger.

I took a step closer. "I am on my way to meet the advance guard of the American army," I told him. "I have orders from General MacArthur that anyone who interferes with me or my men will be punished. Put up your arms."

Again he refused. "You are outnumbered," he nearly shouted. "Surrender your weapons at once!"

Three years before I had refused to surrender, and I had not undergone the rigors of the intervening years only to surrender now. But the situation was dangerous. The Huks were heavily armed, and we were indeed outnumbered. What was more, the lieutenant seemed about to lose control. He was trembling and his eyes were wild. Somehow the situation had to be defused.

"I will not surrender my arms," I began carefully, "and neither will you. The war is almost over. There is no need for us to fight. MacArthur will be here in a day or two, and if you interfere with us you will have to answer to him. We are going to Meycauayan. Let us pass."

The lieutenant glowered at me for a long moment and then vaguely nodded his head. Without turning I quietly told my chief of staff, Colonel Bautista, to lead the men out of the village, and I remained where I was, facing the lieutenant. When they had cleared the trail, he barked an order to his troops to go on. Then, with a final glance at each other, the lieutenant and I turned our backs and rejoined our men.

It had been a tense, dangerous encounter, and it drained me. My system was nearly shot, and I realized that my nerves

could not take much more. Cadizon slipped back along the line
of men, and I put a hand on his shoulder to support myself.

"Just a little farther now," he said to me.

When we arrived in Meycauayan that noon, the whole town was
waiting for the Americans. I instructed the local guerilla commander to send patrols out to scout the Manila road in both
directions to be sure that it was clear of Japanese, and then I
had Guillermo set up our radio and let Krueger know that we
were waiting with guides to take Beightler into Manila.

At about two o'clock the advance guard of the Thirty-
seventh Division marched into Meycauayan, led by our men.
The people met them at the edge of the town, cheering and
throwing flowers to them as they came. They were weary, dirty
young soldiers, but there were smiles on their faces and they
waved and hugged the girls as they came by.

Their uniforms were nothing like those of the old army I
remembered, and their weapons were unfamiliar. The iron-
brimmed helmets were gone, the khakis had become a baggy
green fatigue, and there was no leather, only the drab pouches
and cartridge belts that hung bulking from their shoulders and
waists. In my three years of exile the face of the army had been
transformed, the last romantic trappings of the old world being
stripped away and replaced by this looser, more utilitarian
aspect.

I waited at the town square with my staff for the captain of
the lead detachment. He walked up to me, the straps of his
helmet swinging, a carbine over his shoulder, and saluted.

"Welcome to Manila," I said, "or pretty damn near to it."

"Are you Major Ramsey, sir?" he asked.

I was surprised he knew my name.

"Oh, hell, Major," he grinned, "everybody knows about you.
They told us to keep an eye out for ya. General Beightler wants
to meet you. He's right behind us."

The captain wanted to know the situation up ahead, as he
had orders to push on straight into Manila. "We're in a race with

the First Cav," he said, "and the general is determined as all hell to get there first."

I looked over his footsore soldiers. "If the First Cav still had their horses," I remarked, "you wouldn't stand a chance."

I told him that I had assigned a detachment of local guerillas to take him into the city, and that our people reported no Japanese between Meycauayan and Balintawak in the northern suburbs. The captain thanked me, saluted, and waved his men to move on.

As the advance guard was clearing the town I spotted a jeep swinging onto the railroad bridge and turning at top speed toward us. There were pennants flapping from the fenders bearing the single star of a brigadier general.

The jeep scudded to a dusty halt at the town square, and a photographer and reporter jumped out. After them came General Beightler in a new, neatly pressed uniform, scoured shoes, and a gleaming helmet.

I was standing among my headquarters staff and bodyguards dressed in the same threadbare khakis and crushed hat I had worn and slept in for weeks. My only insignia of rank was a hand-sewn major's oak leaf stitched to my collar, and Beightler brushed right past me shaking hands and congratulating the colonels and lieutenant colonels of my staff. "Where's Ramsey?" I heard him ask as he shoved through the crowded little square.

"General Beightler?" I called after him.

He turned, faced me, and frowned.

"You're Ramsey?" he asked doubtfully.

"Yes, sir."

Beightler raised an eyebrow at my appearance, then yelled to the reporter and photographer. "Over here, snap it up!"

They dutifully pushed their way to us, and Beightler struck a pose beside me. The photographer jabbed his camera at us, clicked once, swiveled it and clicked again. The reporter scribbled some notes.

Beightler grabbed my hand. "Congratulations," he said. I

was not sure whether the congratulations were for my work or for having had my picture taken with him.

"General, I've got some pretty hungry people here," I told him as he strode back to his jeep, "can I get some supplies from you?"

Beightler climbed aboard. "No, sorry, Major," he said. "I've only got enough for my own boys. You go on back to General Griswold at corps headquarters."

"Well, sir, how about some rations?"

"Sorry."

He barked at the driver to get going, and they sped off in a swirl of dust.

I was furious and disgusted. My men were starving, but in his rush to make headlines the general would not spare us a mouthful of food. We had paved his way, we had saved him lives and time, and if he won his race to Manila he could thank us for it.

A convoy of jeeps was entering town, and I stepped in front of the lead one. Inside were a driver and two lieutenants.

"Turn around," I ordered the driver.

"Hey, Major . . ." one of the lieutenants began, but I cut him off.

"Turn this jeep around, dammit!"

The young driver nodded. "Where we going, sir?"

"Corps headquarters," I snapped. "By the way, what corps is this?"

"Fourteenth, sir."

"Get going."

We drove back along the lengthy double line of troops slogging toward Manila. The farther we went, the more the route thickened, and we began to pass trucks, artillery, and tanks. I was back within my own army but I was too angry to enjoy it. I was going to get my men what they had earned, and it was going to be today.

Fourteenth Corps headquarters was in a sugar mill at San Fernando some forty miles north of Meycauayan. I grabbed the first sentry I saw, gave him my name, and told him I wanted to see General Griswold. He returned in a minute and led me into the cramped offices of the mill that served as the general's field headquarters.

The sentry snapped to attention at the door. "Major Ramsey, sir!" he shouted over the din of radios, reports, and typewriters. Everything stopped. General Griswold came forward to greet me.

"Major Ramsey, welcome back," he said, and he put out his hand.

I thanked him and got straight to the point. My people were starving, I told him, and they needed clothing, supplies, weapons, and ammunition. "They've been at this for three years," I said, scarcely able to contain my anger. "It's their country, and they're anxious to finish the fight. But they have nothing."

Griswold heard me out in silence. When I was done, he turned to a staff officer waiting at his elbow.

"Open your supply depot," he told him, "and tell the quartermaster to give the major's people anything they want—food, weapons, clothing, supplies, anything."

"Yes, sir!" the officer snapped. He was about to hurry off, but he stopped suddenly. "General, sir," he said, "where are the major's people?"

Griswold smiled at me. "Everywhere, I gather," he said.

I returned to Meycauayan that evening accompanied by a truck loaded with supplies. In my absence my staff had taken over several abandoned houses for use as my headquarters, the largest of which, a two-story bungalow, had been set aside for me. I was impressed with its opulence. The downstairs room housed the radio and my command post, which consisted of a desk and chair, the first I had had during the war. Upstairs were my personal quarters, a washroom with a sink and toilet, and a bedroom with an iron-frame bed.

Everyone was giddy with the new sensation of having our headquarters in a town, with wooden houses, beds to sleep on, regular meals, and the freedom to come and go without the fear of raids. Mona Snyder, who had everything organized and running efficiently by the time I got back, told me that a radio signal had arrived from Claro Camacho. His First Pangasinan Regiment had met the Americans when they landed and had been incorporated into the Sixth Army. Now he was on his way back from the north to join us.

That evening during dinner an angry message came in for me over the radio. Captain Contreras handed it to me, looking puzzled.

"It's from General Beightler," he told me. "He says he wants one of our men arrested."

"Which one?" I asked.

"It says: 'The man with the severed heads on his jeep.' "

"My men don't collect severed heads," I grumbled, "and what's more, we've never had a jeep." I was about to expound on my opinion of Beightler when a jeep pulled up in front of my headquarters, driven by Claro Camacho. Hung from each headlight was the severed head of a Japanese.

I confronted him as he jumped from the jeep. "What in hell have you been up to?" I demanded.

"I captured it from some Japanese," he said. "It's got a mobile radio that still works."

"I'm talking about the heads," I snapped.

"Oh, those . . . that's the Japs I captured it from."

"Did you drive by General Beightler's headquarters on your way here by any chance?" I asked.

Camacho rolled his eyes in understanding. "Is that who it was?" he said. "I heard somebody shouting after me, but I was in a hurry to get here."

"Well, he's still shouting," I said, and I showed him the message.

"Claro, this isn't like you. What the hell did you think you were doing?"

He took a deep breath, and his whole expression changed to

one of deep sadness. "Just before the landing," he began quietly, "they captured my brother. They tortured him to death."

I remembered his brother well, a fine, selfless young man who had been eager to join the guerillas. He and his family had risked their lives to care for me on my trip north. Now he was gone.

"I'll get rid of the heads," Camacho said. "I'm sorry, Major."

"I'm sorry too," I said. I told him I would take care of Beightler, but that nothing like this must happen again. "We're not guerillas anymore," I added. "This is the American army now, and they don't understand these things."

He nodded. "Does that mean I'll have to salute you?" he asked with a little smile.

I waved it off. "It's too late to start that now," I answered. "What matters is, we've won. And you've got your country back. Congratulations."

"And to you, Major," he said. "It's your country too now."

Encounters

The First Cavalry entered Manila on the evening of February 3. The Thirty-seventh Infantry arrived early the next morning, delayed by a roadblock at Balintawak. There was some resistance in the suburbs, but the two columns brushed past it and aimed for the heart of the city. Advance units of the First Cavalry were able to capture the Malacanang Palace quickly, but when they attempted to cross the bridges into the southern part of the city they were repulsed with heavy machine-gun and artillery fire.

The Japanese had chosen to make their stand in the walled city and government buildings on the south side of the Pasig

River. Admiral Iwabachi had ordered that all major buildings be mined, and that they be destroyed rather than let them fall to the enemy. Thus, as the Americans began fighting their way through downtown Manila, building after building exploded in flames. Blocks, streets, and then neighborhoods were blasted into rubble, and from the rubble the Japanese marines and sailors continued to fight back. The American troops had to search them out from street to street, building to building, and floor to floor, killing them one by one as they refused to surrender.

Thousands of civilians were caught within this mad, suicidal stand, and they too became victims of it. Consumed by ritual hysteria, the Japanese shot down Filipino men, women, and children in their homes, their businesses, and even in the hospitals. Hundreds of civilians were advised by the Japanese to take shelter in public buildings, which were then blown up. At Manila General Hospital patients were locked in wards and even tied to beds, while the Japanese mounted artillery pieces on the top floor and fired at the Americans. In all, over a hundred thousand civilians were killed in the battle for the city.

General MacArthur was determined to spare as much of Manila as possible, and so he initially forbade air strikes or artillery bombardments of neighborhoods and public buildings. But as American casualties mounted and the suicidal nature of the Japanese resistance became clear, he reluctantly gave permission for the artillery to open fire.

Before long all of downtown Manila was a smoldering ruin. Three-quarters of the factories, four-fifths of the residential areas, and all of the business district were destroyed. And still the Japanese fought on. It would be four more weeks before the last marine was dragged from the rubble and killed.

I had been at my headquarters in Meycauayan for three days when I received a radio signal from General MacArthur's command post at San Miguel in Tarlac Province.

"The boss wants to see you right away," Colonel Guillermo told me.

I had not expected to be asked to report to MacArthur personally, and the summons took me by surprise. In my three-year relationship with him through couriers and by radio, I had come to share the Filipino people's near-worship of him. His promise to return had sustained me just as it had them, and like them I had lived for the day when he would fulfill it. But that I would someday actually meet him had never occurred to me.

It was ninety miles to San Miguel over a road crowded with American troops and torn by the passage of scores of tanks, and it took us all day in Camacho's jeep to reach it. As the time dragged on I became more anxious, more impatient, and more conscious of my haggard, down-at-heel appearance. Surely my years in the jungle had stripped me of all pretense or awareness of fashion, but now I began to feel like a beggar summoned before a king, and this awareness did nothing to ease my nervous anticipation.

It was dusk when we arrived outside the whitewashed sugar central that served as supreme headquarters of the southwest Pacific forces. I gave my name to a sentry at the door, and he saluted and passed me in. The duty officer seated at a desk in the lobby asked whom I wanted to see.

"General MacArthur," I replied.

He took a long look at my scarecrow frame, shapeless green fatigues, and crumbling boots, and shook his head.

"You'll have to speak to the headquarters commandant first." He jerked his thumb at a phone on the corner of his desk. "You can call him on that; name's Colonel Finley."

"Not Colonel Glenn Finley?" I asked.

"Yeah, I think his first name's Glenn," the officer replied.

It seemed an impossible coincidence. Colonel Finley had been my professor of military science at Oklahoma Military Academy. It had been he who had taught me polo, and it was polo that had brought me to the Philippines. I picked up the phone.

"Colonel Finley," said a gruff voice.

"Is this Colonel *Glenn* Finley?" I asked.

"Yes," the voice rumbled.

"Colonel Glenn S. Finley?"

"Yes, dammit! Who's this?"

I nearly stood to attention. "Ed Ramsey, sir," I replied.

There was a second of silence, and then the voice came thundering through. "The hell it is—you're dead! Get your ass up here!"

I hurried up the stairs to Colonel Finley's office. He was waiting for me at the door.

"Well, I'll be goddamned," he said.

He had not changed. He still had the massive square head, white mane, and bushy moustache that I remembered from OMA, and he had lost none of his old army brusqueness. He ushered me into his office and sat me down next to his desk.

"Do you realize," he began, "that your name is on the monument to the dead at OMA?"

"You're kidding," was all I could say.

Finley shook his head. "Saw it myself," he assured me. "Attended the ceremony. Very touching. You'd have been impressed." He waved at me with the back of a big hand. "Well, this is going to cause some bookkeeping problems."

I asked if my mother knew that I was alive.

"No," Finley said. "Few people did, evidently."

"Can you let her know?" I asked. Finley assured me that he would see to it that the Red Cross contacted her. He then insisted that I tell him the story of my war but I demurred, saying that General MacArthur had sent for me.

"Oh, he'll be hours," Finley said. "He's in a staff conference, and you know how those things are. We'll talk while you wait. What would you like? Anything. You name it."

"Well, it's going to sound funny . . ." I began.

"Go ahead, I have the key to the old man's fridge."

"The truth is, Colonel, for three years I've been craving one thing . . . ice cream."

Finley punched a button on his intercom. "Lieutenant, get in here!" he bellowed.

A young lieutenant in spectacles rushed into the room.

"Major Ramsey would like some ice cream," Finley thundered at him. "Get him as much as he wants."

"Yes, sir!" the lieutenant answered, pattering out like a cadet. "What flavor would the major like, sir?"

"Anything will do," I replied. It was amazing; Finley ran MacArthur's headquarters exactly as he had run the ROTC at OMA. I felt strangely at home, despite the five intervening years and the ten thousand miles.

The lieutenant was about to turn on his heel when Finley's voice stopped him.

"What size boot do you wear?" he demanded.

"Eight and a half, sir."

"Ed, what size are you?"

"Eight and a half."

"Lieutenant, give the major your boots."

For just a moment the cadet lost his composure. "*My boots*, Colonel?" the lieutenant nearly squeaked.

"Yes, dammit!"

In an instant, the lieutenant was on the floor, undoing the laces. I tried to refuse, but Finley would not hear of it.

"You can't go in and see the boss like that," he said.

I took the lieutenant's boots and handed him mine. He thanked me, regarded them squeamishly, and left the office in his socks.

For the next two hours I ate ice cream and told Finley the story of my three years as a guerilla. He listened in silence for the most part, asking an occasional question and nodding with avuncular empathy and understanding. I was still one of his boys, one of his cherished cadets, and despite his legendary gruffness he made no effort to conceal how strongly he felt for the war I had fought, with all its vagaries, all its hidden suffering, all its commingled victories and defeats.

It was strange to hear myself talk of it as if it were truly over. Even as I spoke I felt myself becoming detached from the tale. It had taken years for me to understand my war and to reconcile myself to it. It was a war that had penetrated to the deepest parts of me, forcing me to redefine myself as a soldier and as a man. Now, if it was over, who would I become?

The intercom on Finley's desk buzzed and the lieutenant's voice informed him that General MacArthur was free. Finley led me to MacArthur's office, an arm around my shoulder.

"You don't know how much what you've done means to him," Finley said. "You helped to save his boys' lives, and to him that means everything."

The door opened as if by magic and Finley passed me in, patting my back. From across the wide room a voice said, "So, you are Ramsey."

"General MacArthur," I replied, "it is an honor to meet you."

"No, Major," the voice came back, "the honor is all mine."

General Douglas MacArthur was the most impressive man I had ever met. He was tall and broad, with a massive head and keen, penetrating eyes. He wore the neat, familiar khaki uniform in which he had so often been photographed with an easy power and presence. He seemed to me truly larger than life, dwarfing my emaciated frame and making me feel like a mendicant in my wrinkled green jungle fatigues. Yet in a moment he had put me completely at ease, leading me to a big sofa alongside his desk and sitting me at one end while he took his place at the other.

He began by congratulating me on an extraordinary job and thanking me for the assistance I had rendered him.

"You were always in my thoughts," he said. "It was you and your people who kept the spirit alive."

"We never doubted that you'd come back, sir," I said.

He nodded his thanks. "I am sorry it took so long."

He told me that he was especially grateful for our success in avoiding civilian casualties during our operations, and he thanked me for our help in keeping his own casualties low. Then he plunged into a probing round of questions about the situation in Luzon in general and the guerilla movement in particular.

He wanted to know how many guerillas there were and whether they could all be counted on for loyalty. I told him that my command numbered some 38,600 men and women and 3,700 officers. "And so far as I am concerned," I added, "they are a tower of strength, loyal to the last person in the barrios."

He responded with an appreciative smile and then fired a series of questions at me. Who were the key commanders? Who was likely to be of use in the postwar government? What did my people say about Manila? How many Japanese were left? How many prisoners of war? What were the conditions inside the prisons? Were the Japanese likely to murder the prisoners? Did we have people inside who could help?

I tried to answer his questions as concisely as I could so as not to take much of his time, but it became clear that the general was in no hurry. He was eager for any scrap of information that might advance his plans and save lives, and he searched and examined me to extract it. His questions revealed his depth of understanding of the situation in the Philippines, and I took pains to keep up with him, satisfying his thirst for details.

Next he turned to the puppet government and its leading personalities. "I am under great pressure from Washington to weed out collaborators," he said, "but I intend no injustice to men who aided the resistance."

He then ran through a list of names, asking my assessment of the loyalty of each one. I answered him as frankly as I could, adding that some may have had secret contacts with the resistance of which even I was unaware.

"Of particular concern to me is General Roxas," he went on. "He is considered a leading candidate for president, but there are some who would like to see him shot. What do you think?"

"General Roxas saved my life," I responded, and I related the story of my trip to Manila, when Roxas alerted Mona Snyder to the fact that Baba had located me. I assured him that Roxas had been in touch with my people from the beginning and had provided invaluable information to us.

"I am very glad to hear you say that, Ramsey," MacArthur said, "for I know Roxas well and cannot believe that he is a traitor."

We chatted on, and before I knew it an hour had passed. When MacArthur had exhausted all his questions he asked whether there was anything I needed. I explained that General Griswold was seeing to the supply of my troops, but that I was still concerned about their integration into the regular U.S. forces.

"I'm anxious that my people know that their service is recognized and that they'll be treated as equals by the U.S. Army," I said.

MacArthur assured me that he would attend to it, and he instructed me to report any inequities to him personally.

"There's another thing, General," I continued. "I've brevetted a lot of officers during the past three years, including some lieutenant colonels and colonels . . ."

"You haven't made any generals, have you?" he laughed.

"No, sir," I replied, "but I'm anxious that their commissions stand up."

"Do you vouch for these people?" he asked.

"Every one of them, sir."

"Then you have my word on it," he said.

I started to thank him, but he cut me off. "It's little compared with what you've done for me, Ramsey. You've helped me keep my promise to the Filipino people. The debt is mine, as well as that of every man who came ashore in Luzon."

He walked me to the door and took my hand. "I thank you all," he said. "I am here by the grace of God and your good work. Please, tell your people that for me."

The fighting continued in Manila through February. On the 24th, General Griswold contacted me at Meycauayan with disturbing news. Several hundred Japanese soldiers had escaped from the city into the fish ponds to the north, the same sunken territory through which I had made my way to the coast for the trip to Mindoro a year before. They were terrorizing civilians and threatening Griswold's lines of communications, and the general wanted to know if we could help.

In reply I offered to use my four regiments in the area to sweep the Japanese from the fish ponds, and I asked Griswold to support them with two mortar units of the Fourteenth Corps. On the night of February 27, the combined force of guerillas and mortar platoons commanded by my chief of staff, Colonel Bautista, began their drenching, dangerous slog across the tidal marshes.

The plan was to catch the Japanese up in a broad, tightening net sweeping toward the sea, but the men had not gone far before they began to come across the bodies of Filipino civilians. They had been hunted down and murdered by the fleeing soldiers, their bodies mutilated in horrible ways.

The discoveries shocked and infuriated my men. For the next four days they scoured the ponds, wading in places up to their armpits, searching shacks, culverts, hedgerows—everywhere the Japanese might have hidden—and killing every one they found. By the time they emerged at Manila Bay they had left a dozen of their own dead among the ponds, and six hundred enemy corpses. Not a single Japanese soldier was left alive.

Breakdowns

General MacArthur made good on both of his promises to me. All of the commissions I had issued to my guerilla officers were upheld, and in April 1945 the Sixth Army announced plans for a processing and training center for our guerillas. Construction and stocking of the camp, which would handle the forty thousand troops of my command, was an enormous undertaking, but MacArthur had given me permission to use his name in requisitioning materials and manpower. That name had a magical effect, and supplies flowed into the camp in embarrassing quantities.

I placed my chief of operations, Colonel Luis Villareal, in command of the processing center, and together we set about completing the integration of our forces into the Sixth Army. Troops were being rushed to northern Luzon for the assault on Yamashita's Shimbu strongholds, and MacArthur was determined that, as far as possible, Filipinos would complete the liberation of their homeland. Our task was to train and equip them as quickly as possible, and then send them north to the battlefront.

I worked all through April and into May traveling from one regiment to another, directing them to the processing center, overseeing their training and supply and liaising with Sixth Army command. Although food and medicine were no longer in short supply, I found myself growing weaker. I now weighed scarcely ninety pounds and still suffered from dysentery and, increasingly, from fatigue.

To keep me going, Dr. Campa woke me every morning with nitroglycerine pills, then gave me triple bromides during the day to calm me, plus a heavy sedative at night. My frenetic pace was rapidly taking its toll on my remaining strength. Yet I felt I could not relent; there were scores of problems and controversies to be resolved, and I felt that it was my responsibility to ensure that my people were taken care of. I refused to slow down, and under the influence of the drugs I soon lost the ability to do so.

It was a dangerous situation, but I was used to danger and so assumed I could handle it. This particular danger, however, was different, an internal physical and mental pressure that was scouring my insides, already weakened by war, and tearing me apart. Nonetheless, I preferred it to the alternative, which was confronting the knowledge that my war was over. It was easier to go on abusing myself than to adjust to that new reality, along with the implications it contained for my identity and sense of self. And so I went on propping up my psyche with drugs and matching a pace the fury of which was far beyond my resources.

On May 9, 1945, my twenty-eighth birthday, my fourth of the war, I woke to the sounds of a native band and the sight of colored streamers rippling from the trees outside my window. Mona, in a fresh khaki uniform with gleaming captain's bars, beamed and looked mischievously content. My bodyguards and entire staff were assembled outside, in clean uniforms with shiny insignias and boots, singing me congratulations.

"Someone might actually mistake you for soldiers," I called to them from my window.

The party lasted all day and far into the night. Around noon sirens screeched across the bridge and a caravan of stately black sedans pulled up at my headquarters. From the largest of them stepped General Roxas, slight, dark skinned, with severe black hair streaked with gray, and now—with the death the previous August of Manuel Quezon—the leading candidate for president of the new Philippine republic.

Roxas embraced Mona and then saluted me, shook my hand, and hugged me as well. He had brought with him a dozen ministers and senators, all of whom expressed their gratitude and determination to be photographed in my company. Before he left, Roxas told me that he had recommended to General MacArthur that I receive the Distinguished Service Cross, and that I be promoted to lieutenant colonel.

The Sixth Army staff was represented by several generals, and there were formal congratulations from MacArthur, Krueger, and even General Beightler—who for the occasion I was inclined to forgive. Other dignitaries from the government and military continued to arrive during the day, and though it was a delight to me, I found it almost as wearing as my duties. Two or three times I had to take Campa aside and appeal for help. He braced me with chemicals and warned me sternly that we had to talk, but I would not be robbed of this celebration so long overdue.

There were presents: bright fauvist paintings of me and General MacArthur produced by my propaganda staff, a samurai sword captured from an officer and engraved with my name, and, as usual, a cake baked by Mona. Though the danger was over, I had seen little of her since the liberation. My frantic schedule had left me with scant free time, and I had felt compelled to conserve my fading emotional strength for my work.

The band played into the night, and I danced with Mona under a bulbous moon and fiesta lights strung among the trees. We consumed quantities of brandy and rum, and before long the world was swirling around me. It recalled to me my days as a cadet, the heady nights in San Diego, and the sultry Manila evenings, and for a moment it was almost as if the war had never been.

Then morning came. Dr. Campa came to wake me as usual, but when he did I started trembling. He got me to my feet, but I collapsed and lay shaking on the floor so violently that he had to lift me back onto the bed. I was incoherent, but a part of my brain was still clear and watched myself in wonder. Dr. Campa called for Camacho and Cadizon, and together they carried me out to my staff car. I was laid on the backseat, my head lolling, moans gurgling from my throat. *Is this a nervous breakdown?* I asked myself.

Mona climbed in beside me, while Camacho, Campa, and Cadizon crowded onto the front seat. I heard them shouting at soldiers to clear the bridge, honking the horn madly, cursing and ordering trucks and tanks off the road ahead. The whole time, Mona kept my head cradled on her lap, stroking my hair and soothing me with her voice.

"Be calm," I could hear her say. "Be still now."

I wanted to answer and tell her that I was alright, but my consciousness had shrunk to a pinpoint deep within my mind, and when I tried to speak, all I could do was groan.

They took me to the general army hospital in Manila, and for the next few days I remained in bed in a private room. I kept telling myself that I must get up, get dressed, and go back to work, but I could not get the rest of me to cooperate. It was a frightening detachment from myself, a scattering of my strength so that there seemed to be no center. Then, gradually, the pieces of me began to reassemble themselves. It was like sensation returning to numbed limbs; slowly there was the tingling reassertion of control, the growing confidence that I could master myself again.

After ten days they released me, but General MacArthur had forbidden me to return to work. A house was rented for me in one of the few undamaged residential districts, and for the next week I remained in Manila. I felt awkward and embarrassed at my collapse, and I scolded myself that others had gone through as much as I and had managed to hold together. The shame was the worst part of it; the feeling that I had been weaker than I was meant to be.

I strolled through Manila looking for the landmarks of my prewar visits, but there was nothing but rubble. The devastation was appalling.* Nearly nothing was left of the city center that once had buzzed with polyglot activity, its evenings ripe with scent and humanity. Manila was a scattered skeleton, its ribs and bones and broken teeth denuded and burnt out. A few people picked among the ruins for possessions, and some, in tears, for bodies. It was a crushed, cadaverous landscape, like Tala without the lepers. Like my own insides.

At the end of May I returned to Meycauayan, feeling tender and freshly patched. For a week I tried to get back into the routine, but everything I did was wrong. I snapped at my staff for my own mistakes and suffered the sympathetic glances of Mona and Dr. Campa. They urged me to take it easy, even to apply for

*After Warsaw, Manila was the most thoroughly destroyed city of World War II.

leave, but their solicitude only made me resentful. They were telling me I had had enough; I could see it in their faces. But I could not find it in my heart to stop.

The second breakdown was worse. I was sitting at my desk doing paperwork when suddenly the words melted into one another and I watched the pencil start shaking in my hand. The spirit dissolved within me. It was coming, and there was nothing I could do about it except to withdraw into that pinpoint back in my brain from which I watched in safety while my nervous system fell to pieces again.

Cabral stepped over to my desk, and when I raised my head to ask him what he wanted, I was crying. The tears were rolling down my face but my voice was saying, "What is it, dammit, what do you want?"

"Major?" he said, and then: "I'll get Dr. Campa."

It was strange and ugly to be so helpless. I lay in the hospital bed day after day, wondering how I had become so weak. I could do nothing for myself, had no energy or ambition, not even any shame. I let everyone else care for me and took their kindness as a right I had earned by my incessant sadness. There was no heart left in me, nothing more to be touched. I was alone, the loneliest person in the world, loneliness itself.

And yet deep within me was that pinpoint of clear light. Everyone was safe, I told myself; no one would be killed now, no one was in danger, there would be no more raids, no hiding out in barrios, no alarms. I had brought them all through, and I deserved this despair. I had held it off with all my strength for three years through thousands of deaths, under a pressure of fear and loss so great I could not have afforded to face it. Gradually I had absorbed it all, and now here it was, laying waste to me.

What kind of war was this? I wondered. What were the rules, who was the enemy, how could I win? There had been so many fronts in my war; which one was I on now?

I looked at the poor thing my body had become, and at the

shambles of my spirit, and I understood that this was a war that was beginning, not ending. It was a war to recover myself, to redefine my being out of the experiences I had had, to make sense out of the very senselessness of war itself.

I was in chaos, collapse, splintered from myself. Yet I had not surrendered. I had not surrendered on Bataan, nor had I succumbed to disease or General Baba or the acid residue of the deaths of friends. I had helped the Philippines to fight for its liberation from fear and torment and death. Now I would have to fight for my own.

Partings

W hen word reached General MacArthur of my condition he decided to intervene personally. The day of my second release from the hospital I received orders from his headquarters directing me to return to the United States. Accompanying the orders was notification of my promotion to lieutenant colonel. Whether I liked it or not, I was going home.

I returned to my headquarters at Meycauayan on June 6. I had already sent my chief of staff, Colonel Amado Bautista, to the army's Command and General Staff Training School in the States, and so I arranged to turn over my command to Colonel Luis Villareal, my chief of operations. I spent the next week overseeing the transition and putting my affairs in order. They were strange gestures, going through three years' worth of paperwork, organizational documents, captured intelligence, lists of promotions, commendations for decorations, orders to my commanders. Many of the men and women named, I noted with a sorrow dulled by my scoured nerves, were dead.

Out of a population of eighteen million, the Philippines had

lost more than a million people during the invasion and occupation. Of my own force of forty thousand, some five thousand had
been killed. One in eighteen of the civilian population dead; one
in eight of my own people.

On June 13 I received a message from Colonel Finley to
report again to MacArthur's headquarters, now located in the
unbombed wing of Manila city hall. "And dress like an officer
this time," he added.

One of MacArthur's staff cars was dispatched for me, and I
rode in relative comfort through the blasted streets of the
capital to the square before city hall. Rubble had been bulldozed
into dunes on either side, and the square was ringed with
security troops. A sergeant in ceremonial braid and shiny helmet opened the door, and I stepped out.

"Colonel Ramsey?" he asked smartly. "You're over here,
sir."

I followed him across the square to the steps of city hall,
where an honor guard and band were waiting. They were the
cleanest soldiers I had seen in years, and they hefted huge flags,
American and Filipino. Six other officers were waiting at the
foot of the steps, and among the faces I recognized John Boone
and Bob Lapham. Both had survived, and both, like me, had
been summoned by MacArthur.

"Looks like they're gonna give us a medal," Boone grinned
as we shook hands. He wore bright new major's oak leaves,
MacArthur having confirmed the promotion I had given him a
year earlier. Lapham, like myself, was now a lieutenant colonel.
"How's Mona?" he asked in his good-natured country-boy manner. I told him she was fine. "She's a captain," I added.

An officer led us into city hall, where General MacArthur
was waiting for us in his office, wearing a simple khaki uniform.
He greeted us warmly and introduced us to his staff, one of
whom was carrying an armful of boxes covered in blue satin.

MacArthur stepped to me first, and the staff officer handed
him one of the boxes. An aide began reading aloud from an
official-looking form: "By direction of the President under pro-

vision of the act of Congress . . ." I heard, and then as Mac-Arthur stooped to pin a Distinguished Service Cross on my shirt, I found myself fascinated by the pink smoothness of his skin and I lost track of what the aide was saying. MacArthur straightened, returned my salute, and shook my hand. "Congratulations, Ramsey," he said, "and thank you."

Lapham, Boone, and I spent the rest of the morning reminiscing. Boone's people in Bataan had assisted the landings in Zambales, saving countless American lives. Lapham's guerillas in the north had been among the first to meet Krueger's Sixth Army and had guided it on the rush to liberate the POWs at Cabanatuan. I asked him about Charles Putnam.

"Sad story," he answered. "He drank, you know. One night he had too much and said too much and they grabbed him."

"The king is dead, long live the king," I said half to myself.

Lapham asked what I meant.

"Oh, just something Putnam once said to me," I answered.

On June 16 a car was waiting in front of my headquarters to take me to Nichols Field. MacArthur had ordered that I be evacuated by air, and so it looked as if I would not be leaving by boat, as I had once dreamed. It was four years almost to the day since I had first seen the Philippines.

I had nothing but a small bag containing a spare uniform, my weapons, the birthday gifts, the DSC, and some papers. Nonetheless, I was still too weak to carry it, so Cabral hurried over to help. I took a last look around my office and walked out onto the porch.

My staff, assembled outside, came to attention when I appeared.

"At ease," I told them.

I took each man's hand in turn, thanked him for his loyalty and courage, and said good-bye. When I had spoken to them all I stood before them and saluted. They returned my salute as one man.

Camacho, Cadizon, Cabral, Acosta, and Cornel were waiting by the car. Through the dark years they had devoted themselves to protecting me, and many times they had kept me alive. I could not say good-bye to them. We hugged one another.

Mona rode with me to Nichols Field. I closed my eyes and lay my head on the back of the seat as we drove off. She held my hand.

"Come to visit me," I told her when we had arrived.

"I will," she smiled. She brought her kind brown face close to mine. "Get well," she said, and she kissed me. "Be happy and well."

The C-54 lifted itself above the bay and took a lazy turn to the east over Manila. This must be what Europe looks like, I thought, canyons of destruction, crater rims of rubble. Beyond, as we gained altitude, were the lowlands, stripped now of Japanese, but where the Huks still conspired. And then came the foothills, the cogon grass plateau, the blue green of Nova-liches and, to the north above the cloying mists, Balagbag. I caught the familiar bulk, the waterfall, the lauan crest of Signal Hill.

"Home," I said to myself instinctively.

Nadine met me at the airfield in San Francisco. She seemed fuller to me somehow, more serious, the old toughness in her having matured to assurance and poise.

"Hello, Buddy," she said as she hugged me. No one had called me that in years, and I felt the tears start into my eyes. Nadine, too, I could see, was fighting them, but as usual each of us refused to be the first to break.

"How did you get here?" I asked.

"Howdaya think?" she chided me. She had borrowed an airplane and flown from Los Angeles. It was a slick red racer, and she loaded me into it. "I'm taking you home," she said.

"Does Mother know?"

"They called her from Washington a few weeks ago, I guess

when you were safe. You're a big hero, y'know. God, how'd ya get so skinny?"

"It's a long story," I replied. I told her I had orders to report to Winters General Hospital in Topeka.

"But we're going home first," Nadine insisted as we climbed into the plane. As I buckled myself in, my hands were shaking. Nadine noticed it but said nothing. "All ready?" she asked. I nodded, trying to return her smile. She took off, snapped the racer into a steep bank, and headed east.

"You okay?" I asked her.

"I've been havin' a swell time," she answered with a grin. "Been ferryin' planes for the army—fighters and bombers. Trainin' crews too. There's only eight of us girls who can fly the really hot stuff: P-38s, P-51s." She took a long sideways look at me. "How 'bout you? You okay?"

"I don't know," I shrugged.

Mother was waiting at the airport in Wichita when we landed. Nadine taxied the plane up to her car, a big new sedan. There was a man waiting with her.

"That's Walt Beech," Nadine told me. "Owns Beechcraft. He's become a great friend of the family. He'll be ticked off when he sees I'm not flying one of his."

Mr. Beech came over and opened the door for me and I climbed down. Mother opened her arms.

"Oh, Buddy," she said. "Oh, my God, Buddy . . ."

After two days at home I checked into Winters Hospital. I weighed ninety-three pounds and was diagnosed with malaria, amoebic dysentery, anemia, acute malnutrition, and general nervous collapse.

"I'm afraid you've got a long fight ahead of you to get well again, Colonel," the doctor told me.

It would take eleven months and all the faith and love I had learned in Luzon, but I was determined that this war, too, I would win.

Medals, Awards, and Honors

American

Distinguished Service Cross—*awarded by General Douglas MacArthur, for heroism in combat*

Silver Star with Cluster—*awarded by General Jonathan Wainwright*

Bronze Star Medal

Purple Heart

American Defense Service Medal with Bronze Service Star

Asiatic-Pacific Campaign Medal

World War II Victory Medal

Distinguished Unit Emblem

Philippine

Distinguished Conduct Star—*equivalent of the Distinguished Service Cross*

Distinguished Service Star—*equivalent of the Silver Star*

Gold Cross—*equivalent of the Bronze Star Medal*

Wounded Personnel Medal

Philippine Legion of Honor—*Degree of Commander*

Sagisag Ng Kagitingan—*(Cross of Valor)*

Philippine Defense Medal

Philippine Liberation Medal with Bronze Service Star

LIEUTENANT RAMSEY'S WAR

Designed by Susan Shankin
Maps and medal illustrations by Randy Miyake
Composed by Folio Graphics Company, Inc., in Century Schoolbook
Printed and bound by R. R. Donnelley in Crawfordsville, Indiana